Gnosis

Gnosis

A Renaissance in Christian Thought

Geddes MacGregor

This publication made possible with the assistance of the Kern Foundation

The Theosophical Publishing House Wheaton, Illinois, U.S.A.
Madras, India/London, Eng.

A Quest Book, published by The Theosophical Publishing
House, a department of The Theosophical Society in America.
Inquiries for permission to reproduce all, or portions of this
book, should be addressed to Quest Books, 306 West Geneva
Road, Wheaton, Illinois 60187

Library of Congress Cataloging in Publication Data
MacGregor, Geddes.
    Gnosis: a theosophical renaissance in Christian thought.
    (A Quest book)
    Bibliography: p.
    Includes index.
    1. Gnosticism.   2.   Bible. N.T.—Criticism, interpretation,
    etc.   I.   Title.
BT1390.M27   230   78-64908
ISBN 0-8356-0522-1
ISBN 0-8356-0520-5 pbk.
Printed in the United States of America

To the President, the Board of Governors, and the Faculty of Hebrew Union College — Jewish Institute of Religion Cincinnati, New York, Jerusalem and Los Angeles, I dedicate this opuscule in deep gratitude for their recent bestowal upon me of the degree, *honoris causa,* of Doctor of Humane Letters.

CONTENTS

PREFACE ix

Chapter
   I.   GNOSIS AND GNOSTICISM ....·.........1
   II.   WHAT IS GNOSIS? 15
   III.   SPECIAL PROBLEMS IN DEFINITION 28
   IV.   CRITIQUE OF A SCHOLARLY DEFINITION 37
   V.   GNOSTICISM AS THE CREATIVE ELEMENT
           IN RELIGION 53
   VI.   SCIENCE, MAGIC AND MONOTHEISM 64
   VII.   THE PERIL OF DE-GNOSTICIZING JESUS 73
   VIII.   HIDDEN MOTIFS IN CHRISTIAN LITURGY 94
   IX.   FAITH AS INDUCTIVE GNOSIS 109
   X.   IS GOD OTHER THAN NATURE? 126
   XI.   EVOLUTIONISM AND GNOSIS 138
   XII.   KARMA, REINCARNATION AND
           THE ANCIENT GNOSIS 152
   XIII.   PRAYER AS THE EXERCISE OF
           PSYCHIC ENERGY 164
   XIV.   HUMANISM AND THE GNOSIS   177
   XV.   RENAISSANCE IN CHRISTIAN THOUGHT 188

BIBLIOGRAPHY 205
INDEX 217

PREFACE

Gnosis is to be understood in a wider and in a narrower sense. The Greek word *gnōsis* means simply "knowledge". Gnosis in the wider sense is as old as is reflection on religion. It is as basic a notion in all religions as is the longing for direct, mystical knowledge of divine Being. Its role in Christian thought should be, for at least three reasons, of fundamental importance to all serious students of religious thought: (1) the discovery of the Qumran scrolls in 1947 and the Nag Hammadi literature that has more recently become available to the general public in English raise questions in the minds of all thinking people about the background of the Christian Way and so about religion in general; (2) even apart from such discoveries, a mood is widespread that is unfavorable to religious dogmatism but favorable to the exploration of what lies behind the dogmas; and (3) the twentieth-century scientific revolution, while it neither supports nor injures a religious outlook, does make more likely to be profitable to open-minded people gnostic and theosophical ways of putting questions about religion.

Gnosticism and theosophy have taken special forms through the ages and both terms are consequently used in narrower senses too. For example, the Christian Gnostic sects that flourished in the second century and are traditionally treated as heretical movements within the Christian Church represent special forms that gnosticism may take, as does also, for instance, the Albigensian movement that for generations decimated the prevailing Christian orthodoxy in Western Europe, especially in what is now Provence and northern Italy. The theosophical movement of the nineteenth century in England and the United States is similarly a form of an ancient theosophical tradition that can recognize no territorial or historical boundaries.

Something similar could be said about the great humanist tradition. For humanism certainly takes many forms, some deeply religious, some not at all. So great is the gulf between those types of humanism that are represented to the general public as alternatives to religion and those that are fundamentally religious (e.g., the Christian humanism of the Quattrocento and indeed the humanism of Socrates) that some historians of thought have even proposed different names for them. One scholar, for instance, would call the former types "hominism" to distinguish them from the other, richer, more open-minded kinds. These know no bounds, historical or geographical. Their exponents, in echoing the famous line of Terence, *homo sum: humani nil a me alienum puto* ("I am a man: nothing human is alien to me"), include religion as the deepest and most characteristically human of human concerns. (Terence was the son of a Libyan slave. He was born in Carthage about the year A.D. 185 and taken to Rome where his owner, a Roman senator, gave him a liberal education and eventually freed him, so he understood in a special way the meaning of humanism in its richest sense.) At the outset of the present book we shall similarly see the importance of distinguishing special, narrow uses of the term "gnostic" and the ancient gnosis that is at the root of all religious quests.

The place of gnosis in the Christian tradition is a complex and fascinating question. Christianity, cradled in a half-hellenized Judaism and nurtured in the cosmopolitan Mediterranean world, has in turn cradled both modern science and special forms of humanism. It claims uniqueness: the answer to all religious quests. Is the answer in any sense a gnostic answer? I think it is, and if so we may be on the verge of a theosophical renaissance in Christian thought. For, in the widest sense of the terms, theosophy and the ancient gnosis are the same.

Geddes MacGregor

I

GNOSIS AND GNOSTICISM

> *"I tell you most solemnly,*
> *we speak only about what we know*
> *and witness only to what we have seen."*
> —Jesus, *as recorded in John 3.11.*

Everyone who knows anything at all about the history of Christian thought has heard of the Gnostics who flourished in the second century of the Christian era and claimed to possess a special kind of knowledge (*gnōsis*) of the spiritual chemistry of the universe and an esoteric insight into the workings of the divine nature. These sectaries expounded wildly speculative views and indulged in fanciful and sometimes grotesque interpretations of Scripture. Some even mingled magical formulas with their teaching. (We shall look briefly, later on, at some examples of this second-century Gnosticism.) They flew the Christian banner; but churchmen, alarmed by their extravagances, dubbed them heretical. Their teaching was probably the major cause of the Church's hardening itself into an institution with a more rigid doctrinal system and a more orderly ecclesiastical structure than Christians had generally found necessary in the first century, when the organization of their society had been comparatively fluid and their attitude to doctrine more permissive. These Gnostic sects were very numerous. Scholars today might identify ten or at the most twenty of them; but Epiphanius (*c.* 315–403) reported the existence of sixty such sects.

Prominent among the opponents of these sects was Irenaeus (*c*. 130–*c*. 200), who conducted a bitter campaign against them. Historians of Western thought, including both Christians and Jews, have generally followed second-century opinion and denigrated them accordingly. Perhaps more can be said in their favor than has generally been said; yet it is difficult to see how the Church could have done otherwise than her instinct dictated, for these sectaries would have eventually destroyed Christianity, swallowing it up in the infinite ideological chaos of their own vagaries.

Unfortunately, the disrepute of these sectaries led to a denigration of *all* gnostic ideas, though there is no doubt that much that is incontestably orthodox from a Christian standpoint has a background that reflects attitudes of mind such as were the underpinnings of the outlook of the Gnostics the Church branded as heretical. To many of us, indeed, the ideas that most conspicuously derive from such roots are the most interesting, have been the most fruitful, and show greatest promise for the deepening of spirituality in our own time. The great Christian catechetical school at Alexandria, for instance, favored ideas whose roots are remarkably similar to those of the second-century sectaries, in *some* respects. This is reflected in the fact that even today those Christians who for one reason or another dislike or distrust gnostic ideas in general disapprove of the Alexandrian tradition, while those who tend to be attracted to such ideas favor the Fathers of that early Christian school.

How then are we to distinguish "the second-century Christian Gnostic sects" from "gnosticism in general"? What is the relation between them? These questions have been much discussed by scholars in recent years. I would not disguise my opinion that much of the discussion has been merely semantic. Nevertheless, important historical and theological problems do exist. They are not only important for historical specialists but of the greatest significance for the spiritual life of society today. To condemn all gnostic ideas because of the vagaries of these early Christian sectaries is, as we shall see, somewhat like repudiating conservationism because one dislikes conservative Republicans, or renouncing work because of one's distaste for the British Labour Party.

Gnōsis is a word that, in classical Greek, signified "knowledge" in the most general sense. The more special, philosophical kind of knowledge is called *epistēmē*, from which we get the modern technical term "epistemology". The adjective *gnostikos* in ancient Greek meant "good at knowing" or, as we might say, "knowledgeable" or "apt at learning". When Christian Fathers such as Clement of Alexandria and Origen used the term *gnosis*, they had no need to borrow it from the Valentinians or any other Christian Gnostic sect, or from any pagan source. It was in the Bible. Moreover, in the Septuagint (that version of the Bible translated into Greek about the middle of the third century B.C. for the benefit of Greek-speaking Jews), the word *gnōsis* took on a special meaning: not knowledge in general but the specifically religious kind of knowledge or insight such as the Hebrew prophets enjoyed. The use, however, is even more ancient. (The Hebrew word is *dahat*.) Isaiah, for instance, envisions an idyllic state of affairs in which the country is "filled with the knowledge of the Lord" (*hoti eneplēsthē he sympasa tou gnōnai ton kyrion*).[1] The Lord tells Hosea that he wants, not holocausts, but knowledge of God (*epignōsin theou ē holokautōmata*).[2] Elihu complained that Job talked without knowledge (*en agnōsia rhēmata barynea*).[3] Philo of Alexandria, a contemporary of Jesus and one of the greatest Jewish thinkers of all time, quoted the word *gnōsis* in biblical texts and frequently used it to describe a specifically religious or mystical kind of knowledge. Both the heretical Christian Gnostic sectaries and the Fathers of the Christian Church follow Philo in his dependence on the biblical use of *gnōsis*. Paul himself uses *gnōsis* in that good sense, and when Irenaeus attacks the Gnostic sectaries, what he decries is their claim to a knowledge *falsely so called*, or, as we might say, pseudo-knowledge.

The rabbis distinguished, though they did not entirely separate, two traditions: the Halakah and the Haggadah. The former consisted of biblical commentary designed to deal with legalistic issues arising from the application of biblical teaching to everyday life, while the latter, the Haggadah, treated the Bible in such a way as to present the acts of God in history as prototypes of the history of the individual man or woman. As we all know, the Jews looked forward to the coming of the messianic kingdom, and out

---

[1] Isaiah 11.9. *Gnōnai* is the second aorist infinitive of the verb *gi-gnōskō*, to know, perceive.
[2] Hosea 6.6.
[3] Job 35.16.

of the tradition of the Haggadah arose the literature we call
Jewish apocalyptic, the authors of which claim a sort of esoteric
knowledge of the working out of God's secret plan for humankind. The Christian Apocalypse or Book of Revelation is in the
tradition of that *genre* of Jewish literature.

Of course the whole history of the Jews reflects the exercise of
faith. The Hebrew people, in a way unique in the annals of
mankind, survived by faith. The anonymous Christian author of
the letter to the Hebrews affirms and celebrates that historical
fact in what Christians commonly account the biblical *locus clas-
sicus* on the subject.[4] What he commends in the great patriarchs of
old is what he would commend in the early heroes of the Christian
Way, and what, indeed, we would all commend wherever we see
the like in any people: they walked in trust, *without* knowledge of
the details of the divine plan. They trusted God, content not to
ask for reasons. We all do this to some limited extent with any
leader we truly trust, perhaps a father or a teacher or loyal friend,
and if we believe in God our trust in him must be unbounded.
Nevertheless, such faith implies a *kind* of knowledge. It is not
entirely blind, either in the case of our parents and the like or in
the case of God. When we stumble along a road in the darkness of
night we are apt to say it is "pitch" dark; yet we do see dimly
markers even in that intimidating circumstance. The gnostic
tradition that is closely associated with the Wisdom literature of
the Jews (as *gnōsis* is associated with *sophia*, wisdom), purports to
go beyond faith to knowledge, penetrating more closely even "the
mysteries of God."

For Christians, knowledge of God is a gift supremely obtaina-
ble through knowledge of Jesus Christ, in whose Person are
discoverable and in whose life are displayed even the secret treasures of God. What else, indeed, could Christians mean by calling
him "the full and final revelation of God"? If that be not gnosis,
what could be so called? Paul, in the greatest passage in all his
writings, contrasts our present imperfect knowledge with the full
knowledge that comes through *agapē*, love;[5] but in doing so he
brings out most clearly the all-important fact: the Christian Way is
nothing if not a gnosis. True, the gnosis to which Christian faith is

---

[4]Hebrews 11.

[5]I Corinthians 13.

said to lead is indeed a very special kind; yet we must conclude that Christianity, if it be of any value at all, must provide a kind of gnosis. As we shall see later, this is the *motif* of the whole Christian mystical tradition in all its extraordinarily multifaceted variety, from Evagrius Ponticus (346-399), in whom the idea of Christian gnosis probably first attained its full development, and the Pseudo-Dionysius (*fl. c.* 500), who is generally accounted the culminating point of Greek spirituality and the father of the medieval mystical tradition, being also much quoted by Thomas Aquinas, down to the Christian mystics of recent times and our contemporary age. Not only Origen but also both Gregory of Nyssa (*c.* 330 – *c.* 395) and William of St. Thierry (*c.* 1085 – *c.* 1148) see the soul going on from faith to knowledge, which William in his Latin way calls *scientia.* The symbolism of Chartres, with the *scientiae* of the *trivium* and *quadrivium* under the presidency of the Lady Philosophy, who is identified on the one hand with Holy Wisdom (*Hagia Sophia*) and on the other with the Blessed Virgin Mary, is too obvious to need exposition here. If Christian fears of mysticism and humane learning cannot be assuaged in the exquisite symbolism of Chartres, they cannot be assuaged anywhere.

The history of Christian thought, however, is peppered with warnings and protests against the dangers of the mystical tradition that has developed within the Church. No less has the Church feared the Christian humanists, who have been, not least in the Quattrocento, singularly religious in spirit and intent.[6] Antagonism to these traditions has been notable in recent centuries too. We need but note eighteenth-century contempt for the mystical element in religion and, nearer our own time, the distrust of forms of Christian humanism such as Henri Bremond called *humanisme dévot.* Such fears persist, and not only among so-called "fundamentalist Protestants." These mystical and humanistic traditions are in fact not so much rivals to the mainstream of Christian theology as complementary to it. The notion that one has access to a body of knowledge not accessible to the masses always tends to alarm and annoy some, and indeed the alarm and annoyance are often justified, since the claim is often false. Yet the fact that some bankers are embezzlers should not in itself cause us to abandon banks. The fact that many spiritistic

---

[6]I have considered the relation of such humanism to Christian faith in *The Hemlock and the Cross* (Philadelphia: Lippincott, 1963).

mediums are phony no more warrants the conclusion that all
psychical research is false than the practice of hi-jacking justifies a
belief that air travel is intrinsically evil. Much mysticism is indeed
misguided, to say the least, and much humanism vehemently
hostile to religion; but some mysticism is profoundly religious
(some of us might say it is the essence of all religious attitudes) and
no educated person who is truly steeped in the tradition of
humane learning (the liberal arts, as the medieval people called
them, because they were the arts proper to free men, contradistinguished from slaves) can honestly write off all forms of
humanism as hostile either to Christian faith or any other religious commitment worth the consideration of spiritually-minded
men and women. Some churchgoers say they see nothing salutary
or advantageous in prayer, generally because they have never
fully engaged in it; but that is no reason to stop the practices of
meditation and prayer that the masters of Christian spirituality so
earnestly commend to us and that are so much a part of all
religions, being known to all masters of spirituality to result in
infinite healing of body as well as soul, apart from anything else
they may accomplish.

The reputation of the Christian Gnostics of the second-century
has turned whole generations of people against the very word
gnōsis, as if the term were plague-infected. Even the modern term
"agnosticism" is historically a nineteenth-century protest against
gnosis. It was a neologism invented by T. H. Huxley, who tells us
how, as an undergraduate, he was reading about the second-
century Christian Gnostics and felt that, unlike them, who
seemed to claim to know everything there could ever be to know
about the universe, he knew nothing, so that the term "*a*gnostic"
would best fit in describing his mind. The term became popular
among those who felt threatened by other people's claims to
knowledge of God. It remained so till nearly the middle of the
present century, when intellectual fashion dictated that antipathy
be switched from truth-claims to meaning-claims. The vogue
among the enemies of religious thought was then changed accordingly; but gnosis is still prominent among the targets of
hatred, for it is at the core of all experience of the interior life
apart from which there could be no religion worth talking about
except, perhaps, by some anthropologists and other specialists in
primitive human behavior. So gnostic notions that are imported

into Christian thought today usually have to be bootlegged under a banner such as Jung's by way of disguising their nature.

Modern biblical and patristic scholarship, illumined by twentieth-century discoveries such as the Qumran and Nag Hammadi literatures, has become involved in disputes about what has been traditionally recognized as Gnosticism, on the one hand, and, on the other, what the Germans call *die Gnōsis*. It is abundantly plain that gnostic developments were already under way long before the second century dawned. The problem is one of distinguishing between the highly dogmatic and fanciful doctrines of the Valentinians and other Christian Gnostic sects on the one hand, and, on the other, the general climate of thought in which *die Gnōsis* was ensconced as part of the intellectual furnishings of the minds of all thoughtful people. Scholars ask: whence did that gnosis come that is to be differentiated from the traditional second-century kind that we have all been for long reading about in text books? What terminology might we profitably use to distinguish between the two phenomena?

That Jesus and Paul could no more have visited a gnostic temple or school than we could visit a Marxist or Freudian one today is clear enough. Whatever it is that has convinced us of the presence of an element clearly distinguishable from the "Christian Gnosticism" of the text books yet apparently with some common roots, it was not a structured movement or an organized religion. There is not the slightest evidence of anything of that kind. There is ample evidence, however, of a climate of thought that may be very properly called gnostic in terms of its presuppositions and its talk. Nevertheless, as soon as we say that, we naturally ask: how, then, are we to define "intellectual climate"? How can one define anything so vague? Is it not indeed so vague as to elude all definition? Is there any religious idea in the intellectual ambience of people in the time of Christ that could be called *non*-gnostic? Is it merely a term that functions in every religious system somewhat as does the term "value" in modern economic theory, specifying no school of thought, hinting at no particular stance, betraying an inclination neither to Keynes nor to Galbraith?

Rudolf Bultmann, for example, sometimes talks as though there were a definite movement in the first century that is to be called *die Gnōsis*, though he makes clear that, whatever it was, it was not a Christian growth only but had an alien ancestry, being furthermore an open rival to emerging Christianity.[7] Neither he nor any other scholar can well doubt, though some are still inclined to do so, that the ideas we have in mind and propose to label "gnostic" were widespread before the time of Christ and influential in the emergence of Christian thought. What is perhaps most in question is: were not these ideas, or at least many of them, present in, say, Stoic or Platonic thought? For example, the notion that the soul is a lonely pilgrim in a temporary body that is at once its instrument and its foe is one that, by and large, Plato adopts and expounds. Then are we to call Plato a gnostic? Surely only in the sense (ridiculously vague) in which we might call him or almost anybody else a socialist. If we call Plato a gnostic, is there any serious speculative philosopher in antiquity or in modern times whom we could not equally well so designate? As applied to any pre-Christian thinker, at least in the three centuries immediately preceding the birth of Christ, the term "gnostic" could then serve as a synonym for almost any sage, prophet or rabbinical teacher. It would be applicable to Lao-tze and Confucius, to Dante and of course Goethe, and even to Socrates who, insisting that he was the most ignorant man in Athens, said so with gnostic tongue in cheek. Plainly, we must do better than that.

Late pre-Christian Judaism, even in Palestine itself, was much penetrated with ideas from the Gentile, Hellenistic world. (As we shall observe later, there were some special reasons for this.) So the ground was already prepared in such a way that Christian thought simply could not have developed apart from the *gnōsis* in which it had its roots. Then how different was Jewish *gnōsis* from, say, the Egyptian or Greek kinds? Was it a mere adaptation, as the light Palladian architecture of Italy was modified in England in a heavier form better suited to northern skies? More importantly,

---

[7]In English the German term *die Gnōsis* is often translated "Gnosticism". In view of the pre-empted restrictiveness of this latter term as used in Christian text books, that practice leads to further confusion. I propose to adopt the convention of using upper case ("Gnosticism") to specify the movement that flourished in the second century and is dubbed a Christian heresy and by contrast lower case ("gnosticism", "gnostic", "gnosis") to denote gnostic attitudes and developments in general. In English this is practicable. In German it is not, since all German nouns take upper case.

perhaps, how widespread within Judaism were gnostic ideas? Judaism was the religion of a very particular people. Proselytes were few compared with converts to some other religions. The Jewish outlook in Palestine was culturally and in other ways different from that of neighboring peoples and Jews were dispersed all over the Mediterranean world. How then could Jewish *gnōsis* be typically Jewish? Yet if it were very atypical, how could it be so influential as to color in a special way not only Jewish thought but that of the Christianity it cradled?[8]

Perhaps we might throw some light on these questions by considering how a sociologist a thousand years hence (especially if we have the stomach to postulate an intervening nuclear holocaust) might view the beliefs of twentieth-century Christians. On the one hand, he might see the social activism that plays such a notable role in what passes for the business of the Church in so many of its assemblies today. When he inspected extant records of the parochial life of the Church, he would note, no doubt, the pot-luck suppers, the badminton evenings, the rummage sales, and the Sunday school picnics. He might garner, perhaps, leaves from our services books suggesting formalized beliefs in various seemingly supernatural entities such as the Holy Ghost and the Virgin Mary, indeterminable locations such as Heaven and Hell, and unchartable movements such as descents to Hades (which, since he would probably have read about them in Homer, would lead him still further up the garden path of scholarly puzzlement) and ascents to Heaven, which might well puzzle him even more, not least if he happened to be familiar with some of the developments in twentieth-century aeronautics. He might very well conclude from all this that the Church in the twentieth century was an odd sort of club for those not affluent enough to attend the more socially exclusive ones. But then, on the other hand, he would probably also come across, if he were diligent enough, references to some twentieth-century people's religious experiences, mystical ecstasies, and reports of their intense interest in spirituality, in

---

[8]For a study of ideas imported in Christian thought from Jewish gnosticism, *see* Oscar Cullmann, *Le Problème littéraire et historique du roman pseudo-Clémentin: Etude sur le Rapport entre le Gnosticisme et le Judéo-Christianisme* (Paris: Félix Alcan, 1930). His chapter on the writings entitled *Kērugmata Petrou* is especially interesting: "Les Prédications de Pierre et le gnosticisme juif" (pp. 170ff.).

prayer, and in the interior life. He would find hints about claims to a deeper understanding and fuller knowledge of divine things than is enjoyed by the bridge-playing, cocktail-partying, real-estate-speculating, triviality-mongering masses, and even by run-of-the-mill churchgoers. Perhaps he would simply hand the latter part of his discoveries to a colleague with religious inclinations and working in some other field, who would then conclude (against him) that a very lively form of spirituality flourished throughout the Church in the twentieth century. This colleague might even instigate scholarly inquiries into the origins of this strangely unexpected movement within the Christian Church of the twentieth century and so spawn all sorts of lively controversy among the learned. Both the sociologist and his colleague in the other field would be wrong. Yet like the blind men in the old Indian fable, they would both be, of course, partially right.

With these intimidating warnings before us, what, then, do we find? Gershom Scholem makes the point that, while certain kinds of Jewish mysticism (*e.g.*, Merkabah) are impeccable in their orthodoxy from a Jewish standpoint, not least in their strict monotheism, other gnostics who cared little or nothing for Jewish orthodoxy would borrow from such gnostic enterprises and dispense with their monotheistic flavor.[9] (The procedure is familiar in the history of ideas and may be likened to that of a cook who, in preparing a dish, takes the curry out of the recipe, which some account an improvement while others say the dish has been ruined.) If that be the case, as seems plain enough, we may expect that both the orthodox and heterodox forms of gnosis have a common ancestor.

It is likely, moreover, that the ancestry goes back far beyond any verifiable point in the history of religions, for the simple reason that it is embedded in religion itself and emerges in a primitive form, at least, as soon as religion becomes reflective. It would then assume as wide a variety of forms as there are types of religion. For if there be any *gnōsis* at all it springs from either real or pretended encounter with divine Being. Whether spurious or genuine, it is obviously going to be at least as adaptable to circumstance as have been, for example, Buddhism and Christianity in

---

[9]J. Philip Hyatt, ed., *The Bible in Modern Scholarship* (Nashville, Tenn.: Abingdon, 1965), p. 268, referring G. Scholem, *Jewish Gnosticism, Merkabah and Talmudic Tradition* (1960), 2nd.ed., (New York: Block, 1965).

their institutionalized forms. Nothing in all this determines, of course, the answer to questions about whether religions are all fundamentally "saying the same thing", as the *Religionsge-schichtlicheschule* generally supposed, or are not.

In the story of Christian mysticism and spirituality we find something similar to what Scholem describes out of his Jewish background and study. Spanish mystical literature is extraordinarily rich and diverse. At least something of it is known to most educated people through the writings of John of the Cross and Teresa of Avila: the former because of his poetic genius, the latter because of her strength of character and unusual personality. Such writers are careful not to incur the charge of pantheism (or whatever such tendencies were called before the term was invented by the deistic Irish writer, John Toland, in 1705) by using terms such as *hilo de amor* to describe how, in the soul's final union with God, God and the soul are bound together with a cord of love yet without the soul's divinization or fusion with the divine. Other writers, however, with no interest in such precautions, can easily adapt and have in fact adapted such Christian mystical literature to their own use, so traducing, however reverently and with whatever good intentions, the authors' meaning. Some may take it to be an improvement; others will regret it. Again, within the Christian tradition itself there have been mystics whose views have been suspect among the orthodox. Neither medieval Christian mystics such as the Dominican Meister Eckhart (*c.* 1260– 1327) nor later ones such as the German Lutheran Jakob Boehme (1575–1624) can be accounted orthodox from even the most permissive Christian stance; yet they are recognized as part, if on the fringe, of the Christian mystical tradition. Once again, in contrast to all such colorful forms of mysticism stands the ancient Benedictine tradition of contemplative prayer, a more restrained and sober form of Christian mysticism that Dom Cuthbert Butler felicitously insisted on calling "Western Mysticism" in contradistinction to "Mysticism in the West."[10] It is represented chiefly by Augustine (354–430), Gregory the Great (540–604), and Bernard of Clairvaux (1090–1153). In a very different vein is the Salesian tradition, which takes its name from Francis of Sales (1567–1622). Developed in seventeenth-century France, it was

---

[10]Cuthbert Butler, *Western Mysticism*, 2nd ed. with "Afterthoughts" (London: Constable, 1927).

designed as an urbane spirituality and for developing the interior life of persons following the ordinary pursuits of a cultivated, worldly society rather than those of the cloister. All of these methods have followed their own individual lines and in accordance with the customary Christian principle that discourages *seeking* a mystical goal while it encourages the welcoming of mystical insight when it comes. Each accounts itself capable of providing the *gnōsis* of God, which for any mystic is the highest bliss on earth.

Even today, not all scholars are willing to concede unequivocally the existence of a pre-Christian gnosticism, despite the innumerable pointers to such a state of affairs. For them, therefore, the questions raised in this chapter could be of no interest. Their skepticism is unsurprising. All scholarship is in its very nature cautious, and biblical scholarship perhaps more than ordinarily so, since biblical scholars are peculiarly liable to the charge of trying to squeeze opinions out of evidence that is too meager to satisfy everybody. Biblical scholars tend, therefore, to be peculiarly exacting in their demand for hard, textual evidence for what may seem to many too plain to need further demonstration. Jung expressed the opinion, shared by many hardly less eminent in the history of gnostic ideas, that "the central ideas of Christianity are rooted in gnostic philosophy."[11] Yet some scholars question whether a gnostic element is to be found even in the followers of Simon, mentioned in the Book of Acts.[12] The question seems important to them because they doubt whether even Simonianism provides evidence of the existence of a pre-Christian gnosis.

Two works that have appeared within the last decade reach opposite conclusions on the question whether Simonianism was gnostic or not. Karlmann Beyschlag thinks it has nothing to do with gnosticism.[13] Gerd Lüdemann, noting that everything in the Simonian tradition has parallels elsewhere, suggests a connection with the Helen-Ennoia figure, which he thinks was authentically gnostic, and that Helen in her original form was attractive to the

---

[11]C. G. Jung, *Psychology and Alchemy* (New York: Pantheon Books, 1953), p. 35.
[12]Acts 8.9.
[13]K. Beyschlag, *Simon Magus und die christliche Gnōsis* (Tübingen: Mohr, 1974).

Simonians because she was seen as a Pythagorean symbol of the soul fallen from the moon.[14] When two such careful scholars, both working with approximately the same materials and using much the same methods, reach such opposite conclusions, the reason is likely to be that either there is not enough evidence to justify either conclusion (in which case they should not have claimed to arrive at either) or else (which I suspect to be the case) no evidence could possibly persuade anyone to change his or her mind on this subject when it has been already made up. That is to say, the partisans may be already *for other reasons* so convinced of their position that neither is likely ever to be refuted by any kind of textual evidence.

This does not mean, of course, that either is merely prejudiced in the commonplace sense of the term. What it does mean is, rather, that their total view of, and their fundamental insight into, the question is so radically different that what appears to be the same methodology is in fact not precisely the same. If one were to start off with a positivistic outlook on science and were rigidly to adhere to it, there could be no conceivable way in which one could ever see what is obvious to anyone who did not labor under that methodological disability. If one has a more creative insight than is available to a strict positivist, there is likewise no imaginable way in which one could be "converted" to the more limited view dictated by positivistic trammels. So it is with the question before us: if the New Testament seems to you to be saturated with gnostic presuppositions prompting questions to which it purports to be providing an answer, nothing could change your view, not even the discovery of a first-century manuscript of Acts with an additional apostolic proclamation such as: "Brethren, Christ is risen indeed, thereby being the fulfilment of the limited gnosis we have all so far enjoyed and that is being abused by some." You would but set in motion yet another long and intricate but fruitless discussion. You would consider, for example, possible meanings of the term *gnōsis* as used in this imaginary text. If, however, you were already convinced, as apparently is the distinguished Dutch scholar, Arend Theodor van Leeuwen, that the presence of a gnostic element in the climate of thought in which the New Testament literature emerged is too obvious to need much dis-

---

[14]G. Lüdemann, *Untersuchungen zur simonianischen Gnōsis* (Göttingen: Vandenhoeck und Ruprecht, 1975).

cussion, then the discovery of such an imaginary text in such a hypothetical manuscript could tell you nothing you did not already know.[15] You might well feel, indeed, that your time could be put to better use than in prolonged rejoicing over the *trouvaille*. To the color-blind, even the color-sighted must always seem claimants to a sort of clairvoyance.

The more basic question, however, remains: what is the ancient gnosis, especially in the form in which it determined the presuppositions and affected the thought of the apostolic and other early Christian workers? The fact that Paul and others felt it their mission to attack some forms of it does not mean they were not also heirs to a gnostic outlook. To this question we now turn in our next chapter.

---

[15]Arend Th. van Leeuwen, *Christianity in World History: The Meeting of the Faiths of East and West* , translated by H. H. Hoskins; (New York: Scribner's, 1964), p. 138: "Wherever the apostle [Paul] opposes Greek wisdom to the wisdom of God in Jesus Christ, he is directing his polemic against Gnosticism."

II

WHAT IS GNOSIS?

He who binds his soul to knowledge,
steals the key of heaven.
—Nathaniel Parker Willis,
The Scholar of Thibèt Ben Khorat

Both the Greek terms *sophia* (wisdom) and *gnōsis* (knowledge) are used in the Bible, occurring in both the Old Testament and the New. From *sophia* we get, of course, the word "theosophy". The relation between the two terms has been discussed by scholars without definitive results. C. K. Barrett, for instance, a noted British biblical scholar, has argued that, at least within Paul's first letter to the Corinthians, *gnōsis* has to do with practical knowledge, knowledge of matters relating to morals or customs, while *sophia* relates to speculative questions. The French biblical scholar J. Héring, however, reaches exactly the opposite conclusion, aligning *sophia* with ethical teaching and *gnōsis* with metaphysical and theological questions. In Paul the two terms seem to be in fact usually interchangeable, and in the Septuagint such distinctions as may be found do not turn out to be, in the long run, fundamental. It is true that *sophia* can sometimes signify that kind of wisdom that gives the heart and mind whatever is needed for the right conduct of life.[1] More often, however, it means the highest

---

[1]E.g., I Corinthians 6.5; Acts 6.3; James 1.5.

intellectual gift, the gift that gives insight into the secret purposes of God. That is what the great Wisdom literature of the Bible is about.

Gnōsis, though it may be sometimes used in some special sense, has a fundamental significance that is so similar to *sophia* as to make any attempt to draw a radical distinction between them somewhat artificial. *Gnōsis*, like *sophia*, is what theosophical writers from time immemorial have been talking about. For all ordinary purposes, therefore, we may identify gnostology and theosophy, the theosophist and the gnostic. Nevertheless, we must at no time forget that besides the broad, general use in which they are synonymous, both terms have also been used to designate special movements. Theosophists would be among the first to perceive such a distinction between, say, the nineteenth-century movement initiated by H. P. Blavatsky and others, on the one hand and, on the other, theosophy as an ageless pursuit. As many philosophers were pantheists centuries before the term "pantheism" was invented by John Toland in 1705, so of course ancient sages in India and Egypt and Greece were theosophists thousands of years before anybody ever used the term. We have seen, and we shall see again, that much the same is the case with gnosticism. Our principal concern in this study, however, will be with the wider use of these terms. If we were to say, for example, as well we might, that Clement of Alexandria is more gnostic than, say, Clement of Rome, we could equally well say he was more theosophical. So closely are the terms related in the history of ideas.

We have seen that a sharp distinction must be drawn between the teachings of the second-century Gnostic sects that churchmen feared so much and the *gnōsis* that is not only a fundamental and perennial category in the history of religions but a familiar concept in the literature of the Judaism in which Christianity was cradled. We must now try to see what specific content is to be given to that term *gnōsis*, so as to avoid its becoming too vague to have any useful meaning.

First we should recall the battle-cry of Tertullian (*c.* 160–*c.* 220): *Quid Athenae Hierosolymis?* "What has Athens to do with Jerusalem?" As we might put the question today: "What has 'secular' philosophy to do with the Bible and the Church?" This question of Tertullian's spawned a controversy that became classic in Christian tradition. Its interest for us here lies primarily in the fact that it may presuppose the currency of that claim to *gnōsis* that is familiar to us in the writings of the Alexandrians and other early Christian literature, including indeed the New Testament itself.

Tertullian, influenced as he was by the Montanist view also current in his time, with its pentecostalist emphasis, stressed the irrational element in Christian faith. Why do I believe the claims the Gospels make, attesting that Jesus Christ is the answer to all religious quests? Why do I accept the testimony of the early Church that he is the unique Son of God, the full and final revelation of God to humankind? Tertullian answers: *credo quia impossibile*, "I believe because it is impossible"; *credo quia ineptum*, "I believe because it is absurd." By this paradox he meant that the central doctrines of the Christian faith are too astonishing, too humanly inconceivable to have been fabricated by some professional religion-monger eager to make a name for himself by concocting a new religious system, for they are much too far-fetched, much too incredible to human reason and remote from human expectation. They come as a complete surprise, and their surprising character is their very self-authentication. The importance of this insight, not only in Christianity but in other religions too, cannot well be exaggerated. It has played a crucial role in much of the most deeply Christian thinking throughout the ages, not least in that of Blaise Pascal (1623–1662) and of that other extraordinary religious genius, Søren Aaby Kierkegaard (1813–1855). No doubt it has no less an important future. Nevertheless, it is by no means the last word in Christianity, as Kierkegaard himself presumably recognized when he called himself a "corrective". It is only an aspect, only an ingredient, however important.

Recognition of the importance of the concept of gnosis for Christians comes early. Clement of Alexandria (*c*. 150–*c*. 215) specifically notes that Paul himself does not entirely despise the gnosis that Hellenistic philosophy provides, though he deems it to be only an introduction to the higher gnosis of the Christian Way. Philosophy teaches only "the elementary doctrine"; the true gnostic, "having grown old in the Scriptures," is he who has attained that deeper gnosis that comes through *agapē*, love, the fundamental principle of the Christian life.[2] What is wrong with people like the Christian sectaries of the second century is not that they talk of *gnōsis* rather than *pistis*, faith; it is, rather, that they pretend to a knowledge they do not possess, a knowledge to which they have not even come near reaching. We might put this into modern language as follows: they are like students who call themselves "advanced" because, though they cannot yet spell English properly, they have dabbled in learned disquisitions on Coleridge and Shakespeare, or, never having mastered the multiplication table, they have picked up something of the vocabulary of calculus and they parade their superficial knowledge as if they were great mathematicians.

This better perspective on gnosis was eventually transmitted to Western Christian thought in Augustine's perception that faith *by its very nature* seeks understanding, a notion echoed centuries later in Anselm's (*c.* 1053–1109) celebrated phrase *credo ut intelligam*: "I believe in order that I may understand." Augustine, during his life before his conversion, had been for nearly a decade a devotee of the Manichees, then a fashionable philosophy of the day with many gnostic elements in it. Augustine, after his conversion, claimed to perceive that it made exaggerated promises of gnosis (*scientia*).[3] Now he saw the necessity of faith; but he also saw faith as the necessary introduction to genuine gnosis. Faith, as the Alexandrians had seen, is an indispensable ingredient in the process of attaining knowledge of God and, more especially, in acquiring the ability (so important in a Christian diagnostician!) of discerning true gnosis from false. Faith is the basis of all human life. Whether we call ourselves "religious" or not, we walk by faith in something or other. Faith, then, is totally indispensable to the seeker after the divine. The Christian has found that the secrets of God are given in scriptural revelation, secrets undiscoverable to human reasons alone. This

---

[2]Clement, *Stromateis*, 7. Clement put forward a "true *gnosis*" against the "false *gnōsis*" of the heretics. He called his perfected Christian "the gnostic" and denied to the heretics the right to the name. Cf. E. F. Osborn, *The Philosophy of Clement of Alexandria* (Cambridge: Cambridge University Press, 1957), p. 14.

[3]*Confessions*, 6.5.

is by no means a notion peculiar to Christianity; but it does play a very important role in all intelligent Christian thinking. We must listen humbly, in awe and with love, to what is revealed to us by God, believing with all our hearts and minds what he is saying when he speaks to us so clearly and dramatically through his Word, if we are to make any headway in the gnosis of the Lord.

Faith is, then, as a later school of theologians would have put it, the correlative of revelation. This is reflected in the liturgical interchange of versicle and response. "Christ is risen," proclaims the priest, announcing the affirmation of the Word; "He is risen indeed," respond the faithful, as faith's attestation to the revelatory Word. Yet faith is no more the end of the story than the hypothesis is the end of the scientific inquiry, indispensable as are both in their respective domains. *Pistis* seeks *gnōsis*; faith seeks understanding. What is wrong with those who make false claims to gnosis when in fact they know little or nothing of the mysteries of the divine nature is that they have been too proud to walk in the first instance in the way of faith. It is a common disease: children want to run before they can walk. We must not pretend. We must be patient and humble enough to walk in faith. Kierkegaard's "knight of faith" is indeed the very paradigm of all Christian living. To affect the possession of gnosis when one has never known the agony and the joy, the loneliness and the assurance, of walking humbly in the darkness, each step lighted by only a feeble little lamp of faith, is as odious as it is futile. It might even be called (Kierkegaard would be ready to do so) the height of irreligion, worse even than gross unbelief. It is like saying "of course" instead of "thank you."

Still, faith cannot be an end in itself. It is a disposition, an expression of love and trust. The whole value of my faith lies in the fact that it opens up to me the way to a genuine knowledge of God, a gnosis that would otherwise have remained closed to me. Through faith in my teacher I learn not merely the informative lesson he has to teach me; I learn to know *him* and *what it means to be he*. Through faith in my mother I learn not only whatever she has to tell me; I learn to know her as she is in herself and what her motherhood means, *not to me, but to her*. Through faith in God I learn to know the very nature of God, at least in respect of his relationship to me, and the knowledge of the ways of God to man evokes awe and love such as I have never known in all my seeking.

In short, faith and knowledge, *pistis* and *gnōsis*, traditionally contrasted as though they were two virtually incompatible approaches to God, are, on the contrary, two aspects of the same cognitive process. As soon as I humbly accept the revelation of God that is given to me, I already, by its light, see dimly something of the divine secret. I already see something of the suffering of God before I know the depths of my own suffering. I already understand tragedy before it touches my own life. I know, as I knew, in however feeble a way, something of the nature of my mother when I was so young and so feeble as to be able only to grasp at her for sustenance and protection. As I walk in faith, however, the prospect enlarges. I do not know where precisely I am being led; yet that is the beginning of true gnosis. The exercise of my faith is like the exercise of my mind: it leads me to understand what it is to be a consciousness. It teaches me that self-knowledge that leads to gnosis of God. The boy or girl in the school laboratory who makes halting first steps in conducting a scientific investigation, under the teacher's eye and without much maturity of understanding of what is going on, has already begun to grasp the nature of the universe better than someone who leisurely reads clever little articles about space in popular science magazines. Authentic faith results in authentic gnosis of God.

We have been considering, so far, faith and *gnōsis* as elements in all developed forms of religion, and we have recognized the unique roles they have played in the biblical thought undergirding all Christian experience. Where the emphasis on faith becomes so strong as to be, or at least to seem to be, distorted, we may conveniently speak of a fideistic type of Christianity, notwithstanding the fact that the term "fideism" may seem to have been pre-empted for a special, restricted use in comparatively recent theological debate. (I have in mind here French Protestant theologians such as Auguste Sabatier (1838–1921), whose thought is in the tradition of Kant and Schleiermacher.) Likewise we may claim the right to speak similarly of a gnostic type of Christianity wherever we discover a strong emphasis on claims to mystical or other kinds of knowledge of God. For many, however, that would be far too broad a usage to qualify for gnosticism in even the widest sense they would allow.

Among notable scholars who insist that gnosticism, however loosely or restrictively defined, can never be a mere syncretism, is

Hans Jonas,[4] who writes: "A Gnosticism without a fallen god, without benighted creator and sinister creation, without alien soul, cosmic captivity and acosmic salvation, without the self-redeeming of the Deity—in short, a Gnosis without divine tragedy will not meet specification."[5] Jonas is referring, of course, to doctrines such as that of the Demiurge and the alienation of the cosmos from the divine. Such doctrines are typical of the forms of gnosticism most familiar to us in text books of Christian Church history.

In fact, of course, much if not all of even that spectrum of gnostic ideas is obviously quite prominent in canonical Christian Scripture; for example in the antithesis that Jesus makes between his Father and "the Prince of this world." Indeed, in the Christian baptismal formula, still in use wherever ancient liturgical treasure has not been completely destroyed by ignorant minds and imprudent hands, the candidate renounces the world and the flesh along with "the Devil." Surely these ideas are a development (healthy or otherwise as we may be inclined to suppose) of basic elements in the wider history of religious ideas. So basic are they, indeed, to all spirituality that apart from them religion degenerates into a rather poor joke. Were there no tension at all between the forces of good and evil, what function could religion have? There would be no need for any doctrine of the fall, or of any fall, cosmic or otherwise, and certainly no need for salvation.

The metaphysical dualism that is such a widespread outlook in the history of religions can hardly be said to be a surprising way of looking at things, as things first appear to ordinary men and women faced with the contrast between the realities of daily living and their emerging ideals. A primitive African tribe has entertained the belief that, while God made the world perfectly, he has, unfortunately, a half-witted brother who goes around in his footsteps messing everything up. Nor can we deny that this is the way the world often looks. We need not be astonished, therefore, to find that established in even the most orthodox thought, Jewish and Christian, is at least a modified dualism: Lucifer (Satan, the Devil, the Evil One) stands in opposition to God much

---

[4]Hans Jonas, *The Gnostic Religion* (Boston: Beacon, 1963).
[5]J. P. Hyatt, ed., *The Bible in Modern Scholarship* (Nashville, Tenn.: Abingdon, 1965), p. 293.

as does the evil spirit Angra Mainyu to Ahura Mazda in Zoroas-
trian thought. Though, in traditional Christianity, God, as Pantokrator, is represented to be in full control of the situation, he
gives Satan a considerable rope, and with him, of course, the
hordes of *daimones* and other evil powers (*dynameis*) who war
against Michael and the other good angels that are on God's side.
(Why God, being omnipotent, does not work with a tighter rein
on these demonic forces is a classic problem for theism and is
nowadays generally called, for short, the problem of evil.) The
world, enslaved as it is to these evil powers, must be redeemed. All
this is in the most orthodox traditions of Christian thought and
has played a notable role in popular Christian life and worship
throughout the ages. It is in line with a very ancient gnostic
tradition.

Such ideas, however, can be and have been developed in various ways. Exponents of one type of gnostic development are
often extremely hostile to exponents of other types that look, at
least superficially, very similar. Hostility of this kind is common in
all human activities, not least religious ones. Family feuds are the
most bitter of all quarrels. Controversy is often most fierce among
traditions that seem to have the closest ideological ties. It is unlikely that, say, a Baptist and a Greek Orthodox Christian would
have any very significant occasion for quarrel. They are too far
apart in their understanding of their common Christian heritage.
Among two Baptist sects, however, hostility can be very sharp
indeed, as it can be also between one exarchy of Eastern Orthodoxy and another. Again, to the casual outsider, Rome and
Constantinople look so close in ethos that one may wonder why
they should ever have quarrelled at all; yet the schism between
them is very deep and in fact far more ancient than the official
date, 1054. Indeed, from the standpoint of, say, an Athonite
monk with little knowledge of the West, Rome and Geneva are
easily bundled together in his thought as "Western" and therefore more or less in the same condemnation. So those who are
most seemingly allied through an interest in gnostic ideas are
likely to be most sharply critical the one of the other. Were it
otherwise, gnosticism would be too vacuous to be the occasion of
critical discussion.

What Christians and Jews deemed odious in the kind of Gnosticism Paul decried was its arrogant pretentiousness. The Israelite

"knew with the heart." Hebrew has no word that corresponds
exactly with "intellect" and "mind". In Hebrew, "to know" is "to
experience" and the New Testament writers understand *gnōsis*
almost entirely in Old Testament terms. In primitive modes of
conceptualization "to know" is "to feel" or "to understand
through intimate feeling" as when it is used, for example, of
sexual intercourse: "to know a man" or "to know a woman" is a
euphemism for sexual intercourse.[6] To make known is to cause
another person to experience.[7] This usage lies behind theological
uses of *gnōsis*: one knows the saving deeds of Yahweh through
experiencing them and by acknowledging that he is the doer of
these deeds.[8] So in the New Testament, "to know" is to accept
commands by obedience, to accept the will of God and to obey.[9]
The enemies of Christ will know how he loves the faithful when
they experience his vengeance.[10] To know "even as one is known"
is that mutual knowledge between God and the believer, in which
one accepts God with the same unreserve as God accepts the
believer.[11] In the Johannine writings the experiential character of
knowledge is dramatized even more: knowledge and love grow
together and are interdependent. They mutually enrich one
another.[12] To know God *is* eternal life.[13] John also associates
knowledge with faith.[14] Against all this is set the arrogance of
merely intellectual pretention to the knowledge of the divine:
how can one profess to know the divine on the same terms as one
knows the theorem of Pythagoras, the number of angles in a
triangle, or the best time to plant pansies? That would be like
trying to put my knowledge of my mother or my wife on the same
level as my knowledge of the Dow Jones Average for today or the
weather forecast for tomorrow.

---

[6]E.g., Genesis 4.1, 17, 25; Numbers 31.18, 35; Judges 21.12 ff.
[7]E.g., Psalms 77.15; 98.2; 106.8.
[8]Deuteronomy 11.2; 8.5; 29.5; 1 Maccabees 4.11; Sirach 36.4; Isaiah
41.20; 43.10; Hosea 11.3; Micah 6.5.
[9]Luke, 19.42, 44; Romans 10.19; Acts 22.14; Colossians 1.9.
[10]Revelation 3.9.
[11]I Corinthians 13.12.
[12]I John 4.7f., 16, 20; 2.3ff.; 3.6.
[13]John 17.3.
[14]John 6.69; 8.31f.; 10.38; 16.30; I John 2.13 f., 21; 5.20.

Gnosis of God is unique because God is unique. I cannot assimilate God as I can hope, if I am fairly intelligent, to assimilate facts about geology and chemistry. Why? Kierkegaard, in his dramatic way, provides the awesome answer: God is "pure subjectivity." By that he does not mean that God is only a subjective experience. He means God is confronting me, judging me, as the objects of my studies in chemistry and geology are not. My hope of understanding him is nil unless (a) he first deigns to reveal himself to me and (b) I approach him in that humble faith that is the only effective prelude to *this* kind of knowledge, that is, knowledge of the divine.

Christianity is not the only religion to recognize this peculiarity about knowledge of the divine; but by its very nature it recognizes it in a very definite way. That is why Paul and others who proclaim the Christian Gospel out of the background of their Hebrew heritage are so severe in their denunciation of the "false gnosis", the gnosis they see as empty of faith and love. Such pseudo-knowledge, they are saying, in effect, is as unlike authentic gnosis of God as is a science-fiction -reading whiz-kid's understanding of nature unlike that of a trained and experienced scientist. Faith and love are as indispensable to gnosis of God as are scientific method and scientific experiment to the understanding of science. All religions, however, recognize in one way or another that "knowledge of God" can be spurious as well as authentic. Faith, too, can be spurious, of course, and surely one need but read a little of the history of Western civilization to learn that much of what purports to be Christian love can be as remote from *agapē* as ever could have been the second-century Gnostics from gnosis.

All the great religions recognize, moreover, each in its own way, that true knowledge of God is attained through what may usefully be called "getting the feel of God." By that I do not at all mean that religion is simply a matter of feeling. I mean, rather, that one can know God only through confrontation, as one knows nature only through direct exposure to its effects. John Macmurray used to tell a story that illustrates the point. He wanted to learn to ice-skate, so in typical academic fashion he took out of the university library a number of first-class books on the subject. He carefully read them over the course of several months. Eventually he donned his skates, moved on to the ice and within seconds fell flat on his face. A fellow-skater picked him up and said reassuringly: "You must get the *feel* of it. Then you'll skate very well." This is obviously true of sailing, skiing, flying, and even driving a car or riding a bicycle.

Primitive peoples often have a sensitivity to nature that most of us have long lost. They have made friends with nature even to the point, not surprisingly, of worshipping it. In some ways they may be said to know nature better than do physicists or biologists as such. Never having seen a Bunsen burner or a burette, never having dissected a frog or tested the specific gravity of water, they understand and cope with nature in all the manifold guises that come habitually within the range of their experience. Similarly, men and women who have never heard of psychology have coped with people far more ably and successfully than professionally trained psychologists are ever likely to do. We may call such expertise, if we like, instinctual; but if it be instinct it is an instinct very different from the kind we attribute to dogs and cats, for it is highly informed through a very special and a very specifically human experience. It is a higher kind of consciousness that brings with it an authentic gnosis of nature or of people as the case may be. We may go so far as to say that no one who resented nature or despised people could be able to make any headway in genuine knowledge of nature or people respectively. If we are "to get the best out of people," we must approach them with a certain degree of openness and trust, risking disappointment and failure at every step. We can no more get to understand people through hostility toward them than a lion-tamer can control beasts toward whom he shows fear. Only through certain attitudes can one remain master of such situations.

From all this the importance of attitude in our quest for the divine should not be difficult to see. Even the slightest pretentiousness in our talk of the divine immediately raises an insuperable obstacle to our real knowledge of God. Thomas Aquinas, greatest of all medieval Christian thinkers, is said to have declared, toward the end of his life, that he had learned more "at the foot of the Cross" than in all his study of books. That did not mean that he, of all people, disparaged learning. It meant, rather, that the least suggestion, half-conscious though it be, that we are being clever in our "handling" of theological questions is ruinous in the development of any relationship that might ever lead to any genuine gnosis of God. Thomas, scholastic philosopher *par excellence* though he was, was also mystic enough to understand this fundamental truth about all religion.

Kierkegaard, in his very different way, asks us in one of his many satirical parables, to imagine a global war (such as had never yet occurred in the nineteenth century in which he lived), on account of which Europe's rulers jointly issued a rescript commanding all priests and other clergy to engage in a massive, *official* supplication of heaven. A prodigious exhibition of worship is arranged, with a choir of a hundred thousand professional musicians and a vast team of a million clergy all bawling for all their worth till the noise (Kierkegaard mischievously suggests) must surely have penetrated the heavenly gates. God, however, is not in the least interested and certainly not at all moved by all this official hubbub, knowing as he does that such official demonstrations are merely elaborate ceremonious insults. Yet when a poor man hobbling down Main Street sighs to God in the sincerity of his heart, *that* concerns God indescribably and moves him subjectively. That is most certainly, then, the way to gnosis of God, as all the great sages and prophets from the earliest times have seen, however dimly, each in his own way. It is what some of the mystics have called "walking with God as a friend."

While this gnostic and mystical element is to be found in all developed religions, it is by no means to be so identified with the religious consciousness as to deprive it of all specific meaning. On the contrary, many elements contribute to the complex phenomenon we call religion (ritualistic, legalistic, emotional, ethical and theological, for example) that do not at all necessarily lead to the kind of knowledge of the divine that we have been considering here. So indeed there are plenty of non-gnostic elements in all religions; yet at the same time of course we can see gnostic elements in Plato and the Stoics as well as in Amos and Jeremiah, to say nothing for the moment of the vast gnostic elements in the religions of Asia.

Gnosis, like all that is precious, has many imitators and the imitations take many forms. If we allow that the second-century sectaries represented a deviant form of gnosticism, I think we should also be prepared to recognize that what they were trying to do was not *entirely* misguided. At any rate, however we esteem them, the restriction of the term "gnosticism" to them, with perhaps some extensions of it to movements that seem to have anticipated some of their special tenets, would seem to be as unwarranted and as methodologically futile as confining the term "mysticism", for instance, to, say, twentieth-century Zen or the

Spanish mystics of the sixteenth-century Renaissance. The use of the wider understanding of the term that I am proposing in no way diminishes, of course, the importance of such scholarly evidence as may point to the existence of a form of gnosticism about the time of Christ that may be properly considered the lineal ancestor of the second-century outgrowths that have brought genuine gnostic quests and attainments into popular disrepute. Gnosis remains, whether in its mystical or in any other forms, at the heart of all religious awareness and of all spirituality. Surely it is at the center of the Judaeo-Christian tradition in its adoring awe and loving worship of him who desires of his people, as one of the Hebrew prophets declared eight centuries before Christ, "the knowledge of God (*epignōsin theou*) more than burnt offerings."[15]

---

[15]Hosea 6.6.

III

SPECIAL PROBLEMS
IN DEFINITION

Hold thou the good: define it well:
For fear divine Philosophy
Should push beyond her mark, and be
Procuress to the Lords of Hell.
—Tennyson, *In Memoriam*

We have seen that the ancient gnosis has taken many forms, so that we need not be put off by those that seem too weird or too extravagant to command our respect or even elicit our interest. After all, weirdness, hypocrisy and fraud occur in lush profusion in all forms of religion. Corruption in religion is so widespread that it provides no clue at all to the truth or falsity of one form over another. Its occurrence, therefore, in expressions of the ancient gnosis, whether in Christianity or elsewhere, says no more for or against a gnostic outlook than it says for or against religion at large. Since we all know that exponents of the most impeccable orthodoxies have been sometimes notable scoundrels and often as culpably stupid as they are wicked, we have no cause for surprise, to say nothing of righteous indignation, if the ancient gnosis should spawn, as indeed it always has and presumably always shall spawn, a vast array of charlatans.

We have also seen at the outset of our study the fundamental importance of distinguishing the ancient gnosis from the tenets of the Christian Gnostic sectaries. We have learned that we are not to expect to find in all gnosticism features that are accidental to some expressions of it. While we know that certain doctrines (mind-matter dualism and the demiurge, for instance) seem to be characteristic of the forms of gnosis with which historians of Christian thought have been for long familiar, we must question whether even such characteristics are so essential as to warrant our excluding as non-gnostic all attitudes in which such ingredients are not conspicuous.

Most scholars, however, naturally do insist on specifying certain definite characteristics as qualifying for the gnostic label. Very difficult problems indubitably remain. Were they but problems of a purely technical sort we might well ignore them in the present study and leave them to textual experts and other specialists. Since they are in fact of much practical importance in applying the basic premises I have proposed to the interpretation of any document one might wish to test for gnostic elements, we cannot ignore these problems.

Those scholars who are not disposed to rule out entirely the existence of a Jewish or pagan pre-Christian gnosticism yet (being jealous of the uniqueness of the Christian claim) are disinclined to concede that ancient gnostic attitudes influenced the rise of Christianity in any fundamental way, may nevertheless go so far as to admit that some form of gnosticism must have antedated, at any rate, the Johannine Gospel. This is the cautious position taken, for example, by a Scottish scholar, Professor R. McLachlan Wilson.[1] Even this much he concedes reluctantly and only after sympathetically reporting C. K. Barrett's view that even John the Evangelist is not a gnostic at all. Wilson admits, however, that because of John's terminology a problem remains. This admission conforms to his recognition of "a sense, a broad and comprehensive sense, in which John *can* be called 'Gnostic'."[2] Elsewhere, however, he seems to have inclined to concur in the view of some of the older scholars in this field who thought Christian Gnosticism to have arisen as an "attempt to express Christianity in Hellenistic terms, without the safeguards which Paul and his fellow-laborers imposed upon their work. Speculations of a Gnostic type, as has been said, were already current before Christianity appeared on the scene, and there were in later

---

[1]R. McL. Wilson, *Gnosis and the New Testament* (Philadelphia: Fortress Press, 1968), p. 48.
[2]*Ibid*, p. 47.

days pagan systems closely akin to the Christian Gnosis."[3] By
contrast we may note here the remarks of Professor James M.
Robinson in his introduction to the edition of the Nag Hammadi
library of which he is the general editor. After noting "the long-
standing debate among historians of religion as to whether Gnosticism is to be understood as only an inner-Christian development
or as a movement broader than, and hence independent of, and
perhaps even prior to Christianity," he goes on to state specifically: "This debate seems to be resolving itself, on the basis of the
Nag Hammadi library, in favor of understanding Gnosticism as a
much broader phenomenon than early Christian heresy-hunters
would lead one to think."[4]

The discovery of the Qumran scrolls some decades earlier was
attended by much interest in view of the likelihood felt by some
that these manuscripts would tell us of a gnosticism with plainly
pre-Christian roots; yet while some (e.g., K. Schubert) saw certain
passages in the *Manual of Discipline* as proof of a pre-Christian
Jewish gnosticism,[5] others (e.g., H. J. Schoeps and K. C. Kuhn)
who had been at first inclined to see a pre-Christian Jewish
gnosticism in the Qumran literature, altered their position, now
preferring to view the Qumran documents as evidence of mere
syncretism and to go on to observe that syncretism is not at all the
same as gnosticism. Schubert, too, had second thoughts, seeing in
Qumran an ethical dualism and an eschatological concern that
were in his opinion in marked contrast to the metaphysical
dualism of the gnostics.

The demand for a clear distinction between gnosticism and
syncretism must not go unheeded. The syncretist is a mere collector of religious ideas. He pastes them together as one pastes
interesting newspaper clippings in a scrap book. In such a miscellany there need be no governing theme, indeed not even a common motif, unless it be one that a psychoanalyst might unearth
out of the compiler's psyche. The syncretist gathers religious
ideas as a lover of butterflies gathers specimens for his collection.
"See here," he says to his admiring friends, "see what I got
yesterday. Isn't he a beauty? Have you ever seen anything quite

[3]Wilson, *The Gnostic Problem* (London: Mowbray, 1958), p. 68.
[4]James M. Robinson, ed., *The Nag Hammadi Library in English* (San Fran-
cisco: Harper and Row, 1977), p. 6.
[5]*Manual of Discipline* iii.13 - iv. 28.

like it?" Then someone may perhaps suggest that the one the
collector acquired the previous August was even more gorgeous,
evoking the collector's retort that it belonged to a different
species, so that its beauty was of a correspondingly different kind.
That is how the syncretist deals with religious ideas. "I've found a
tribe," he tells his friends, with the air of a collector, "that has
definite cultic practices yet no place for anything such as prayer."
If he is more than an anthropologist he may even suggest to his
co-religionists the idea of setting aside a day on which ritual is
performed, psalms and hymns sung, but prayers forbidden.

Unless the syncretist is a *mere* idea-collector, however, he is not
content to go on simply filling scrap books. He wishes to weave
them into a pattern, perhaps somewhat like that of a huge tapes-
try or Persian rug. Yet he has no principle to guide him in his
weaving. "Whatever are we going to do with the Eskimo's
Torngarsuk?" he muses. "He's an interesting character, a sort of
devil-god. I'd hate to lose him." Then he will perhaps be able with
some ingenuity to find a niche for Torngarsuk, dangling him
from Lucifer's tail, with a bodhisattva glancing compassionately
toward the Sufi dervish who is whirling around the diabolical
cluster. The syncretist could go on like this for ever and sometimes seems inclined to do so, because he is really somewhat like
the child in the nursery who amuses himself by cutting off the
heads of Bluebeard and Little Bo-peep and transposing them to
the other bodies. It is a childish pastime that may be psychologi-
cally beneficial at a certain stage of early childhood; but it is not to
be confused with the imaginative activity that develops later and is
the special gift of the poet and artist. The poet or novelist does not
do just whatever he pleases, as does the child in the nursery. He
has to express a motif, a theme. He does not (unless he is a bad
poet or novelist) simply sit back and let his ideas freely drift forth
in arbitrary association with one another. He organizes them
according to a principle. Syncretism is very properly denigrated
because the syncretist does not organize his ideas or at any rate
does not do so well.

The ancient gnosis that I would call the perennial gnosticism
does have a motif, a theme, a principle that governs the judg-
ments the gnostic makes and that gnostics have always made
about religious ideas, practices and beliefs. Gnosticism indeed
constitutes a specific understanding of what religion is about, and
the ancient gnosis that this understanding is called is perennially

(though by no means always consistently or well) expressed in gnostic movements and tendencies from the dawn of the recorded history of religions down to the present day. It is closely allied to the mystical element in religion. It is by no means equally distributed throughout religion, nor do all religions have a unity that justifies our saying that they are all affirming the same thing. That is where the now unfashionable *Religionsgeschichtlicheschule* that flourished about the turn of the century was in error. The variations to be found in religions are not, as members of that school tended to suppose, merely different ways of doing the same thing, as clothes are different ways of covering up the human body to protect it from climate and adorn it for purposes such as sexual courtship. They are, on the contrary, often different postures, as different as is a totalitarian view of the function of the State different from a democratic or oligarchical one. Before we can fully appreciate, however, the specificity of the ancient gnosis, we must first detach from the term "gnosticism" the accidental connotations with which it has been saddled. These are not confined to the vagaries of the second-century Christian sectaries but are found even in the attitudes that some contemporary scholars specify as constitutive of gnosticism.

The writers who most insistently make such demands include those who exhibit the extraordinary reluctance to acknowledge the existence of pre-Christian forms of gnosticism, Jewish or pagan, that we have noted earlier in the present chapter. They shelter behind a scholarly insistence, admirable in principle, on hard textual evidence. They repeatedly concede the existence of various forms of religion that emphasize gnosis yet affirm that these have nothing to do with gnosticism and do not show that gnostic ways of thought had any important bearing on the thought-patterns of the early Christian writers. As we have already seen in this chapter, they will admit, for example, a *kind* of dualism, but then they will say it is not the kind that qualifies as gnostic. In view of the focus that is to be found so much in the history of religion on the quest for knowledge of the divine nature, one wonders whether *any* evidence could ever force them to concede the existence of a pre-Christian gnosis apart from which Christianity could not be properly understood. Simone Pétrement, for instance, says that texts proving the existence of a pre-Christian pagan gnosticism not only have always been lacking *but always shall be lacking.*[6] How could she or anyone else possibly know this?

We must surely ask a more pointed question still. What is it that so many Christian scholars fear in the suggestion of pre-Christian forms of gnosticism, Jewish or pagan? In all cases I can envision the answer seems to be: injury to the uniqueness of Christianity. Of course that is not a consideration that genuine scholarship can allow, understandable though it be in those who claim, as do I, to be Christian. In due course, therefore, I shall show that on the view I take, the debt of Christianity to the ancient gnosis does not at all injure the proper claim of Christianity to uniqueness. On the contrary, the uniqueness of Christianity cannot be fully appreciated without an acknowledgement of that debt.

Many writers refer, however, to something such as a "vague gnosis" that runs through the history of religions, though they are so fearful of falling into the trap of the old History of Religions school (a trap one should have thought by now thoroughly covered by safeguards) that they say interest in gnosis must be distinguished from gnosticism, whether of the second or any earlier century.

I would toy at this point with a fanciful situation that might help us to see what is at issue. Suppose that for some reason people had grown so accustomed to identifying with Calvinism what we now so vaguely call "Protestantism" that they simply assumed Protestantism to have emerged in Geneva in the sixteenth century as a fundamentally new movement in Christianity. Let us suppose, further, that scholars were not unaware of similar earlier movements, including those led by Wyclif, Huss and Luther. By professional convention, however, they had come to treat such earlier references to the need for reform as having only a distant, not at all an essential, connection with Geneva and the rise of "the Protestant faith." (All this is, of course, a ludicrous perversion of history.) Ordinary people would pay little attention to the scholars' researches; but when they did the scholars would assure them that though these seeming precursors of Protestantism before the time of Calvin did seem to use some of the language of Protestantism, one could very easily show that they were not really talking

---

[6]S. Pétrement, "La notion de gnosticisme", in *Revue de Métaphysique et de Morale*, LXV, 1960, p. 389.

about the same thing at all. Far from it. They did not properly appreciate, for example, the nature of grace and predestination as Calvin expounded these dogmas, though they used the words. They talked of parishes, too; but it was not the Genevan model they had in mind, so they were not really talking about parishes at all. They would point, perhaps with an air of triumph, to the indisputable fact that Lutherans do not like to be called Protestant, so how could their kind of activity, whatever it was, be related to either the Reformation or the seventeenth-century aberrations it was later to spawn? At any rate, if there were a connection it must be a tenuous one.

Then, on the other hand, a century or so after Calvin, there had been another movement that historians call Puritanism. This movement, scholars might argue, must have developed out of a false interpretation of Calvin's teaching. It splintered into numerous sects with grotesque deformations of the authentic Calvinist teaching. Some of the more indefatigable scholars might postulate some connection with the earlier, pre-Calvinist movements, such as the Waldensians and the Anabaptists, but they would do so timidly and in face of vehement opposition from their colleagues, who would point out the slimness of the evidence and the paucity of the corroborative texts. Reform "in general" must not be confused with "the Reformation", which, they would assert, could be clearly dated from the middle of the sixteenth century at Geneva.

Lest some think the analogy too far-fetched to be useful, I assure them that it is only minimally a caricature of attitudes; I have discovered in some of the hardier Calvinists I have known, whose misunderstanding would have shocked Calvin as much as the rest of us. What is wrong with them is not mere narrow-mindedness; nor are they to be charged with dishonesty. It is simply that they have failed to recognize two fundamental facts: (1) that reform is a perennial as well as an essential activity in all religion and (2) that it is expressed in a wide variety of forms, some violent and arrogant, others gentle and persuasive, others again resolute and practically effective. The ancient gnosis is likewise not only a constant feature of all authentic religion that has developed beyond a very primitive stage in human history; it is the very essence of all enduring religion, though it expresses itself in so many different forms, some pure and exhilarating, others vicious, fraudulent and even cruel. All expressions of the ancient gnosis are therefore connected. If the claims of Christianity to uniqueness are unjustified, then whatever gnosis it expresses is a false gnosis. If Christians are justified in claiming the uniqueness they do claim for their faith (in which I concur), it is because of the unique gnostic *answer* Christianity claims to give to the ancient gnostic quest. Christianity, I would contend, can no more be understood apart from the ancient gnostic quest that lies behind it than bacteriology can be understood apart from the history of medicine that antedated its emergence.

Contrary to what one might argue, that is *not* to say nothing about gnosticism. An historian of any discipline may plot its beginnings where he chooses. In the history of medicine, for instance, one might well contend that Hippocrates has nothing to do with medicine as understood and practiced today, which begins with some comparatively recent figure such as Pasteur. So also modern logicians might well say (some virtually do say) that since Aristotle's logic is too primitive to be worthy of the name, and other systems such as Mill's and Bosanquet's are quite outmoded, we must put the beginnings of logic as we know it today somewhere about the beginning of the present century. So one may say that gnosticism *as one wishes to circumscribe it* begins in the first or second or any other century one cares to choose. By contending that, on the contrary, medicine began as soon as men and women found the possibility of healing, and logic began whenever and wherever people tried to discover the "rules of thought" we are certainly not "saying nothing" about medicine and logic respectively. To maintain that gnosticism has permeated religion ever since people began to be reflective about their cultic and religious practices, were curious about human destiny, and attained awareness of the importance of psychic realities, is likewise by no means "saying nothing" about it, though of course it is unlikely to be saying enough.

How the ancient gnosis took the particular form it did take in the immediate background of the time of Christ is a highly technical problem. It is also of surprisingly little importance for an understanding of the proposal I am making that basic New Testament teaching reflects a special type of gnostic answers to a gnostic quest. That is why the early Christian writers, including Paul, are so severe in their denunciation of what they account "false gnosis." The second-century sectaries no doubt misread and misunderstood the nature of the Christian answer, which is a

very subtle answer to what was, after all, already a very subtle
conglomeration of religious questions posed in the course of a
gnostic quest that had many labyrinthine passageways. We all
know what so easily happens in our own time when people unprepared for a Christian answer are suddenly confronted by one,
as a result, for instance, of vigorous but too precipitous missionary enterprise: they tend to rush into strange interpretations,
over-allegorical or over-literalistic, that lead them into devious
paths and sometimes singularly barren dead-ends.

A more careful determination of the meaning we are to assign
to gnosticism is therefore essential to the conduct of our inquiry.
Can we draw up a list of qualifications that would justify our
calling a text gnostic or otherwise? If not, we are forced into
acquiescing in the charge that our understanding of gnosticism in
general is so vague as to have practically no defining qualities in it
at all. Is the gnosis then merely something that all genuinely
religious people applaud with the same patriotic, if perfunctory,
fervor that Americans in general are supposed to accord to
motherhood and apple-pie? I am sure it is not. I am equally
convinced that it does not necessarily have the characteristics that
scholars have traditionally expected of it.

With these considerations in mind let us proceed to our next
chapter in which, after critically examining, step by step, a list of
sixteen specifications proposed by a well-known contemporary
scholar, we shall see what insight we may gain into the nature of
gnosticism by comparing it with modern existentialism, a movement with which educated people today are all at least to some
extent familiar. The comparison may provide surprisingly illuminating results.

IV

CRITIQUE OF A
SCHOLARLY DEFINITION

> *This earthly existence is a time of testing*
> *[Prøvens Tid], of examination. All this*
> *nonsense about achieving is another priestly*
> *invention for money, a kind of earnestness*
> *to do away with God. No, neither you nor I*
> *have anything to do with playing Providence or*
> *with wanting to achieve. You and I are being*
> *examined our whole life long. So it naturally*
> *follows that you must work in one way or another*
> *quite differently from the way they work*
> *who are "achieving"; but you are freed from*
> *all pride.*
> —Kierkegaard, *Papirer*

A prominent contemporary scholar, in a paper entitled "Towards a Definition of Gnosticism,"[1] recognizes that "a short definition" is impossible. He goes on to specify a list of sixteen characteristics that he would take to be qualifying. I propose to list these briefly and, in support of my general contention, comment on each one in turn.

---

[1]T. P. van Baaren, in *Le Origini dello Gnosticismo*, ed. U. Bianchi (Leiden, 1967), pp. 178-80.

First, however, we must note that some experts would frown on so long a list of specifications and would be content to cite only a very few, such as the mind-matter dualism and the notion of the demiurge that may be accounted a corollary of it. We have already noted in an earlier chapter a shorter, though quite specific list by Hans Jonas. Jean Daniélou, who took the one essential feature of gnosticism to be the mind-matter dualism, perceptively observed that that is always what we should look for, not any of "the various images through which it is expressed."[2] Yet another scholar, still more skeptical of the possibility of definition, suggests that "pre-Christian Gnosticism may be, in reality, nothing more than an unknown something postulated by the science of religions. . . ."[3] My own observation on lists such as van Baaren's is not so much that they are too long but that in specifying so much they exhibit the pervasive character of the ancient gnosis by showing, unwittingly though it be, that little if anything is specified at all. What is exhibited, if anything, is a paradoxical affinity between gnosticism and existentialism. With this observation in mind let us look point by point at van Baaren's requirements.

(1) **Gnosis is not primarily intellectual but is an insight into the total state of affairs and is necessary for salvation from our present plight.** The notion of attainment of a non-intellectual kind of knowledge is typical of all forms of mysticism. The mystic's claim is always precisely to the kind of knowledge van Baaren specifies. The notion of salvation from our present plight is no less characteristic of existentialist approaches to religion.

(2) **Gnosis is related to certain ways of understanding time and space.** All metaphysical stances, religious or otherwise, are inseparable from the spatio-temporal view they entail. Neither the mystical nor the existential approach provides an exception; nor, of course, does gnosis.

(3) **Gnosis is essentially secret, not available to all comers.** The occult or secret character of gnosis, often thought to be peculiar to gnostic and theosophical attitudes, is found in all

---

[2]Jean Daniélou, *The Theology of Jewish Christianity,* tr. J. H. Baker (London: Darton, Longman and Todd, 1964), p. 73.

[3]Giovanni Miegge, *Gospel and Myth,* tr. Stephen Neill (Richmond, Va.: John Knox Press, 1960), p. 30.

religion, though variously expressed. There is one teaching for "babes in the faith" and another for the more mature. Paul, writing to the Corinthians, tells them that he had had to deal with them "on the merely natural plane, as infants in Christ. And so I gave you milk to drink, instead of solid food, for which you were not yet ready."[4] Novices in monasteries and convents are kept apart from those who have made their first, temporary vows, and the latter from those who have committed themselves for life: the junior class is not privy to the doings of the senior class. In some religions the whole process of training consists of a series of initiations into secret mysteries. Till comparatively recent times the ability to read, being rare, was an effective way of withholding knowledge from those not accounted yet fit to receive it. Even after literacy was fairly widespread, the Roman Catholic Church used Latin for certain passages in manuals of canon law that were not for everyman to read. In the Protestant tradition, the gulf between the popular understanding of the Bible (often crudely literalistic) and the scholarly understanding of it has often been enormous, not least in nineteenth-century Germany but also in twentieth-century America, making the religion of scholars inaccessible to the ordinary person. Religion by its very nature entails initiation procedures. The deeper the spirituality, the more hiddenness it entails. Otherwise how could there be any swine to which one might be in danger of casting one's pearls? Yet none of the manifestations of religion I have mentioned here could be considered specifically gnostic.

(4) **Sacred writings such as the Bible are interpreted allegorically. Where the question arises, there is a tendency to disparage or downgrade the Old Testament.** If downgrading the Old Testament be a defining characteristic of gnosticism, how could there be a Jewish gnosticism at all, since what Christians call the Old Testament is the sacred as well as the classical literature of the Jews? Even if the Jewish use of the term *gnosis* does not constitute anything gnostic,[5] and even if, as some argue, Diaspora Judaism was a mere element in the syncretistic mix in the Mediterranean

---

[4] 1 Corinthians 3.1-2 (N. E. B.). Cf. the Abbé Dimnet's whimsical definition of the old Papal Index of Prohibited Books: a convenient device for enabling the learned to write without fear of offending pious ears.

[5] Simone Pétrement, "Le Colloque de Messine et le problème du gnosticisme", in *Revue de Métaphysique et de Morale*, LXXII, 1967, p. 371.

world,[6] we must still account for the unmistakable gnostic elements in later forms of Judaism, such as the kabbalistic and hassidic movements.

(5) **God transcends human thought yet is indisputably good; nevertheless God is revealed to some extent through emanations and intermediaries such as angels.** The transcendence and ultimately incomprehensible nature of God is a fundamental plank of Christian orthodoxy in East and West, as it is of classical biblical Judaism and of Islam. So the Christian Fathers taught and those who seemed to deny it were anathematized by an early Christian council. That God is good is similarly basic doctrine in all these three traditions, though what divine goodness means is a much disputed question among the learned. True, all creation has been traditionally attributed to God; but the intellectual anguish the attribution has caused (classically expressed by Job) shows how deeply conscious monotheists have been of the problem of evil. For monotheists this problem is still the most intractable in the philosophy of religion, despite the great ingenuity that Christian and other theologians have brought to bear upon it. Nor should one forget that, as what we call pantheism emerged in India unself-consciously at a very primitive stage, long before Indian thinkers had been able to try to sort out traditional Hindu beliefs and the philosophical presuppositions pertaining to them, so in the West a monotheistic view emerged at first not as a well-thought-out position but, rather, as an improvement on the polytheistic outlook of more primitive times. The good-evil dualism that is held to specify the gnostic outlook appears in Judaism and Christianity, covered with only a very thin veneer: Satan stalks the earth and has it to a tragic extent in his grasp, but only because God gives him enough rope to exercise his fiendish power. (The power of the demonic has been vividly recognized in biblical literature, in the Christian Fathers, in the medieval schoolmen, in the Reformers, and down to our own day in theologians such as Paul Tillich.) But why should God give his Adversary (as Satan is often called) so much rope? Why, indeed, any rope at all?

---

[6]E.g., R. McL. Wilson, *The Gnostic Problem* (London: Mowbray, 1958), pp. 256 ff.

(6) **The world is regarded with pessimism, being the work of a demiurge or other such being who has created it or brought it about in ignorance of God's will or even against his will.** I see nothing in the mainstream of Christian tradition to suggest optimism about the world *as such*. On the contrary, the elect are gathered *out of* the world, saved from the destruction toward which it is presumed to be headed. According to Augustine, whom the Reformers follow closely at this point, humankind is a mass of perdition, and in this as in so much else he is surely as loyal to the New Testament as anyone could be. There is no evading the fact that "the world" has very negative connotations in all orthodox Christian teaching. Hence its place, along with the flesh and the Devil, in the triad of entities to be formally renounced at Baptism. We are *in* the world and we should be (as the anonymous epistle to Diognetus said of the Christians in the Roman Empire) its leaven; yet we are not *of* the world. The world is our prison.[7] We make the best of it as no doubt one should do if one were incarcerated in the State Penitentiary. So powerful is habit that one might even eventually come to think of such a prison as home and develop a sort of nostalgia for it, encouraging recidivism. Yet all along we must know of course at the bottom of our hearts if not at the top of our minds that it is not really our home and that pretending to ourselves that it is must be accounted perverse and neurotic. The New Testament writers, who were expecting the end of the world any day, certainly could not have regarded the world very positively. We know indeed that they did not. A few centuries later, when Rome, mistress of the world, fell, a very thoughtful and temperamentally optimistic person could look forward, as did Augustine in his *De Civitate Dei*, to a transformation of the world (the "earthly Babylon") into the Church (the "heavenly Jerusalem"); but the world as such could not be seen and never was seen as good in itself, its divine creation notwithstanding. True, writers we call clearly gnostic do emphasize that "the world" is evil; but everybody who thinks at all about God and the world recognizes that evil, however it arises, does rule the

---

[7]On the prison motif so characteristic of modern existentialism, *see* Victor Brombert, "Esquisse de la prison heureuse," in *Revue d'Histoire Littéraire de la France*, March-April, 1971, in which the Yale professor considers, *inter alia*, in this long article, how freedom can be as burdensome as non-freedom.

42 Gnosis

world, whether or not under the permissive Providence of God. One need not be a gnostic to perceive that the world is at least under the viceregency of the demonic.

(7) **Man is a mixture of spiritual and material components. The spiritual ones are the cause of his longing to return to God**. This is an old way of expressing a basic truth discovered in all religions that have any sort of moral development in them at all. People learn the need to cultivate what we call the inner or interior life. Indeed, every form of humanism that has any religious content to it, such as the humanism of Socrates and that of Confucius, recognizes that there are certain thoughts and actions that degrade men and women and others that elevate them. Surely these propositions are as unspecific as any in the history of human thought. I can think of no great philosophy or religion to whose adherents the two propositions before us would not seem to be fundamentally platitudinous, noble platitudes though they be. That is not to say, of course, that all would be content with the mode of expressing the platitudes.

(8) **Human beings are of three kinds: (i) those who possess full gnosis (the pneumatics) and are therefore capable of full salvation; (ii) those who have faith (pistis) and have a limited capacity for salvation; (iii) those who are wholly absorbed by the cares of the world and are consequently incapable of salvation.** For whatever reason, psychological or otherwise, this triadic arrangement is a widespread idea. Plato uses it in the *Republic*. It has counterparts in medieval thought, for example in the ordination to the Holy Ministry of the Church: bishops, priests, and deacons traditionally represent a hierarchical deployment of the plenitude of the sacerdotal office. Even in the academic world today we have assistant, associate, and full professors. In capitalist societies the triadic arrangement is an economic commonplace: the rich, the middle class, and the poor. No doubt in other societies similar triads emerge, as in the U.S.S.R., where it takes the form of official members of the Party, other citizens, and the inmates of slave camps. Of course what van Baaren specifies here is how the Christian Fathers of Alexandria saw humanity; but though they were certainly more disposed to gnostic influences than were some others of their time, few if any would dub them gnostic *pur sang*, in the sense van Baaren wishes to specify.

(9) **Gnostics make a clear distinction between pistis and gnōsis.** Not only, however, is the distinction between *pistis* and

gnōsis universal in Christian thought and common elsewhere; it is eminently conspicuous in precisely those circles that are *least* disposed to gnostic influences, for example, the heirs of the Reformation. If there be anybody in the whole history of Christian thought to whom the term "gnostic" could *not* be conventionally applied, it is surely Kierkegaard, who spent his entire literary life (an extraordinarily prolific one) in expounding the distinction and its implicates for the individual.

(10) **The mind-matter dualism generally leads to a severely ascetical manner of life, though it can also lead to a libertinism that is the very opposite.** There is indeed some truth in the notion that an extreme mind-matter dualism may issue in either of these results: uncompromising "mortification of the flesh" or wanton dissipation. To some extent, however, this is true of all forms of religion that have anything to say of human conduct at all. It is well-known that religious people do tend to be, on the one hand, severe, restrained, disciplined, sometimes even to the point of self-cruelty, or, on the other, notably gentle, easygoing, broadminded. The enmity between the rigorists and the laxists, between Shammai and Hillel, is a familiar phenomenon in all religions. The rigorists are notoriously hard to live with, but dependable, while the laxists are undependable but often socially delightful. What van Baaren specifies here is only an extreme case of a universal phenomenon. All religions recognize that the flesh, whatever good may or may not be said of it, can be a snare. Gluttony and lust can make beasts of men and women. Even the least religiously-minded person can sometimes reproach himself with the reflection: "I did make a pig of myself at that buffet dinner." All of us who know anything about the history of sexual mores recognize the fact that attitudes to sex tend to swing from the restrictive to the permissive and back again. The early Victorians were not at all so prudish as were the late Victorians. There is nothing here that could specify a peculiarly gnostic outlook. The phenomena have little if anything to do with gnosticism at all.

(11) **Gnosticism is a religion of revolt.** In all religion there is a notoriously conservative, not to say ideophobiac, element, and at the same time a revolutionary one. The same churchpeople who will fight to their dying breath over a hymn tune may well be in the vanguard of some social action. It would come as no surprise if we were to discover that those who fought for the abolition of slavery in the United States had fought just as fiercely for the

retention of some quite insignificant piece of church furniture or apparel. Many of the highly developed religions of the world, notably Buddhism and Christianity, were conceived in terms of revolt, then became later on instruments of an Establishment. Wherever an existentialist outlook prevails in religion, however, the old shibboleths are weakened, the old legalisms brought into question, the old gods dethroned. All that might be shown under this heading, therefore, would be some sort of affinity between gnosticism and existentialism, an affinity we shall presently consider.

(12) **Gnosticism appeals to the desire to belong to an elite.** Religion is widely known for its elitist tendencies and often reproached for them by those who account themselves its foes. Nor could it be otherwise. To be elect is to be elitist willy-nilly. To be saved is to be in one way or another singled out. The Jews were a chosen people, a people set apart by God from all other peoples. Japan, one of her poets tells us, is not a land where men need pray; it is itself divine. Even those religions that claim to be thoroughly internationalist (Buddhism and Christianity are classic examples) have elitist structures: the monastic way is for those who are willing to follow certain counsels of perfection. To be a Christian at all, however, is to be set apart. Nowhere is this more emphasized than in the evangelical wing of the Reformation heritage. A religion without elitism is inconceivable. It would be no more a religion than would a non-three-sided figure be a triangle. So elitism in no way specifies any particular religious phenomenon, persuasion, movement, or thrust.

(13) **Where the question arises, the tendency to distinguish sharply between Christ as "heavenly Saviour" and "the man Jesus" is prominent. Hence the docetism that was a popular outlook in first-century Christian thought.** The distinction between the Christ and Jesus the man is by any reckoning a thorny question for all Christian thought. There are many solutions, some that have won ecclesiastical approval and some that have been denied it. The enormous literature called "christological" is largely about that very question: the relation of the "Jesus of history" to the "Christ of faith." True, the official position of all orthodox Christians is the one associated with the findings of the Council of Chalcedon in 451: the doctrine of the two natures, the divine and the human, in the Person of Jesus Christ. In fact, however, people have generally tended to emphasize the one or

the other. The Nestorians, who tended to emphasize the human, were persecuted and mostly fled eastward to India and elsewhere. Some branches of Christianity, such as the Coptic Church to this day, have officially adopted a Monophysite position, emphasizing the divinity rather than the humanity. In the Middle Ages, the official position notwithstanding, the divine side was stressed in the popular imagination (consider, for example, Michelangelo's *Last Judgment*), while in some other periods of Christian history the human side was exalted. Docetism (the notion that Jesus was a spiritual vision, not a reality in the flesh) was indeed an appealing solution to some in the first century. There are several historical reasons for this. The "Jesus of history" and "Christ of faith" question will be considered much more fully in a later chapter. Meanwhile, let us simply recognize that the difficulty, though acute in those whose outlook would generally be called gnostic, is by no means peculiar to them.

(14) **Where the question arises, Christ is accounted the turning point in the cosmic process. As evil has come about by the fall of a former aeon, Christ ushers in a new aeon, a new age, by proclaiming the hitherto unknown God.** That Christ is the turning point in human history is an axiom of all orthodox Christian theology and few even among the heterodox would entirely repudiate the notion. It is reflected in the universal Christian practice of dating B.C. and A.D. and is proclaimed in the New Testament, not least by Paul.[8] That the fall, whether cosmic or human or both, has brought about a radical corruption is also a familiar Christian doctrine. The only tenet mentioned under this head that might raise a Christian eyebrow is the suggestion that the God whom Christ fully revealed and that the apostles proclaimed had been entirely unknown. Yet many would be willing to say that Christ, through his life, death and resurrection, made the nature of God known *as it had never been known before*. So at most this proposed qualification would not qualify much.

(15) **In connection with the Person of Christ is often found the notion that as Redeemer he is himself redeemed. He has achieved par excellence the redemption he makes available to others, his chosen ones.** At last we have a specification that looks more promising than any of the others so far examined, for the notion that the Redeemer has been himself redeemed is certainly

---

[8]E.g., 1 Corinthians 15.22; Romans 8.22.

alien to traditional understanding of Christian doctrine. We must
note, however, the use of the adverb "often". The notion is not
presented as a universal feature of forms of gnosis flying the
Christian banner. The practice of polygamy often occurs in the
history of Judaism; but certainly no one would account it a defining characteristic of Jewish life, though it was not *officially* prohibited till the tenth century of the Christian era.

(16) **Salvation consists in the complete emancipation of the
spiritual from the corporeal. This is expressed in the myth of
"the ascent of the soul."** This last item in van Baaren's list has
affinities with the seventh, already considered. It is a strong way
of stating a truth universally recognized in all developed religion.
It may also sound archaic to some modern ears, but no more so
than the typical language of the ancient world, Christian or
otherwise, on the nature of salvation. What do the Spanish and
other mystics mean when they talk of "the ascent of the soul"? It is
a phrase very typical of mystical literature. The Flemish mystic
Jan van Ruysbroeck speaks of a seven-stepped ladder. John of the
Cross goes out on a dark night (*una noche oscura*) and leaves his
cares, the cares of this world, "with the lilies and forgetting them."
In this tradition of Christian mysticism, the dark night of sense
that precedes illumination and the more advanced state called the
dark night of the soul both symbolize, each in its own way, precisely such a severing of the soul from the senses, which not only
ensnare men and women but (as all empiricist philosophers must
also agree) constitute the gate to such knowledge of the world as
we may claim to possess. So to renounce the world of sense–
experience and attempt to take off on a mystical flight beyond it,
even if for but a Pascalian half hour, is what all Christian mystical
traditions in one way or another purport to do. It is surely to do
precisely what this last alleged peculiarity of gnosticism is supposed to do. Moreover, it reflects a mood typical of much Christian spirituality that would not be at all generally accounted
gnostic, a mood that is found, for instance, in many popular
evangelical hymns as well as in the Catholic liturgies.

By examining in some detail so long a list of alleged characteristics of the gnostic outlook, I hope I have shown that it does almost
nothing to specify anything more than what is either common to
religion in general or else is not radically if at all alien to widely
accepted features of Christian spirituality. We are therefore
thrown back on a much wider and more useful way of under-

standing the nature of the ancient and perennial gnosis. That is not to say, of course, that the forms gnosticism took in New Testament times, whatever they were, had no greater specificity. Every form in which the ancient gnosis has ever been or ever can be expressed must have some individuality of its own.

Walter Schmithals, in his *Gnosticism in Corinth* argues persuasively that even the cosmic dualism so often accounted an indispensable feature was not present in all systems commonly called gnostic. He also contends that the "false teachers" in Corinth were Jewish gnostics, Jews who were especially proud of their Jewish ancestry. That they were heretical from a traditionalist Jewish standpoint seems obvious, since Judaism without the Law (which gnostics of every sort tend to downgrade) is certainly not Jewish orthodoxy. Yet Mesopotamia, where gnostic influences seem strong, was also, after the Exile, a second home of the Jews. So we may conclude that "Jewish gnosticism existed alongside the proper 'orthodox' Judaism. . . ." The Judaism of New Testament times, Schmithals reminds us, "was in no respect second to Christianity in complexity and this fact helps us to understand Christian beginnings."[9] What eventually triumphed as "Christian orthodoxy" was a hellenistic phenomenon, sometimes, alas, with some anti-Jewish overtones.[10] The earliest Christians, including Paul, all moved, however, in Jewish circles and thought like Jews, and whatever gnostic tendencies they may be supposed to exhibit must reflect that Jewishness. Paul's proclamation of the Christian "Good News" was *atypical* of Jewish gnosis; nevertheless, formulated as it was, as an answer to his Jewish gnostic contemporaries, it must be accounted a form of gnosis, though a distinctive one, as also is John's.

If one looks at the motifs of twentieth-century existentialism, one will find in them remarkable parallels to what seems to be constantly found in the innumerable forms in which the ancient gnosis was objectified. The prison motif, for instance, which permeates modern existentialism, as we have already noted, is a

---

[9]Walter Schmithals, *Gnosticism in Corinth*, tr. J. E. Steely (Nashville: Abingdon Press, 1971). *See* especially the concluding summary, pp. 293 ff.

[10]*See* Eldon Jay Epp, "Anti-Semitism and the Popularity of the Fourth Gospel in Christianity", in *Central Conference of American Rabbis Journal*, 22, 1975, pp. 35-37.

constant element in all forms of gnosticism that have been sub-
jected to historical and analytical scrutiny. We are imprisoned by
circumstance and have to find our way out. The cause of the
imprisonment may be a matter of metaphysical speculation. The
fact of the imprisonment is taken to be axiomatic. Sometimes the
image may be that of a bog in which we are sinking. We must be
rescued. We cannot do it entirely by ourselves. Our need for a
Saviour is absolute; but practically speaking we also need helpers.
Both these notions (Redeemer and angelic or other intermediaries) dominate gnostic literature so much as to be accounted part of the general prison motif. In modern religious
existentialism, contradistinguished from nihilistic forms such as
Sartre's, trust in a Redeemer or Saviour is typical, for despite the
extreme emphasis on freedom of choice (and indeed from one
point of view because of it) one must seek a helping hand to
enable one to get oneself out of the mire. Those familiar with the
karmic principle in Indian thought will not fail to recognize at
once the ideological likeness among karmic, gnostic and existentialist symbols of the human predicament.

All modern existentialists from Kierkegaard onward give cen-
trality to the notion of *Angst*, a uniquely poignant form of anxiety.
It is variously translated into other languages: in French usually
angoisse, in Spanish *agonía*. It points to yet another dimension of
the prison motif: the homesickness so characteristic of the ancient
gnostic quest, with its emphasis on pilgrimage. Being pilgrims, we
are not at home anywhere, however accustomed we may be to our
prison. We are exiles. The exilic theme is very characteristic of
both the gnostic and the existentialist. As the writer to the Hebrews reminds his readers, "here we have no abiding city." We
have fallen in a state that might also be likened to an alcoholic
stupor: we cannot walk straight or see clearly. So we are alienated
from reality. All these images of the human condition are as
existentialist as they are omnipresent in all forms of gnosticism.
With the world, *jeté là, comme ça,* in Sartre's phrase. I find myself

> a stranger and afraid
> In a world I never made.[11]

I yearn for redemption, whether I take the remedy to be that of

----

[11] A. E. Housman, *Last Poems*, xii.

the nihilists such as Sartre or that of the religious existentialists such as Kierkegaard and Marcel. Whether or not I find that Jesus Christ perfectly fills the role of Saviour, I am in no doubt that I need to be saved from my predicament.

Modern existentialism is notoriously hospitable to very disparate attitudes toward religion. Heidegger, to whom Sartre is much indebted, is plainly both existentialist and gnostic. He is certainly not a Christian, though, as John Macquarrie has shown, his understanding of Being might be treated as susceptible to a Christian interpretation: a very gnostic one.[12] Gnosticism, like existentialism, has been expressed in many forms and no one who has understood how deeply the best modern Christian theology is indebted to existentialist insights need have much difficulty in perceiving that all that is vital in Christianity, contradistinguished from the trivia of its externals, is gnostic and existentialist. Deeply convinced Christians have come to see Christian existentialism as the most authentic expression of the most basic Christian stance. There is no reason why they should not similarly view a Christian gnosticism.

As the late Jacob Taubes pointed out in a perceptive article a quarter of a century ago, it is in the doctrine of man that gnosticism may be most easily distinguished from other views, including many in the mainstream of Greek thought. He reminds us that Spengler pointed out the fundamental differences between Greek and gnostic attitudes through the idea of limit. "The Greek idea of space depended on the presence of bodies. The limit (*peras*) was conceived as a center force pulling and holding things in form. The body formed in space by the center force was also inwardly formed—like the whole *cosmos*. The form of a thing was determined by its inner limit. In the Gnostic vocabulary the entire structure was turned around: the *peras* pointed to the finiteness of things. *Determination* was made a negative characteristic. The limit became a wall that separated inside from outside. It was to be *transgressed* and *transcended*."[13] The Greeks temperamentally hated the *apeiron*, the infinite, the boundless, as they loved what they found to have form (*morphē*). In gnostic thought the cosmic

---

[12] John Macquarrie, *Principles of Christian Theology* (New York: Charles Scribner's Sons, 1966), pp. 105 f.

[13] J. Taubes, "The Gnostic Idea of Man," in *The Cambridge Review*, I, 2 (winter), 1955.

realm was transcended by the transmundane self. So the gnostic's whole understanding of the nature of man was transmogrified.

Taubes goes on to say: "The *cosmos* is like a prison, but there is a chance to escape from it: there is an exit, there is a way of redemption.[14] The deprivation of all the positive attributes of the *cosmos* was not simply pessimistic lamentation about a general state of affairs, but a revolutionary act permitting the existence of a beyond: Gnosis provided a way to salvation. It created the modern idea of salvation. It is true that the *cosmos* became a cave, and that the sense of limit as block or a wall became real, but also a great hope was born that this wall could be broken." Taubes affirms that "The fundamental unity of all Gnostic language is to be seen through the Gnostic idea of man."[15]

If my findings are substantially correct, not only can we see a gnostic *element* in most of the great religions; we can also understand the profound traditional Christian suspicion of a false gnosis while not hesitating to speak of a true gnosis that Christians generally might identify (as do I) with the fundamental *kerygma*, the Good News that the New Testament writers proclaimed to an audience for the most part accustomed to sophisticated forms of Jewish and other pre-Christian gnosticism.

The existentialist and gnostic attitudes have another striking feature in common: they both cut across ideological boundaries and religious systems. Martin Buber was as thoroughly Jewish as was Kierkegaard profoundly Christian, and both are so typically existentialist as to make a comparison of them an all-too obvious topic for undergraduate term papers. Many have seen in Zen conspicuously existentialist motifs. There is no form of religion really worth talking about that is not in one way or another susceptible to gnostic and existentialist interpretations.

Nor can the origin of either gnosticism or existentialism be dated as one might claim to date, say, the Exodus or the Enlightenment of the Buddha or the flight of Muhammad. Even to more debatable beginnings, such as the rise of the doctrine of transubstantiation or the roots of the Reformation we can set some limits (if only, in such cases, the Last Supper and the conver-

---

[14]Here is indeed the cardinal gnostic hope: *there is an exit*. It was a stroke of genius on Sartre's part to affirm, as a *nihilistic* existentialist: no exit. *See* his *Huit Clos*.
[15]Taubes, *ibid*.

sion of Augustine, respectively!); but to gnosticism and existentialism no historical limit can be set at all, unless it be the emergence of human thought, whenever that was. When twentieth-century existentialism first appeared in Germany in the decade after World War I, it was not long till Kierkegaard could be seen as its precursor: its great uncle if not its grandfather. When the "new" movement crossed into France, the French recognized at once how deep were its roots long ago implanted into French thought. Pascal was but an obvious example. Soon people came to see what Kierkegaard himself had seen in his own way, that the outlook of Socrates two and a half millenia earlier had been notably existentialist. The case can be made for other ancient sages too. Gautama's protest against the institutionalism of the India into which he was born is but one. Biblical scholars have not been slow to see that the life and outlook of the early Hebrews was such as to promote the existentialist view so characteristic of classical Hebrew thought and so much a part of the Jewish heritage and experience today. A similar timelessness pervades the gnostic outlook in all the forms in which it is expressed. The awareness of individual responsibility, the inner assurance of the individual's capacity for free choice and of the individual's power to attain an understanding of his relation to the cosmos and a knowledge of his potential destiny: all these are gnostic motifs and also common existentialist coin.

For the ancient gnosis is not and never was taught exclusively or even principally out of a book. The gnosis is attained basically through experience of life and (as is a familiar gnostic view) over the course of millions of lives. Books may help, as books on mothercraft may help a prospective mother though it is not primarily from them that she learns what motherhood means. Books and teachers are at best but midwives to gnostic awareness. When Bianchi and others suggest that gnosticism always appears as a parasite on a living religion, they surely fail to see that their slur on gnosticism could apply equally well to existentialism and be equally ill-founded. It is a well-known paradox that many of the most illustrious gnostics, mystics and existentialists tend to be peculiarly well-rooted in a particular institutional religion while not only transcending it but dramatically vitalizing it. Clement of Alexandria, Teresa of Avila, Pascal, Kierkegaard and Berdyaev are examples that spring readily to mind. None could be less parasitic on their respective traditions. On the contrary, without men and women of this caliber the traditions out of which they have sprung would have dried out long ago. The truth is, indeed, the other way round: it is the gnostics and the existentialists, the mystics and the religious humanists, to say nothing of the heretics, to which the Church is indebted for its survival. Too often the parasites are the institutions that survive through sucking, however inefficiently and therefore in the long run fruitlessly, from those superabundantly life-filled sources.

V

GNOSTICISM AS THE CREATIVE ELEMENT IN RELIGION

Philosophy always buries its undertakers.
Etienne Gilson, *The Unity of Philosophical Experience.*

Gnostic and theosophical elements are found in all religions and are as old as speculative religious thought. Gnosticism, in the general sense, is the creative element in religion. It is born as soon as priests and other functionaries weary of simply performing the appointed rituals and reciting from the holy books and seek to understand what lies behind the ritual acts and sacred literature. Of course that occurs at a very primitive stage of religious and cultural development and the level of the gnostic quest is correspondingly low; nevertheless, it is a beginning of religious thought. Priests are not necessarily and perhaps not even usually learned; but even the most uncreative among them are moved by boredom—if nothing else—to do something more than perform the ritual and read the books. Arguments over legalistic minutiae may occupy their attention for a while; but to a creative mind such occupations soon prove as wearisome as the ritual repetitiousness.

Imagination, at such an early stage, has free rein and is likely to run riot. Claims to knowledge are likely to exceed attainment. To protect such extravagant claims, the sages and others who make them resort to the device of secrecy: the methods by which the knowledge is alleged to be attained are available only to persons who have been initiated into secret societies or occult orders, and these persons are bound under oath not to reveal the secrets. The priesthood itself, or an inner circle of priests, may constitute such an esoteric society. Only when philosophical critique is possible and takes place, as was the case in Athens in the time of Socrates, for example, can such claims be effectively challenged and intellectual correctives introduced.

All human thought, notably philosophical and religious thought, has two indispensable components: the speculative and the critical. The former is the imaginative, creative element, the latter the logical and analytical. Without the critical element, speculation runs wild; without the creative element, analytical critique, having really nothing to do, merely hones its tools and makes them more elegantly useless. In short, only through free discussion can progress in religious thought be made and true *gnōsis* attained. Such progress cannot even be begun without imaginative, creative speculation.

The forms that gnostic speculation took in the Mediterranean world about the time of Christ could not have been very varied, for Hellenistic civilization was rich and ideas were being exchanged more readily (with the rise of cities and the influx of foreigners into them, as well as with the increase in trade and commerce) than had been the case in earlier, less cosmopolitan circumstances. The form it took among the numerous second century sects whose teachings have been commonly labelled "Christian Gnosticism" seems to have been well defined. The adherents of these sects had definite religious tenets and, though the teachings varied, they had also much in common, including no doubt the requirements listed by Hans Jonas and cited in our preceding chapter.

Each sect, nevertheless, had its own distinctive peculiarities. The Valentinians, for instance, provided an extremely elaborate account of the gods who had come down to them in ancient priestly Egyptian speculation. Their founder, Valentine, grafting Christian elements on to his special arrangement of such ideas, produced a system with an "ogdoad" or hierarchy of eight powers or divine emanations. In this system, the infinite abyss of being, called "Bythus", existed from the beginning. It is conceived as pure "thereness". Then Bythus, in the course of self-reflection, perceived the notion of himself in the form of absolute silence, called "Sige". The word "Sige" happens to be grammatically feminine, so it was easy to attribute to it sexually feminine qualities. At any rate, through the union of Bythus and Sige was begotten Nous (understanding). Nous was a twin to Alētheia (truth), a word which in Greek is also fortunately feminine. Nous, through intercourse with his twin sister Aletheia, produced a son, Logos (rational discourse) who, having also a convenient twin sister Zōē (life) was able through union with her, to produce Man who, however, also required a consort: Community or Ekklēsia. So we have the first eightfold deity or "ogdoad" of the Valentinian system. That is only a superficial glance at one aspect of its ramifications; but it is all we need here to give us some idea of the character of the sects that provoked such alarm among churchmen.

No doubt a family resemblance ran through these numerous sects, including even the Marcionites. The latter, however, followers of Marcion, repudiated entirely the God of the Old Testament, whom they identified with the Demiurge and whom they accounted fickle, despotic, ignorant, and cruel—an entirely different deity from the God whom Jesus came to reveal. Their teachings are so distinctive that some scholars prefer not to include them among "the Gnostics." Therein lies, I think, a clue to the nature of the confusion that has attended the treatment of gnosticism as a background to the New Testament: if the qualifications for being called "Gnostic" are made so narrow that not even Marcion meets them, then we are plainly talking as arbitrarily as if we were to confine the term "socialism" to, say, the Fabian Society that flourished in England in the latter part of the nineteenth century, or perhaps to the earlier "Christian socialists" of the 1840s, the time of Maurice and Kingsley. The term "gnostic" ought to be applied to all speculative thought about religion, good or bad, that purports to lead to deeper insight into the divine nature or greater knowledge of the ways of God to man. For us in the West the forms such gnostic speculation have taken in our traditions will be of special interest, of course; but we shall see gnosticism as a universal element in religion and, some of us would add, the most central.

Gnosticism, by its very nature, rules nothing out and is therefore capable of encompassing novel and interesting ideas that can lead to religious truth; but it is not well-equipped to exclude falsity. One might say of it what one says of a great city: you can find everything in it, good and bad, ugly and beautiful. Analytical methods of philosophy and theology, being critical, are much more restrictive and much less indiscriminately hospitable to all comers among religious ideas. By the same token they will exclude ideas that may be of great importance for the development of religious thought. This is obviously the case with what is traditionally called "dogmatic theology", which presupposes a body of revelation sufficient for the needs of the institution to which it relates and beyond which members of the institution are supposed not only to have no need to go but to have a duty not to go. In such a restricted climate of thought, to seek for more is to trifle. The gnostic, by contrast, is always on the outlook for enrichment. Exposed as he is to an endless ideological stream, he develops a kind of resistance comparable to the sales resistance that we all develop when we are bombarded by marketing techniques in our economically free society. Yet the gnostic would not have it otherwise.

The gnostic movement that pervaded the religious thought of the Mediterranean world into which Jesus was born was confident in its high esteem of the spiritual elements it saw in man and the universe. Its way of expressing this confidence was to contrast that spiritual or psychical realm with the "material" world, to the detriment of the latter. From this perspective, everything spiritual or psychical seems good and everything material bad. To call this a spirit-matter or mind-matter dualism is useful enough labelling so far as it goes; but it can also be misleading, not to say anachronistic. The ancient gnostics were intoxicated with· the discovery of the value of the spiritual or psychic element in man and the universe. They had not yet reached the stage at which thinkers have found it necessary to go beyond that particular perception and see that the situation is more complex. Yet I believe the gnostic insight at this point, even in its more primitive forms, is essentially right: the psychic realities *are* the more important, though it is no doubt a most unfortunate mistake to suppose they are separable from the "material" world as is cheese from the cheese dish that contains it. The fundamental truth, however, remains. That is why Jung, who makes so much of the emphasis on the psychic realm, on archetypes and the collective unconscious, is properly called neo-gnostic. He sees what the gnostics of every age, in the West as in the East, saw so well: the great verities about the universe are to be found in its psychic realities.

The ancients, knowing nothing, of course about quantum physics or the velocity of light, naturally contrasted two aspects of existence as they found it: on the one hand the psychic realm, spiritual, luminous, golden, mercurial; on the other, the material world, solid, dark, carnal. This oversimplification exposed the typical gnostic of the first century of the Christian era to precisely the kind of critique that the writer of the Epistle to the Ephesians directs against such an outlook. In urging his readers to put "God's armor on so as to be able to resist the Devil's tactics," he warns them that "it is not against human enemies that we have to struggle, but against. . . the spiritual army of evil in the heavens."[1] The mind-matter dualism has already broken down: if there are evil spirits as well as good "in the heavens," how can the spiritual be presumed to be so essentially good and the "carnal" so fundamentally evil? Again, if spirituality be intrinsically good, how could it have changed to evil as in the Lucifer story in which the highest and most glorious of the angels becomes, by his own act, the lowest and worst of beings?

Let us put the whole question in another perspective. When we are very young children, our greatest psychological need apart from an atmosphere of love and tenderness is for a copious flow of imagery. We can never get enough of it, for our imagination is alive and running riot in fancy. We welcome all images indiscriminately: gallant knights and snorting dragons, fairy godmothers and one-eyed ogres. We need them all. We also personify objects: tables, chairs, trees. As we grow older our needs change. Now we need, rather, to achieve an economy of the imagination. Our wilder fancies must be set aside, making way for a more disciplined use of our imagination. We have to throw out some images while conserving others and logically classifying them. We simply cannot accommodate and use all the images we allowed to be poured into us in our earlier years.

This necessity comes upon civilizations in various ways and at various stages of their development. Two examples in the history of ideas should suffice to illustrate the necessity. Toward the end of the Middle Ages in Europe, William of Ockham taught the

---

[1]Ephesians 6.12. Most modern scholars question the traditionally assumed Pauline authorship of this letter.

principle of verbal economy, the principle that it is futile to use more elements for what can be done with fewer.[2] At the end of the thirteenth century, the Golden Age of medieval Christian scholasticism, the scholastic method had degenerated into a caricature of itself. Though I have never come across any actual instance of the legendary discussion of how many angels can dance on the point of a needle, which is so often cited in scorn of the later forms of medieval scholastic discussion, it does typify the absurd sorts of question that the scholastics did raise in the degenerate last stages of the period before the Reformation and Renaissance. The scholastic method, which had done marvelously well in marrying religion and science in the thirteenth century, the century of Bonaventure and Aquinas and Duns Scotus, had led nowhere during the two succeeding centuries. Ockham's "razor", as logicians call it, was a necessary remedy. It was, indeed, the only way out. Another example is the fate of the early nineteenth-century Romanticism. The nineteenth century was a century of extraordinary creativity and growth, culturally, ideologically and in many other ways, and its glories were very largely due to the Romantic Movement. That same movement, however, led nowhere in itself; that is to say, without the reaction that set-in it would have issued in an intellectual and cultural nihilism. Inevitably other movements came to the rescue, such as forms of neo-classicism. Yet Romanticism did for the nineteenth century what gnosticism had done for the age in which the New Testament was in process of formation.

The nineteenth-century Romantics exalted the category of feeling. They did do in various ways, of course, and they often exaggerated, as the gnostics and other theosophical writers have often been forced to exaggerate to get across their point. Without them, however, the nineteenth century would have been barren indeed and the twentieth ideologically even more barren than it is. The Romantics, after a long period in which Reason and Nature were alternately deified, proclaimed the case for feeling. Inevitably, their protests were often ill-considered and rarely well thought-out. Imagine ourselves, however, at a stage in human

---

[2]*Frustra fit per plura quod potest per pauciora.* The form commonly quoted is: "entities are not to be multiplied without necessity" (*entia non multiplicanda praeter necessitatem*), which, however, is not to be found in Ockham's extant works.

history in which we had no well-developed psychological vocabulary for, say, ideas of action. Perceiving action, nevertheless, as a focus of value, we might go on to denigrate inaction as disvalue, so giving the impression that all action is good and all inaction bad, which, though of course thoroughly misleading, might well be the best means at our disposal of calling attention to the value of "doing something" and the evil of "sitting down." The so-called dualism of the gnostics, like the Romanticist exaltation of feeling in the nineteenth century, should be seen in that light. Such movements are indispensable for the development of the human spirit. They betoken leaps of which there must be counterparts in every renaissance, tomorrow's as well as yesterday's.

We have already distinguished gnosticism as a basic theosophical climate in the Mediterranean world from the special Christian gnostic sects that flourished pre-eminently in the second century of the Christian era. This Christian Gnosticism, represented by sects led respectively by leaders such as Valentine, Marcion and Basilides, taught specific interpretations of Christianity and was, as we have seen, increasingly resisted by prominent Christian teachers. These sects were not merely influenced by the general presuppositions of a gnostic climate, as was practically everybody; they held and taught definite tenets, with vagaries such as those we have found in Valentine. The gnostic notion of a Demiurge who creates the world with all its attendant evils and stands in contrast to the unknowable divine Being, had deep roots in earlier, pre-Christian thought. Also characteristic of the gnostic sects, though already present in first-century Christian thought, was what has come to be called Docetism: a tendency to deny or at least diminish the reality of the humanity and especially of the sufferings of Christ. It had its roots in the difficulties some felt (difficulties fostered by a literalistic approach to what is now called mind-matter dualism) in the notion of the Incarnation of God in the Person of Christ. How could God permit himself to be contaminated by matter, if matter was intrinsically evil? Perhaps, then, Jesus existed only in appearance? Perhaps he miraculously escaped the ignominy of death by changing places with someone before the crucifixion occurred? That *kind* of gnosticism, as represented in such sects and teachers, was anything other than open-minded. It formulated, indeed, very distinct dogmas that included all sorts of fanciful vagaries.

It was these Christian gnostic sects of the second century that alarmed the Primitive Church and eventually forced it into formulating narrowed dogmatic affirmations of its own. The most regrettable consequence was that Christians who in the earliest period had been permitted much latitude in their thought and had been open to various alternative and enriching ways of expressing their beliefs about Christ, the center of their faith, were now forced to take a doctrinal stand. Though the so-called Apostles' Creed that has come down to us today dates, in its present form, several centuries after apostolic times, some doctrinal confession having a resemblance to it seems to have been in use in Rome by about the middle of the second century, when the Gnostic sects were at their zenith. No doubt these early formulations were conceived in opposition to those sects.

Long before the clash between the Church and the Gnostic sects had reached its zenith, the views of the Docetists had alarmed many and the reaction of the spokesmen for what came to be understood as Christian orthodoxy was, in its own way, a protest against mind-matter dualism such as we have already seen in the author of the Epistle to the Ephesians. It is not anti-gnostic; it is against what was, for very understandable reasons, a favorite way of expressing gnostic ideas. Ignatius (c. 35–c. 107), Bishop of Antioch, had vehemently attacked the Docetists for saying that Christ suffered only "in semblance." He called them "godless" and "unbelievers". "They call Christ a semblance," he writes with bitter irony, "because they are themselves mere semblance!" With studied repetitiousness he insists that Christ was truly (alēthōs) born, truly ate, truly drank, was truly persecuted, was truly crucified, truly died, was truly raised from the dead, and apart from Him we have no true life.

Ignatius was right; but perhaps he did not know exactly how right he was. The meaning of his attack on the Docetists, in so far as it has been understood to be anti-gnostic, has surely been much misunderstood throughout the ages. For the orthodox churchmen who made such attacks turned out to have a gnosis of their own to offer. The Alexandrian school, we have already noted, was nothing if not gnostic in its approach to the mysteries of the Christian faith. We must ask, then, the question: was the Church always exactly right in what it kept and in what it threw out? Christians today have before them examples of similar quandaries in which the Church has found itself in later times. The sixteenth-century Reformation and Counter-Reformation provide a good example. In that controversy, as soon as one side stressed one concept the other denigrated it and magnified whatever was its traditional opposite. When the "Protestants" exalted faith, the "Catholics" stressed works. When the "Protestants" seemed to denigrate Mary, the "Catholics" exalted her, sometimes to the point of absurdity. The result, of course, was not only that both sides lost perspective; both succeeded in impoverishing Christian faith. Educated Christians on both sides are now trying to recover the plenitude of that faith; but the recovery must be slow and painful, for the effects of that movement, historically inevitable though it was, have been devastating. Both sides were unsuccessful in their respective aims, so that on the one hand Luther and Calvin would be horrified if they could see what Protestantism has degenerated into, while, on the other, luminaries of the medieval Catholic Church such as its greatest thinkers, Aquinas and Duns Scotus, to say nothing of its artists and mystics, would hardly recognize much of modern American Roman Catholic life and thought to be in their lineage at all.

Anti-gnostic writers such as Irenaeus exaggerated, of course, the vagaries of the gnostic sects whose influence they feared. In an age that was naturally looking for strong leadership and firm institutional anchorage, the appeal of these writers must have been to many irresistible. They had, indeed, an excellent case; but the price was intolerably high, for it entailed the elimination of much of the creative element in Christian thought. True, it could not possibly be in fact entirely killed. It lived on and flourished, not least in centers such as Alexandria. Throughout the centuries it kept re-appearing, like a strong plant with deep roots, in the most unexpected corners of the Church. Nevertheless, the Church's emphasis was now so irrevocably on institutional concerns that spirituality had to find new ways of survival. It did, chiefly in mysticism and the monastic life and, in the later Middle Ages, in the Christian humanism that had deeply religious roots. Much spirituality in the West found expression, however, outside the Church, among the Bogomils, for instance, in the East, and the Albigenses or Cathars in the West. The Albigenses prospered so strongly in the twelfth century, especially in what are now Provence and northern Italy, that for a time it looked as though they would capture all Christendom. One of the chief purposes of the new Dominican Order, which later played a notorious role in the Inquisition, was to oppose and suppress the Albigenses, who were unquestionably committed to a sort of gnostic renaissance. It is doubtful whether the Albigenses would have arisen at all, however, but for the hardening of the institutional arteries of the Church.

Nevertheless, a glance at the voluminous early Christian literature of "apocryphal" Gospels and other such material must surely convince us that some critical restraint was needed to stem the prodigious avalanche of speculative thought that was very early pouring out of the minds of those who wished to be accounted Christian. Such is the nature of gnostic speculation: it flows so copiously and so freely that it cries out for the good offices of those whose business is to put the brakes on its terrifying speed and to channel its staggering volume into more manageable compass. For useful criticism can deal only with speculation that is to some extent already self-disciplined. That self-discipline is what the gnostic learns to achieve as he goes along. The genuine gnostic thinker, like the genuine mystic, welcomes constructive critique of the expression of his ideas and abundantly uses such critique in saying what he has to say. With perceptive critique and understanding analysis his gnosticism becomes more and more developed, as imagination in the arts produces better and better results as the artist learns from the history of art and from the work of others how to refine and purify what his imagination inspires him to do. Only when the critical element in religious thought is bent on the destruction of all gnostic speculation and sets itself against all attempts to understand better the nature of the divine and the ways of God with man (as is, alas, too often the case) is the analytical approach to philosophy and religion unwelcome because useless and futile. The speculative element remains paramount because it is creative.

A final word here may be desirable, though some will think it should go without saying. While the kind of speculation that was warranted and perhaps inescapable two thousand years ago was right for those who engaged in it at that time, it would not be right for us today, for we have the whole corpus of the history of religious ideas to guide us. If we do not learn from it, we shall be merely indulging in wild fancy. We can have no right at all to speculate today in the manner of either the writers of the Upanishads or those of the Mediterranean world in the time of Christ. We can profitably, however, inspect and reassess their insights in the light of all we now know, and surely it will not be surprising if we find that some of their ideas have been too little appreciated. Prejudice, whether of the age or of the place, can effectively blind people to the wisdom of their prophets and teachers and stand as an obstacle to the attainment of that gnosis of God that is the quest of all religions in every society and in every age.

VI

SCIENCE, MAGIC AND MONOTHEISM

Science is for those who learn; poetry, for those who know.
—Joseph Roux, *Meditations of a Parish Priest*

What is the cause of the persistent prejudice in the Christian Church against gnostic tendencies? The prejudice extends far beyond the more extreme forms of gnostic pretension. In the eyes of many, not least Protestants, even the mystical element in Christian experience is suspect. If we can better understand the nature of such fears and assess the extent to which they are warranted, if at all, we may be better able to judge the proper role of the gnostic element in Christian thought and life and how healthy it may be for the well-being of the Christian Church.

Opposition to gnostic ideas today seems to come from two distinct sources. On the one hand it tends to be suspect wherever the monotheistic emphasis is strong, involving the traditional biblical insistence on the insurmountable gulf between the human and the divine. On the other hand, it is associated in the minds of many with primitive magic and ranged accordingly alongside the forces of anti-scientific speculation. If either objection were solidly grounded there would be indeed good reason for Christians to oppose gnostic influences. For true religion can never be against true science, and the concept of the unity of God, so vehemently affirmed in Judaism and Islam, is also basic in all Christian thought.

Historically, gnostic notions have indeed been often allied to magical ones. The reason is simple. Magical and mystical ideas begin in the conviction that there are dimensions of being beyond those to which our five senses provide access. Magic begins as a way of trying to solve the riddles of the universe. It is a primitive kind of speculation about the nature of things; that is to say, it is a primitive form of science that has not yet developed a methodology that makes possible scientific progress. Both magic and mysticism promise a pathway to the better apprehension of the truth about the universe. The magician's profession, however, is obviously attractive to time-servers and charlatans. In this it is not unique: science and theology are by no means exempt even today. In the ancient world it was tempting to construct chemistries of those dimensions of being that magic sought to explore, and no doubt many gnostic systems were evolved out of such beginnings.

Magic continued to play a considerable part in the thinking of many even in the seventeenth century, when modern science may be said to have been born. When Sir Thomas Browne, in his *Religio Medici*, wrote that "I could be content that we might procreate like trees, without conjunction, or that there were any way to perpetuate the world without this trivial and vulgar way of coition,"[1] he may well have had in mind the alchemists' notion of the creation of human beings without the usual reproductive process, a notion that has reappeared today, of course, in the notion of biological cloning, already successfully accomplished with frogs and supposed by some biologists to be at least a distant possibility with humans. A century before Browne, in 1533, an Englishwoman, Mary Woods, was alleged to have given another woman medicine made from the spawn of a trotter to enable her to conceive a child without benefit of male sperm. A treatise issued in 1631 tells us that one may predict whether a patient will live or die, by performing a urinalysis as follows. One inserts a nettle in the patient's urine for twenty-four hours: if it withers, he will die, if it remains fresh, he will live.

---

[1] Thomas Browne, *Religion Medici*, Verulam Club edition (London: Chapman and Hall, Ltd., n.d.), p. 121. The work was originally published in 1642.

The king's touch was firmly believed by many to have thera-
peutic qualities. From 1634 till 1728 the Book of Common Prayer
included a ritual for the purpose. Though the therapy was supposed to be chiefly effective against scrofula, the beneficial effects
could include the cure of epilepsy. Belief in such notions tended
to make the learned suspect all inquiry into what could not be
established by strictly empiricist methods.

On the theological side, the root of the two objections to gnostic
ideas is curiously self-contradictory. On the one hand, there is the
well-known objection that gnostic systems of spiritual chemistry
leave no room for the freedom of the will. This, if justified, would
be indeed a fatal objection, since Christianity is meaningless apart
from a doctrine of human freedom. The medieval astrologers did
indeed seem to teach such an astral determinism, and it was
precisely at that point that the theologians of the day parted
company with them. The theologians had little or no quarrel with
what the astrologers said about the influence of the stars upon
vegetation and other physical phenomena; but they could not
allow the notion that the lives of human beings and all their
actions as well as all the events surrounding them are determined
by the position of celestial bodies, for that, of course, made people
wholly the victims of circumstance. That theological objection to
gnostic elements in Christian thought, if warranted, would certainly be justified. From the earliest times, however, Christian
thinkers have objected, on the other hand, to gnostic notions on
exactly the opposite grounds.

Irenaeus, for instance, complained that a certain Valentinian
of his day strutted about as proud as a cock because of his spiritual
achievements: he thought he had gone beyond heaven and earth
and reached the divine Pleroma. Why would one become so
absurdly and (from a Christian standpoint) blasphemously proud
of oneself? Only because of one's achievements. But how can one
be said to achieve or accomplish anything if one lacks freedom of
the will to do so? The objection to gnostic pride is not merely *akin*
to the objection to the magician's pride in his art of controlling
nature; it *is* the same objection. For as the magician claims to
manipulate the awesome forces of nature and make them operate
as he wishes rather than otherwise, so certain gnostic and
theosophical ideologies do seem to suggest that if only I know
enough I am the master of my fate. Fate becomes, indeed, merely
the stuff out of which I design my destiny as the sculptor sculpts

his work of art out of a chunk of inert marble. Gnostics are charged not only with claiming to know everything but also with claiming to be able, as a result of their knowledge, to do every-thing. The typical churchman is quick to warn them against the arrogance of such pretensions, since we are all but clay in the hands of the divine Potter, created by His almighty power and standing under His inescapable judgment. Who are we to pre-tend to be able to manipulate anything, whether the "laws of nature" or other people's minds? Paradoxically, however, it is the mystics who tend to be humble and the dogmaticians arrogant.

The very self-contradictoriness of these two standard objec-tions to gnostic elements in Christian thought provides a clue to the understanding of how the suspicion arose and has been perpetuated. For the dual objection is not unlike that which the Christian mind has instinctively directed against natural science itself, which until recent times generally appeared in a very de-terministic guise, while the individual scientist and perhaps more especially the technologist must always have seemed somewhat arrogant in the eyes of those who are trained to contemplate with awe and devotion the wonderful works of God. Apart from the speculations of some of the early Greeks such as Anaximander, evolutionary ideas were unknown, so that Christian preachers could expatiate at length about the incomparable beneficence of the Almighty in bestowing on man, for example, his five fingers, so ingeniously designed by the Creator and reserved by him to the human species. The suggestion that man had developed this arrangement over the course of a million years or more would have been universally greeted in Christian circles, right down to comparatively recent times, as a blasphemous outrage. Muslim scientists, who in the earlier Middle Ages were far ahead of either Christian or Jewish thought, had similar and perhaps even more acute difficulties with their own Islamic theologians, who upheld, of course, the extreme predestinarianism of the Qur'ān.

Yet when all that has been noted, we know very well what envy and bitterness have been generated in the hearts of all but the most deeply spiritual of men and women, Christians included, at the thought of anyone's having any special powers of any kind, especially any that have seemed hidden or occult. The persecu-tion of so-called witches is well-known; but any kind of achieve-ment having in it even the slightest *soupçon* of the inexplicable is obviously one that would arouse some degree of suspicion or fear.

The medieval scientists such as Adelard of Bath, the pioneer student in Christendom of Arabic scientific thought in the twelfth century and the most outstanding name in English scientific thought before Grosseteste and Roger Bacon, are distinguished from the scholastic philosophers and theologians chiefly by their preference for experience over books. For that very reason, however, they tended to be suspect in the eyes of scholastics who relied so much on ancient authorities. For unless your experience happens to be also my experience, not only am I unlikely to be impressed by your discoveries about it, I am prone (for such is human nature) to be either envious of your superior range of experience or incredulous of your claims to possessing it.

I am far from suggesting that the Church's caution about the gnostic element in Christianity has always been merely obscurantist. On the contrary, the instinct for caution among the learned in the Church has been warranted, for the Church is a ready prey to charlatans of every kind, and gnosticism is among the avenues that give these free passage. Nevertheless, the Church has been generally far too unwilling to look open-mindedly at many ideas it has so readily dubbed occult and thereupon dismissed as heretical. The notorious popular eagerness for cheap nostrums of every sort (familiar to us today in our pill-oriented society) has contributed to the tendency of traditionalists to see all unfamiliar religious ideas as superstitious. There is superstition in all religion, however, as there is religion in all superstition. What makes the difference is the attitude one brings to bear on the situation.

That true science and true religion, being both grounded in experience, can never be radically opposed but have, on the contrary, a common ultimate goal, is an insight of incomparable importance. At various times in human history the task of reconciling them has become the prime concern of the most worthwhile philosophical thought. In the thirteenth century, in the West, as a result of the recovery of Aristotle, whose teachings were the scientific challenge of the day to Christian faith, the reconciliation was accomplished by the schoolmen, notably Aquinas and Duns Scotus. It was a magnificent achievement in terms of the task as these medieval thinkers took the task to be.

Seven hundred years later, another battle developed between the science and the religion of the day. For though many ancient beliefs had been overthrown, not least among thinkers under the "Protestant" banner, others had not only remained strong but had become probably even more deeply entrenched, for the fewer the tenets a society holds the more focus is turned on them so that they tend to be held all the more vehemently. One of these firm beliefs that almost everybody with pretensions to anything like orthodox Christianity—"Catholic" or "Protestant"—held without question through the first half of the last century was that humanity was a special creation of God, as were other living species such as birds and fish. God had created living beings in order. Man was the crowning act, the work of the last "day" of divine creation, as Genesis recounts. Against this belief came the Darwinian bombshell: the scientific proposal, soon widely accepted in scientific circles at least, that the case was very different. The work of Darwin and Huxley was such a blow to literalistic Christians that for decades many, if not most, simply refused to accept the scientific evidence for biological evolution, and some even today feel they must repudiate it, at any rate among the more literal-minded sects. Yet toward the end of the nineteenth century, when the battle between science and religion was at its height, some of the most perceptive and deeply spiritual writing in the history of Christian thought was done by thinkers who saw that biological evolution, far from demolishing or even impoverishing Christian faith, immensely enriched it. Men such as Henry Drummond, M. J. Savage, Lyman Abbott and James McCosh, all helped their fellow Christians to see the truth. John Fiske called evolution "God's way of doing things." Once again the reconciliation of science and religion had been undertaken. This time it issued, in the long run, in the work of twentieth-century thinkers such as Teilhard de Chardin and the process theologians. On the implications of an evolutionary understanding of the universe we shall have more to say in a later chapter.

What has loomed large in the thought of the most enlightened thinkers of today is the recognition of the fact that, contrary to what has often been supposed, the methodologies of science and religion are closer than at first sight may seem to be the case. What, until the seventeenth century, probably delayed the emergence of modern science more than any other factor was the traditional emphasis on deduction and the absence, until the end of the Middle Ages of any *widespread* appreciation of what inductive methods can accomplish in the attainment of scientific knowledge. But genuine progress in religious thought also suffered from the lack of appeal to experience, since apart from the

mystical tradition, traditional theology worked for centuries from
a priori premisses. True, the range of experience that the natural
sciences dealt with and those that interested religious people were
different; nevertheless, not only did their methodologies seem to
converge more than had been the case in the past; there was
sometimes even a common range of experience that concerned
them. Indeed, but for such growing appreciation, dim though it
often was, Christianity would have all but died out among educated people by the turn of this century as it had almost evapo-
rated in the eighteenth under the influence of the rationalist
philosophy and mechanistic science of that age.

This then brings us to the question of the status of gnosticism.
What advances in methodology can gnostic and theosophical
enterprises claim to have made since, for instance, the time of
Christ? This is an extremely difficult question to answer at all
satisfactorily; nevertheless, theosophical writers today are surely
more aware of intelligent and knowledgeable criticism of what
they propose than were, say, the second-century Gnostics that
caused such alarm among so many Christians at that time. We
recognize today that the gnostic outlook belongs to no particular
age. It is perennial, if only for the reason that it is the creative
element in all religion. It begins with a deepening awareness of
the spiritual realities around us. That awareness is not cultivated
to perfection overnight. It takes not merely many years but many
lives.

In the age in which Christianity emerged, Greek had already
become the international language. Egyptian papyri show that a
remarkable range of literature was copied for reading. The
Greek translation of the Old Testament now known to scholars as
the Septuagint exercised considerable influence on vocabulary.
Words such as *plērōma* that had previously borne only a neutral
significance acquired religious overtones. Words so laden with
new meanings were no doubt bandied about freely. No doubt,
too, many were intoxicated by them and felt instantly superior
just by using them, as all of us have probably felt superior when, as
children, we were suddenly exposed to the high-sounding terminology of a science that was new to us, such as geology or
biology. Paul seems to have detected such an immature pride in
the Corinthian Christians, who thought themselves already advanced in gnosis. He tells them in effect that their gnosis is all
right as far as it goes; but he has a prescription for their develop-

ment of a far superior gnosis through the "three things": faith, hope and love, especially love (*agapē*). In other words: "Don't think you've nothing to learn, for that's the way to block all real progress." A little later he rebukes them: "Some of you seem not to know God at all. You should be ashamed."[2] Paul seems to be telling the Corinthian Christians: "Some of you think you have all the gnosis there is. On the contrary, you seem to lack the most fundamental gnosis, for you are ignorant of God (*agnōsian gar theou*)."

What is particularly interesting in Pauline and other apostolic teaching is that those who are instructing the new Christian communities find a gnostic disposition already there. While they see its inadequacy they do not repudiate it in itself but only when it leads immature people into foolish and unwarranted pride. That gnostic concepts came in half-baked forms and that people got "big ideas" about their own spiritual capacity because of them need cause no surprise. It could hardly be otherwise. Immaturity does no great harm so long as it is kept in check and is not allowed to mislead those whom elsewhere Paul calls "infants in Christ" who have to be fed with milk because they are not ready for solid food.[3]

The Christian message to the Gentiles inevitably includes the biblical emphasis on the unity of God. The Jews had learned this. It is still the central tenet of Judaism, formulated in the Shema, which is the nearest that Judaism comes to a creed: "Hear, O Israel! The Lord thy God is *one* God." The Gentiles, nurtured in polytheistic cultures, could not at first grasp all the implications of this monotheism that Christianity inherited from its Jewish cradle. According to their Christian teachers it was what above all they most needed to grasp. Nevertheless they were already asking the right questions. They were already looking for God. So they could not be *entirely* "carnal". Their progress in sensitivity had already begun, though it had a long way to go.

The development of the natural sciences, after all, took many, many centuries to reach anything like what we would call modern scientific method, with its laboratory experiments and verificational procedures. When we look at what passed for science two

---

[2] 1 Corinthians 15.34.
[3] 1 Corinthians 3.1-2.

thousand or even a few hundred years ago, we may smile at much of it, amazed that people so sophisticated in other ways could be so immature in this. Medicine was particularly backward by modern standards. Not until 1628 did Harvey produce his treatise, *De motu cordis*, showing that the blood in the human body circulates. Less than two hundred years ago even well-to-do people were still using leeches, under their doctors' prescription, for the supposed cure of a large variety of ailments. It is only a little more than a century since Pasteur established the role of bacteria in disease, a discovery that has revolutionized both medicine and surgery as much as printing once revolutionized the distribution of books. Need we be much astonished, then, if the gnostic quest that was in progress in the Mediterranean world at the time of Christ, with its attendant awareness of psychic phenomena and the apprehension of other dimensions of being, should need at least as much time for its development of a satisfactory methodology of its own? If, as I am suggesting, Christianity was from the first an answer to that gnostic quest, and if gnostic speculation provided the creative element in Christian thought, would it be astonishing to find that the full appropriation of such wisdom should take even longer than the development of medical knowledge and scientific method?

VII

THE PERIL OF DE-GNOSTICIZING JESUS

There is much else that Jesus did. If it were
all to be recorded in detail, I suppose
the whole world would not hold the books
that would be written.
—Concluding verse of the Gospel according to John

Christianity emerged in a climate of psychic awareness and, at least on the part of some, of gnostic preoccupation. Little is known for certain about the life of Jesus. When he died, his movement, to all appearances, died too. Whatever happend on Easter Day, it was miraculously revived.

The life of Jesus remains shrouded in mystery. In the nineteenth century, with the rise of new forms of historiography, the quest for "the historical Jesus" became a concern for both the Christian community and the scholarly world. When Hermann Samuel Reimarus had undertaken, in the seventeenth century, a serious study of the historical Jesus, nobody had ever written a life of Jesus except for the one written by Jerome Xavier, a Jesuit and nephew of the celebrated missionary, Francis Xavier (1506–1552). Xavier's life of Jesus had been designed for presentation to a potentate of Hindustan, an account that would give no offence to the ruler. Written in Persian, it was eventually translated into Latin by a Reformed Church theologian, Louis de Dieu, apparently with the specific intention of discrediting the Roman

Catholic Church. Reimarus, by contrast, sought to present Jesus as thoroughly Jewish and to contend that, sharing his compatriots' exclusiveness, he had intended to establish an earthly kingdom and deliver his people from political oppression. The enterprise had failed. His disciples, at first fearful of being implicated in their Master's foiled attempt to bring about an uprising, eventually took courage. Having stolen the body of Jesus and hidden it, they proclaimed his resurrection and announced that he would soon return and that the world would then come to an end. The hope of the parousia, the Second Coming, was the basis of the apostolic religion. In the eighteenth century, rationalists produced a series of biographies of Jesus such as might have been expected of them. Then at last, in 1855, came the first edition of the life of Jesus by David Friedrich Strauss. Strauss's work, written with sincerity and literary skill, was much influenced by Reimarus. It disposed of the miraculous elements in the Gospels and was very influential, not least in the fierce controversy it aroused.

The torrent of critical nineteenth-century studies of Jesus produced negative results. The literature was assessed by that great genius of our own century, Albert Schweitzer, in his work *Von Reimarus zu Wrede*, originally published in 1906 and translated into English as *The Quest of the Historical Jesus*. Scholarly skepticism about the life of Jesus has reached the point that many scholars question whether we can know anything of its details at all. Some people have even doubted the existence of Jesus, though I do not think anyone with any training in sifting historical evidence could seriously entertain that view. Yet, though that is a hypothesis that may be safely ignored, biblical scholarship has left Christian piety with at most a hazy picture of the central figure of the Christian faith.

Biography as we understand it today was unknown not only when the Gospels were written but for many centuries afterwards. When it did emerge in the nineteenth century it was at first handicapped by its use of the model of the natural sciences. It took into account the role of nature in human as in other history; but it failed to a great extent to take account of what is distinctively human in humanity, the element in man that transcends the nature the sciences inspect. That element the ancients would have called divine.

In recent decades, a movement has emerged that may be called a *new* quest. The claim to newness is amply justified: it brings to bear on the quest new methodologies that are capable of encompassing dimensions the old ones could not touch. These methodologies provide a new hermeneutic that takes into account, for example, the results of existentialist and phenomenological types of twentieth-century thought. Associated with this new quest are the names of Rudolf Bultmann, Joachim Jeremias, Günther Bornkamm, Oscar Cullmann and many others. In the United States a well-known exponent has been Professor James M. Robinson of Claremont, California. The literature on the historical Jesus, staggering in the immensity of its volume, has obviously performed a task indispensable to modern scholarship. Even at the best, however, its results must disappoint anyone hoping for a literary portrait of Jesus. Opinions vary widely about the extent of historical skepticism that honesty demands. Some think we have considerable information in the Gospels and lack only the technical details a modern biography would be expected to provide, especially chronological details. Others contend that we have almost no historically reliable knowledge at all. Probably most would hover between these extremes, accepting the view so beautifully expressed by the late R. H. Lightfoot of Oxford at the close of his Bampton Lectures for 1934, that we but touch the hem of his garment.

One of the most important reasons for the patently false pictures of Jesus that have been presented both in ecclesiastical tradition and in the work of imaginative writers has long been recognized: it is the tendency to modernize him. Medieval artists depicted him as a holy man according to the standards of their day: a monk or a mendicant friar. In the eighteenth century, Voltaire satirically proposed, in looking at a picture of Jesus dressed in a habit of a Jesuit, that the Jesuits had so painted him in case men might love him!

The danger of unwittingly modernizing Jesus was noted half a century ago by the late Henry Joel Cadbury of Harvard, who pointed to trivial anachronisms disfiguring biographies of Jesus, such as references to a first-century house in Nazareth with a separate kitchen and upstairs bedrooms for a family of eight persons or more, and then went on to note that an author guilty of such cross anachronisms in mundane details is likely to be guilty of far more misleading ones in the sphere of ideas. Some have thought of Jesus as primarily a social reformer; others have presented him as a Victorian visionary. One biographer has even seen him as a top management executive![1] The tendency is pernicious, of course; but it is eminently understandable. We humans, whom the Bible says are made in the image of God, seem to delight in returning the compliment by making God in our image. So an Englishman's God is an Englishman twelve feet high, a Frenchman's one who speaks a French more impeccable than could ever be heard even at the *Académie*. A century before Socrates, the Greek poet Xenophanes of Ionia had pointed out that if only oxen and lions could draw as human artists do, they would make pictures of their gods in their own likeness. So, too, Jesus, who in Christian orthodoxy is accounted God made man, is seen in the image of those who worship him.

If, however, Jesus himself and his disciples reflected an outlook such as we call gnostic and if the extravagant forms that Christian Gnosticism took in the second century led (as we have seen they did) to a hardening of Christian opinion against gnostic elements in the Church, then of course all portraits of Jesus throughout the ages, popular or scholarly, would be likely to have been vitiated by veiling that gnostic outlook from them. For such a radical modernization would always fatally warp any possible insight into the mind and teaching of him who is the focus of the Christian faith. If the people who sought and accepted Jesus as Master and Lord were already thinking in terms of angels, transfigurations and a vast world of psychic realities, then most church people (learned and unlearned alike, since neither usually shares such a view) could not avoid the peril of modernizing Jesus against which Henry Cadbury warned his generation. If the mental furnishings of people around the cradle of the Christian faith included notions anything like clairvoyance, for instance, and awareness of various states of consciousness, planes of energy, and the like, then those who (in obedience to what they have taken to be Christian orthodoxy) have renounced all such ideas as tinged with the "false teachings" the New Testament warns against, are bound to misunderstand what Jesus and the apostles are saying.

---

[1]Bruce Barton, *The Man Nobody Knows* (Indianapolis: Bobbs-Merrill, 1925).

Not only could they not know the *Sitz im Leben*, the life-setting, in which the New Testament literature arose; they would be even more seriously incapacitated by lack of understanding of the psychic scenery it presupposed.

What exactly do we mean by suggesting the prevalence of a "gnostic climate of thought" or a "gnostic ideology" at the cradling of the Christian faith? We cannot too strongly underline the distinction we have already made between that climate, whatever it was, and the Gnostic sects that so much alarmed second-century Christians such as Irenaeus, leading them to emphasize and develop such heavily institutional concepts as apostolic succession, the episcopate, and the New Testament canon, and to denounce the "false teachings" of the sects who were making elaborate systems of gnosis. That gnosticism can and did run riot is unastonishing. That it should provoke such reactions in the Church is understandable. Wild and wanton developments may issue from any group of ideas and so cause people nurtured on these ideas to take fright. The emergence of Jewish gnosticism comes to many as a surprise. Some have even suggested that a Jewish gnosticism is a contradiction, since the Marcionites and some other gnostic groups were apparently anti-Jewish. How, they ask, could any Jew ever accept the reckoning of the God of his fathers, the God of Jacob and of Isaac, as the Demiurge, as Marcion and other Gentiles did? That is almost like asking how Americans can believe in political and intellectual freedom when it produces men like Charles Manson. No ideology can be held accountable for the deviant forms that it may spawn. If we are to talk, as I believe we must, of a general gnostic attitude, we must rid ourselves of all specifically developed gnostic forms and systems and try to detect, rather, presupppositions.

The emergence of celibacy within Judaism is an example of a promising locus for such detection. Classical Judaism was very strongly oriented towards the family. Marriage was looked upon not only as a great blessing but also as a primary duty. A man who by the age of thirty had not taken a wife was regarded with disfavor if not contempt. That has been a fairly general attitude in most societies. From such a standpoint the choice of celibacy for religious motives, entailing the ideal of total abstinence from all sexual activity, is obviously such an extraordinary decision that its emergence, for instance among the Essenes and other groups in

Judaism about the time of Christ, demands explanation.[2] No one would choose such a life who shared the old, traditional outlook. The choice was likely to be made only through acceptance, conscious or unconscious, of a gnostic type of claim to religious insight, for example that the created world is not as wholly good as Genesis suggests and that instead of conforming to it we should be striving to purify ourselves by fasting and mortification of the body so as to fit ourselves for a higher plane of existence. It also encompasses the principle of the sacrifice for some higher end of what is most valued: in this case the family, the propagation of children for posterity. Sacrifice, to be genuine, must be sacrifice of the best we know. In the Christian Middle Ages the two qualities people most admired were holiness and chivalry, and they killed off their knights in war and forbade their holy men to procreate families.

The Gospels are full of allusions that imply special attitudes of mind that are not ordinarily to be expected of people of any race or class at any period of human history. Let us take, as a random example, the beautiful story of the meeting of the disciples with the Risen Christ on the road to Emmaus.[3] The disciples, talking, as they went, of the seemingly tragic failure of the movement of which they had been part and which had resulted in the ignominy of the crucifixion of their Master, are overtaken by a stranger who joined in their conversation. According to the Gospel narrative, the stranger was Jesus, risen from the dead; yet they did not know it was Jesus because "their eyes were holden that they should not know him."[4]

Jesus then expounds the Scriptures to them, beginning with Moses and the Prophets, showing why Christ had to suffer and what had to have befallen him. Still they do not recognize him. Meanwhile, evening approaches, so they hospitably urge the stranger not to go farther on his journey, as seems to be his inclination, but to stay overnight. The stranger acquiesces. Even now they do not see who he is. At last they sit down to eat. The stranger takes bread and, according to Jewish custom, blesses and

---

[2]Josephus mentions some Essenes who married; but these must have been very exceptional, since Pliny, Philo and Josephus himself all specify celibacy as a characteristic feature of the Essene movement.
[3]Luke 24. 13-35.
[4]Luke 24.16.

breaks it as he gives it to them. Then suddenly their eyes are opened: "they knew him; and he vanished out of their sight."[5]

Even more extraordinary than his sudden disappearance at the meal and before he partakes of it is the circumstance that they could listen to him all the way along the road and not recognize him, seeing in him only an interesting stranger with a gift for biblical exegesis, and that they could then suddenly recognize him during the meal. Could Jesus have been so devoid of personality, so workaday in manner and appearance, as not to be instantly recognizable by his own disciples? Surely not. Then are we to ask what disguise he had worn during the walk and how he had contrived to discard it at the *baruch* of the bread? Even as we formulate such questions we see the absurdity of them. Yet if we rule out the gnostic element in Christianity, as has been habitual for many centuries, the story is so fantastic as to trouble even the most credulous mind. How often must people have asked themselves, under their breath, precisely such foolish questions? Only in the light of the gnostic presuppositions in which the Christian faith emerged do such accounts become intelligible at all, and then they at once captivate heart and mind.

Plainly, stories of this kind presuppose a climate in which what we now call parapsychological phenomena are part of the scenery, a climate in which people are expected to be unsurprised by clairvoyance. We are being told that the two disciples, in their crestfallen mood following their tragic experience of the death of their Master, were still spiritually myopic and were then raised to a higher level of consciousness, able to penetrate another dimension of reality. Such a story, to such hearers, would not in itself raise eyebrows much higher than ours would be raised today by accounts of now well-established phenomena such as hypnotism, telepathy and thought-reading. That is not at all, however, the way in which either uncritical hearers of the Gospels or learned biblical scholars have traditionally read narratives of this kind. On the one side, the skeptics have dismissed such stories as the folklore of an ignorant and superstitious people; on the other, conservative piety, "Catholic" and "Protestant" alike, has called for the exercise of "blind" faith, thereby raising a vast network of philosophical problems about the nature of faith and how it is to be distinguished from knowledge and belief. We have touched on these problems and shall consider them further in a later chapter.

---

[5]Luke 24.31.

Philosophers and others, unless they are willing to open their minds to the significance of the ancient gnostic tradition to which the apostles of Christ were addressing themselves, cannot even ask the right kind of question. As George Berkeley, one of the most penetrating thinkers in the history of Western philosophy, said of the philosophers of his day: they first raise a dust and then complain they cannot see. Theologians also too often blindfold themselves before tackling their task.

Mark tells us that a woman who had been plagued by a haemorrhage for twelve years came quietly up to Jesus from behind him in the crowd and touched his clothes, believing that by doing so she would be cured. She was, and instantly. Then Jesus, "immediately knowing in himself that virtue (*dynamis*, energy or power) had gone out of him," turned round and asked who it was who had touched him. The woman came forward no doubt timidly, admitting that it was she. Knowing "what was done in her," she "told him all the truth."[6] The story is commonly explained away as a relic of an antiquated, magical way of thinking. Today, in circles familiar with the phenomenon of spiritual healing, it would pose no particular difficulties.

All of the Gospel accounts of the Resurrection of Christ abound in details that would be ludicrous apart from gnostic or theosophical ways of thought. To find the sepulcher in which Jesus had been laid empty is startling enough in itself; but John tells us that Mary Magdalene, weeping at the discovery, bends down and finds in the sepulcher "two angels in white" sitting respectively at the place where the head and the feet of Jesus had lain.[7] This is a typically "psychic" mode of conceptualizing. Nobody in any age of history who had not been thinking along theosophical or gnostic lines could possibly even formulate the discovery in those terms. True, there is a strong tradition about angels in all Semitic lore, Islamic as well as Jewish; but to find an angel or "being of Light" (as we might say today) sitting on the place where the head of Jesus had been, and another where had been his feet, presupposes a very special way of thinking. In fact, throughout the centuries writers and other artists have simply ignored the Church's official exclusion of gnostic ideas and have gone on thinking, however individualistically, in such ways. (Perhaps there is an echo of the New Testament presuppositions

---

[6]Mark 5.25-34.
[7]John 20.12.

in the strange painting by Léon Bonnat of the martyrdom of Saint Denis by beheading, which is on the walls of the Panthéon in Paris. The severed head bears around it a halo of light, but rays of light stream also from the trunk from which the head has been severed.) Finally Mary Magdalene turns round and sees a man whom she interrogates. She does not recognize him to be Jesus till he speaks her name. We are to suppose that she made to embrace him, for he told her not to touch him because he had not yet "ascended" to his Father. The same evening, however, when the disciples were closeted in a room, apparently in fear of arrest, Jesus suddenly appeared in the midst of them with the customary greeting: *Shalom elechem*, "Peace be unto you." Yet only a week later he tells Thomas, one of the disciples, who is skeptical, not only to touch him but to put his hand into his hands and side and feel the print of the nails and the wound of the spear. Thomas does so and acknowledges that it is indeed Jesus.[8]

Such narratives do not make any sense apart from the gnostic background we are to presume. No sane person would ask anyone to accept stories of that sort, or indeed conceive of them in the first place, unless he had had some experience of a kind that today would be called "paranormal", and could expect his readers to understand, through their own experience, what he was talking or writing about. If I were to wish to record a psychic adventure today, I would not attempt to do so in a journal of history or in a newspaper column as if it were an account of a street accident or geological occurrence, because my readers would be at best unprepared for and at worst incapable of making the necessary mental adjustments. Unless I were writing in a journal of psychical research or the like, I would find it necessary to forewarn them of the nature of my report. The whole New Testament literature, to say nothing of the vast non-canonical literature of early Christianity, is written by and for people who have attained considerable sensitivity to psychic phenomena. For most people today, blinded by their positivistic tendencies and empiricist presuppositions, the apostolic *kērygma* or proclamation is difficult because grasping its meaning entails such sensitivity and such experience.

In the first century the difficulty was of a different kind. The difficulty was not that such "paranormal" events were occurring, but that they were occurring in such a way as to focus upon him

---

[8]John 20.1-29.

who had been discredited by the ignominy of the Crucifixion. It was the latter that made the paranormal events point to the validity of the apostolic claim that Jesus was the uniquely divine Being who had pitched his tent among men and was now to be hailed as Savior of the world, the full and final revelation of God to man.

To understand that background is to understand why the developing christology had such an appeal. The "Good News" of Christ came to such people as the answer to innumerable questions they had so far been unable to answer. The apostolic message put the whole jigsaw of their experience of psychic realities in place and gave direction to their spiritual quest. Yet as you cannot put a jigsaw puzzle together till you have the pieces, so you could not possibly see Jesus as the answer, in the way the first Christians saw him, unless you had the preliminary psychic awareness and the flashes of clairvoyance. Without the complex spiritual scenery that gnosis enables its initiates to perceive, who could see Jesus as the answer to anything? The appeal of Jesus is strong in proportion to your spiritual awareness. Einstein would not impress you if you knew absolutely nothing of either physics or mathematics, nor would Joyce if you knew nothing of literature.

Paradoxically, the New Testament calls this awareness "faith", which contemporary theologians sharply contrast with every kind of gnosis. Yet faith is a *kind* of knowledge. According to the New Testament writer of the letter to the Hebrews, it is faith alone that "can guarantee the blessings that we hope for" and is able to "prove the existence of the realities that at present remain unseen."[9] But if by "unseen" we are to understand "empirically unseen", what the writer is calling faith (*pistis*) is really a kind of spiritual perception, a clairvoyance that enables those fortunate enough to enjoy it to grasp a dimension of existence that neither the largest telescope nor the most powerful microscope could ever penetrate any more than a slide-rule could measure time. Christian theologians have been right, of course, in their firm insistence that the primary meaning of "faith" in the New Testament is very different from what is commonly understood by the term, which for so many signifies merely a vague sort of willing-

---

[9] Hebrews 11.1 (Jerusalem Bible).

ness to accept a doctrine or theological affirmation that cannot be formally proved. It means, of course, much more, and what it means entails sensitivity to realities inaccessible to physicists, chemists and botanists as such. We shall consider, in a later chapter, the notion of faith as inductive gnosis.

Academic theologians, medieval and modern, have often been so alienated from the perception of the realities of that other dimension of being that they have bypassed the fundamental nature of the life of faith. Christian mystics, however, from the comparatively restrained Benedictine tradition to the more florid Spanish school, from the debonair Salesian tradition that flourished in seventeenth-century France to the mystics of the recent times, have all known in their own way that from their point of view the traditional distinction between faith and knowledge is but a matter of degree. That is not to deny that faith has in it some very peculiar elements; nevertheless, the language of faith and revelation, contradistinguished from the language of the mystics, is always about something that is both concealed and revealed, as the sun on a windy day may be half hid by clouds. Jesus, to whom is so much attributed the language of faith, reproaches those who are willfully "blind" and proclaims that he has come into this world "so that those without sight may see."[10] Those "of little faith" are indeed the spiritually blind.

I am suggesting here that we must get behind distinctions that have become necessary for the scholasticism of formal, official theologies but may in fact fundamentally "modernize" the outlook of Jesus and those who followed him. In a milieu permeated with gnostic or theosophical presuppositions, many were still, of course, only minimally able to perceive a glimpse of the realities of which Jesus spoke. Some, however, were more spiritually perceptive; but even his chosen twelve disciples had to be occasionally reproved for their blindness. The best of all promises set forth in the eight Beatitudes enunciated in the Sermon on the Mount is to the pure in heart: they shall *see* God. We may talk as much as we like about the ambiguities in the term "faith" and the subtle distinctions between faith and sight; but that is because the gnostic or theosophical element in Christian thought has had, from the second century onwards, a bad image and therefore a bad

---

[10]John 9.39.

press. I cannot but think that what Jesus so constantly deprecated was lack of spiritual vision and what endeared men and women to him was that clarity of spiritual perception that we may call clairvoyance. That it was to be achieved, according to his teaching, not through the study of a hermetic literature or of any kind of elaborately conceived chemistry of the spirit but, rather, through that loving disposition that makes possible the acceptance of forgiveness and the openness to new truths, makes it not at all less a gnosis. On the contrary, that is the very nature of all true gnosis. We find difficulty in discerning the divine not because God is too complicated for our human brains to fathom, but because he is too simple for our highly complex brains to grasp. Jesus established himself forever in the hearts of his followers by showing them that the purity of a truly loving heart gives us that kind of knowledge that no amount of learning, rabbinical or otherwise, can ever provide. Nor can there ever be anything static or smug about such gnosis, for the purification of the human heart goes on until all its dross is turned to gold, and that is a very long process indeed, much too long to be achieved in one lifetime.

That part of the Bible we call the Old Testament was familiar, of course, and constantly in the minds of Jesus and the apostles. The New Testament as we know it today was not known as a separate entity in Christian literature till nearly two hundred years after the death of Christ. The importance of this is incalculably great for us. Not only did Paul have no such equipment (which would be a modern Christian missionary's first piece of baggage); none of the great Christian Fathers of the first two centuries possessed any such sacrosanct *corpus* of Christian literature in the form in which it is venerated by Christians today. What they might have had would be papyrus scrolls of individual books. The *codex* or book in the form now familiar all over the world, as distinguished from the old scroll, did not come into general use till later. The old scroll form was far too cumbersome to contain conveniently anything like the whole of the Bible or even the New Testament. It was more suited to contain one book such as that named after the prophet Isaiah or the like.

From very early Christian times the question arose: how should the Bible be read? To what extent should it be read literally? To what extent allegorically? Broadly speaking, the School of Antioch was more disposed to the former way of reading the Bible, while the School of Alexandria favored the latter. Origen, pre-

eminent among early biblical scholars, taught that the Bible might
be read on several levels: the simple, unlettered person could
approach it literally, while the more learned would see beyond
the literal to various possible figurative meanings of the text. In
the Middle Ages the question of the letter and the figure loomed
large in priestly and monastic discussions of the Bible, and on the
whole the tendency was to allegorize, sometimes so fancifully as to
bring about a sort of literalistic backlash; but the medieval mind
was much more inclined to allegorization than is, for example,
anyone influenced by the so-called "Protestant fundamentalists"
of today. The men and women of the Middle Ages were both too
down-to-earth and too spiritually perspicacious to suppose that
any literature containing anything worthy to be so called could be
read only at a literalistic level. If one were to read the Bible
entirely on such a level one would have to suppose that, since
Jesus called himself "the door", one would have to decide
whether he were made of mahogany or oak. The medieval mind
was far too imaginative to go anywhere in that direction; it was
inclined, on the contrary, to err too much the other way, sometimes engaging in wildly fanciful interpretations of the text. It was
when interpretations became intolerably fanciful that voices
would rise in protest: back to the text.

A classic example occurs in the first chapters of the Bible. In the
Educated Christians today, though they may see the Bible as
indeed "the Word of God", know too much about the way in
which it was composed (a very complex process taking something
like a thousand years of writing, editing and compilation, not
counting oral traditions behind the actual writing) to think of it as
written to God's dictation. Nothing so simplistic as that could
possibly be squared with what is known of the construction of the
Bible. They prefer, therefore, to say that the Bible *contains* the
Word of God, the revelation of God to man about the divine
nature and an account of the great acts of God in human history.
That means that while certain statements in the Bible, such as
"Amaziah was twenty and five years old when he began to reign,
and he reigned twenty and five years in Jerusalem," may be taken
as purporting to be as nearly literal as any statement can be, other
utterances have esoteric meanings.[11]

A classic example occurs in the first chapters of the Bible. In the
first two chapters of Genesis we have two very different accounts

---

[11] 2 Chronicles 25.1.

of the creation of the world. The second of these accounts is a much older version of the creation story and very primitive in its conceptualization. God made the earth, but "there was not a man to till it." So God took dust or earth and formed man out of it as a child might make something out of play dough. (Some of the later rabbinical writers enlarged on this notion, suggesting that God took bits of earth from all over the world, using some from, say, India for the legs and some from Babylon for the arms, but reserving for the head the soil of Yeretz Israel.) Then God breathed his *ruach* (breath or air) into the nostrils of the man he had formed, whereupon the "man became a living soul." God then went forth, planted a garden in Eden, and put the man in it. After telling the man what he might and might not eat, God then decided that it was not good for man to be alone. He looked at the various beasts but, finding none suitable to be Adam's companion, he put Adam to sleep and extracted one of his ribs, out of which he constructed a woman. The fact that Adam and Eve are naked does not trouble them till, tempted by "the serpent", they suddenly become aware of their nudity and for the first time ashamed of it. They make themselves aprons of fig leaves, sewn together. Thereafter we find God even taking a walk "in the cool of the day." Adam and Eve, hearing God's voice, are guilt-stricken and seek cover in the heavy foliage of the trees, presumably hoping that God will not be able to see them. So the story goes on, and it is all in the same primitivistic vein, so much so that even a reverent audience today can hardly resist at least a smile.

The other version, with which the Book of Genesis opens, is dramatically different. We know it is a different story for several reasons. It uses, for instance, "Elohim" for the name of God, while the other earlier story uses "Yahweh". The text itself is in fact the product of a period some five hundred years later, and the whole mode of thought is infinitely more sophisticated. To read it literally is to make an absurdity out of it. For instance, the first word in the Hebrew text is *bereshith*, which most English translations render simply "In the beginning."[12] The Septuagint does better in Greek with *en archē*, because that properly removes the notion of an act performed in time. God is beyond time. We might even say "*archetypally* God has been creating . . . ." The

---

[12]The Jewish Publication Society's translation has "When God began to create. . . ."

Greek, however, does less well with the verb, because Greek, like English, has no means of doing with a verb what Hebrew can do. In Greek, as in English, we have to specify the tense and the mood of a verb: the man walked, was walking, is walking, walks, will walk, might walk, and so forth. In Hebrew one may leave grammatical tense and mood comparatively open, so as to say, for instance, something more like: "the man walking", leaving open whether he is or was or will be or might be walking. So the Hebrew text might be telling us that God is, and always has been, creating.

The significance of this for a gnostic interpretation of the text is incalculably great, not least because the whole narrative may now be much more easily aligned to the upanishadic view that the universe is the thought of God, the eternal thought of the eternal Mind. Furthermore, such a view is close to the view developed in early Christian thought that the Logos (identified with Christ who, as Christian thought later develops, is to be identified with the Second Person of the Undivided Trinity) is the Idea in the divine Mind who creates the universe.

The identification of Christ with the eternal Logos, the Idea in the divine Mind, is affirmed in the magnificent prologue to the Gospel according to John. This prologue, consisting of the first eighteen verses of the first chapter of that most patently gnostic of all the four Gospels in the canonical New Testament, is a dramatic expression of the core of Christian orthodoxy, so much so that the first fourteen verses are traditionally read after every celebration of Mass in the Roman rite and in those Anglican churches that follow Catholic usage.

It opens with the words: "In the beginning was the Logos, and the Logos was with (*pros*) God, and the Logos was God."[13] John is writing, of course, in Greek, so we have once again *en archē*. It is *not* that at a certain time, the time at which the universe had its beginning, the Logos existed, was with God, and was God. It is, rather, that *time never was nor ever could be* in which the Logos is not existing, or is not with God, or is not God. For that is the way things are and always must be, at the core of Being. The whole evolutionary process of the universe exists archetypally in the Eternal Mind of God.

---

[13]The Greek preposition *pros* suggests also movement toward God.

Though John's way of thinking and writing, including his repeated use of light/darkness, sight/blindness symbolism, is typically gnostic, he introduces a novel concept: not only is Jesus the Christ, the Anointed One; the Christ is the Logos. Moreover, through the Logos all things come to be; not one thing has its being but through him. In most gnostic systems the creative activity of the supreme God is mediated by a large number of intermediate spiritual beings: angels or powers (*dynameis*). These were considered necessary because of the chasm between the divine nature, which is entirely good and pure, and the world, which is tainted by evil. The intermediate agencies were set in the characteristic cosmology of the age: they ruled over a vast system of concentric spheres arched over the earth and traditionally identified with the planets and other heavenly bodies whose movements, according to the astrologers, determined human destiny. Man, on this ancient view, microcosmically reflects the dualism of the universe (that is, the macrocosm), for while his soul is a spark of the divine fire his body is a mere piece of that dross that is the material world. John is obviously not only familiar with this way of thinking but shares many of the basic presuppositions connected with it. Nevertheless, he proposes a solution to an old gnostic problem: the Logos in the Eternal Mind of God directly creates whatever is created, without intermediary. Angels and other spiritual beings do function of course, as the ministers and messengers of God. They act as God's ambassadors to the prophets and others to whom God wishes to speak. They can function, too, as helpers in human predicaments. (We shall have more to say about that later.) Yet they have no part in creation. Nor is there any need of a Demiurge, since all that has ever come into being has always had its life from the Logos.[14]

I have dwelt on these points at some length in order to try to show the *nature* of John's gnosticism. Thoroughly saturated with gnostic presuppositions, he is none the less critical of some of them. This does not in the least diminish the gnostic character of his thought. On the contrary, it is a reassertion of it. Aristotle, as historians of Western thought have often pointed out, was in a great many important ways very much a Platonist (especially from a modern standpoint), though he radically criticized his master at

---

[14]The New English Bible translates John 1.4: All that came to be was alive with his life, and that life was the light of men.

many points. Hume was by no means less of an empiricist for his departure from the teachings of Berkeley and Locke.

The writer of the fourth Gospel is a Jew by birth and in outlook. While he has before his mind, of course, the opening words of Genesis, the first words of the all-sacred Torah, he also echoes the Stoic doctrine of the *Logos spermatikos*, the generative Logos. Philo of Alexandria, one of the greatest Jewish minds of the day and much influenced by gnostic types of thought, had already tried in his own way to combine Jewish and Gentile notions. He used the Stoic notion of the Logos and identified it both with Plato's Idea of the Good and the Beautiful (*to kalon*) and with the later Hebrew concept of divine Wisdom. In Philo, however, these Gentile ideas are never quite reconciled to the uncompromising monotheism of his Jewish heritage and faith. John, on the contrary, is claiming to answer both the traditional Jewish and the general gnostic quests. Jesus Christ is both the long-awaited Messiah of the Jews and the fulfilment and justification of the ancient *gnosis*.[15]

John's most succinct proclamation of the good news is in the fourteenth verse: the Logos was made flesh; he pitched his tent among us, and we saw his glory as the glory of the only Son of the Father, full of grace and truth. In the Mass, at the words "The Word (Logos) was made flesh," priest and people genuflect, because this is the proclamation of the basic condition of all else John has to tell. It is the keynote of all that follows, the annunciation of the supreme revelation of God to humankind. It does not say *all* gnostic pretensions are false; it tells, rather, of the *gnosis* that is true: John the Baptist had come as a witness to speak for the light; but that light ("the light that enlightens all men") was manifested in the Person of Christ, who "came to his own domain" but was rejected by his own people. He was "a light that shines in the dark, a light that the darkness could not understand." Here is all the gnostic imagery of life and light, the typical gnostic emphasis on intellectual apprehension. All the while the

---

[15]The nature of Johannine Christianity has been much discussed by biblical scholars in recent years. The notion that there were two groups of Johannine Christians, both with strong gnostic tendencies, and that one of these (perhaps the larger) broke off communion with the churches claiming apostolic tradition is eminently plausible, to say the least. *See* E. H. Pagels, *The Johannine Gospel in Gnostic Exegesis* (Nashville, Tenn.: Abingdon, 1973), and R. E. Brown, "Other Sheep not of this Fold", in *Journal of Biblical Literature*, Vol. 97, No. 1, March 1978, pp. 5 ff.

light was shining, yet most people, being in darkness, could not perceive it. It is as if a brilliantly witty lecture were being addressed to a herd of pigs who go on grunting throughout it. One recalls the injunction of Jesus to his followers: "Cast not your pearls before swine."[16] The King passes by and no one notices; that is, no one but for the few who are already sufficiently advanced in the *gnosis* of spirituality to have the power to see beyond the flesh to the spirit.

The same theme runs all the way through the Gospels, even those (the synoptics) that are generally accounted less gnostic. All of these recount the story of the final entry of Jesus into Jerusalem, riding on a borrowed donkey.[17] Only the children cry out their hosannas and throw the palm branches in his way, for only they are not yet entirely blinded by a carnal way of looking at things. Moreover, he who is the light and the life of men is for that very reason the only safe custodian of the spiritual treasures of humankind. For he, the "Good Shepherd," *loves* his sheep, unlike the hireling who is not the owner of the sheep but is merely paid to look after them as an employee.[18] "I am the good shepherd, I know my sheep, and my sheep know me."[19] The strong emphasis is once again on *gnosis*, the mutual recognition. Those who have been diligently seeking the truth are the first to recognize it when they see it. So it must be, for "eternal life" *consists* in the knowledge of God.[20]

Inevitably there had been many gnostic teachers who distorted gnosis to make it sound like a secret, esoteric body of knowledge over which they had control, as the trustees of a corporation have control over its assets. Such a distortion is found in all religions. It is by no means unknown in Christianity, where it has been the occasion of repeated protests. The protest of John Wyclif, for instance, in the fourteenth century, long before the sixteenth-century movements led by Luther and Calvin, was primarily against the notion of *dominium* (lordship), the notion that an officer of the Church has possession of his office as a landowner has possession of his land. No doubt many gnostic teachers spoke

---

[16]Matthew 7.6.
[17]Matthew 21.1-9; Mark 11.1-10; Luke 19.28-38.
[18]John 10.1-15.
[19]John 10.14 f.
[20]John 17.3.

as though they could open and shut the doors of the school of spiritual chemistry. John is saying that though there is indeed a spiritual gnosis, it is guarded by no doors except the doors people erect against it in their own minds: their own mental blocks, as we would say today.

It is impossible, without some background in the gnostic outlook, to understand what John is talking about. But this is true in greater or less degree of most of the biblical writers. That is why, indeed, some people simply see nothing in the Bible but an old scrap book containing a miscellany of the pedestrian literature of an inferior people, while others see it as did George Herbert: "the book of books, the storehouse and magazine of life and comfort, the Holy Scriptures." Of course it is indubitable, from one standpoint, that the Old Testament may be said to be, as John Macy called it, "tribal in its provinciality" and that "its village police and sanitary regulations are erected into eternal laws." But in the hands of a contemporary positivistic linguistic analyst, no religious literature could possibly fare better, neither the Upanishads nor the Tripitaka nor the Zendavesta nor the Qur'ān. For all religions are trying to answer gnostic questions and, without the quest they presuppose, whatever truth is in them is bound to be lost on unprepared hearers. One might as well put a volume of musical interpretation into the hands of a person who is tone-deaf. If he happened to be otherwise intelligent and perceptive, he might do something with it (at the worst one could always at least parse the words and analyze the sentence structure!); but the purpose of the work would wholly elude him, for it would presuppose that its readers had musical problems to be solved.

Paul, whether he knew it or not, was clearly gnostic in his way of thought.[21] Those Christians and others who do not like him are those who do not understand the nature of the gnostic quest. Those who see him as a great apostle of Christianity are those who, though they may never have heard of gnosticism or theosophy and may be indeed very ignorant of the history of

---

[21]Paul accepts the basic gnostic notion of man: our present embodiment (*sōma psychikon*) and the resurrection embodiment (*sōma pneumatikon*). *See* I Corinthians 15.44. As a Jewish writer has put it, Paul divides humanity (I Corinthians 2.10-16) into "the multitude of carnals" and "an elite of pneumatics": Jacob Taubes, "The Gnostic Idea of Man", in *The Cambridge Review*, Vol. I, No. 2, March, 1955.

religions, have been already in their way seeking *gnosis*. Paul, in the Quaker phrase, speaks to their condition.

The story of his conversion to the Christian Way is in every way dramatically gnostic.[22] As he is traveling on the Damascus Road on a mission hostile to the Christians, he has almost reached his destination, when suddenly "a light from heaven" blinds him. As he falls to the ground on account of the brilliance of the blinding light, he hears a voice asking why he is going on this mission: "Saul, Saul, why are you persecuting me?"[23] Saul, as he was still called, asks who is calling him, and the voice replies: "I am Jesus and you are persecuting me." (His companions see the light but do not hear the voice.) Jesus then tells him that he is to get up on his feet and make his way to Damascus, where he will find out what he is destined to do. He is so overpowered by the glare of the light that he still cannot see, so his companions lead him by the hand as he continues on his way. Meanwhile, in Damascus one of the disciples, Ananias, also sees Jesus in a vision and is directed to go to a certain street ("Straight Street") and ask at a specified house for a man called Saul, who at this very moment is praying and has seen in a vision a man called Ananias who is to restore his sight. Ananias protests: he has heard of this Saul as an enemy of the Christian Way. Jesus tells him that nevertheless he has chosen Saul to be the means of bringing the Gospel to the Gentiles. In due course, then, Ananias finds Saul and lays his hands on him, telling him that the Lord has sent him to give him back his sight and fill him with the Holy Spirit. In a moment, something like scales fall from Saul's eyes. He rises, is baptized, takes some food, and feels strong again.[24]

The significance of this narrative cannot escape anyone who is in the least accustomed to psychic phenomena. Nor should we neglect to note that in the early days baptism was called *phōtismos*: enlightenment. Before his mission to the Gentiles gets under way, long before his great missionary journeys to Asia Minor, Greece and Rome, he spends three years in Arabia.[25] The story of the spread of the Christian faith to the Gentile world (an extraordi-

---

[22]Acts 9.1-12.
[23]Paul's name before his conversion.
[24]Acts 9.10-19.
[25]Galatians 1.21.

nary enterprise that was as successful as it must have seemed to many unpromising) is studded with references to the occurrence of psychic phenomena apart from which, if we are to believe the New Testament accounts themselves, the stupendous undertaking of spreading the Good News to the Gentile world could not have even got off the ground.

Indeed, throughout the New Testament accounts of the spread of the Gospel, what dominates all else is the power of the name of Jesus. The kind of thing the apostles claimed to do, the wonders they performed, their fantastic achievements, were not in themselves entirely novel from the standpoint of those among whom they worked. What impressed the converts was that those who did wonders in the name of Jesus not only did them more effectively than anyone had ever before seen wonders done; the wonders they did were accompanied by a psychic radiance and peace the like of which nobody had ever seen at all. The converts were not merely polytheists magically and inexplicably turned toward an obscure little Jewish sect, as the Christian Way at first made its appearance. They were already at least in some measure prepared for the kind of phenomena they saw at the hands of Paul and his associates. What dazzled them was the peculiar brilliance of what confronted them. To try to understand all this apart from the gnostic background of the Christian faith and its expansion in the Gentile world is like trying to understand the merits of solar heating when you have never seen either an open fire or a gas stove.

VIII

HIDDEN MOTIFS IN CHRISTIAN LITURGY

O Christ, whom now beneath a veil we see,
May what we thirst for soon our portion be.
—Thomas Aquinas, *Adoro te devote*

No casual onlooker at the Mass or other liturgical or extra-liturgical Catholic devotion could ever guess that it hides, for example, the motif that *agapē*, the mystical love that is the mainspring of Christian life, is the door to Christian gnosis. Certainly it is the last thing that would occur to anyone dropping into a Protestant service of worship completely unprepared. Christian worship, even while it speaks of the mysteries of faith, skilfully hides the very core of Christian life, disguising the inner reality of which the greatest cathedrals and abbeys are but the shells. All that is most precious in the life of the Church is veiled. On Good Friday, indeed, the ornaments of the church (crucifix, images, paintings) are literally covered with a violet cloth, leaving the church looking desolate and bare, a strident symbol of the motif of the absence of God; but even the Church's most sumptuous apparel is a veil over her inner life. Everything institutional, not least the hierarchical structure, is a means of disguise.

Why? Why such heavy clothing, such elegant disguise, such veiling of life and love in the vesture of decay? One can understand, at burials, why custom should prescribe oak coffins and velvet palls: corpses, even the best of them, are not sights to dwell

94

upon. Merciful are the funereal decencies that discreetly hide the spoils of death. But if Christian life is the way to salvation, as it purports to be, why cover up such a living reality with such a weight of material, gilded or plain? Should not the Risen Christ shine unimpeded in his spiritual glory? To encase the Lord of life in such trappings seems but an elaboration of the primitive Hebrew notion of boxing up Yahweh in an ark. Our hypothetical observer might well suggest: only hypocrisy needs a shroud.

These are, of course, precisely the considerations that have motivated many Christian sects to try to renounce all external trappings and institutionalism. Their attempts, however well intentioned, have been unsuccessful. For, paradoxically, the more spiritual vitality there is in the Church, the more it needs to be "clothed". There are very profound psychological reasons for this. The pursuit of *gnōsis* through *agapē* cannot be conducted in the open. As soon as people try to take the Christian secret out into the open, it vanishes, and Christian life withers and dies. The gnostic motifs hidden underneath the institutional and liturgical trappings disappear and Christianity becomes literally bereft of meaning. People go on talking its language, perhaps for generations; but since they have naturally ceased to believe in what they have caused to disappear, what they are left with is more and more a mere buttress of societal ethics or repository of the archetypes of a forgotten aestheticism. Wherever people are led even a little way toward a gnostic or theosophical interest, the theological affirmations of the ancient creeds can begin to assume profound meaning. The fact that there is so much political corruption in the Church makes the need for "clothing" her treasures all the greater.

Even in the setting forth of these reflections we provide ourselves with a clue to the answer to our questions. For mystical knowledge, which has sometimes grown into the hardiest of plants in God's garden, is extremely difficult to grow and delicate to nurture. Like the *mimosa pudens* that shrivels shyly at the slightest human touch, mysticism dies as soon as the spiritually clumsy lay hold of it. Most of us *are* spiritually clumsy, to say the least, so that the gnostic goal of Christianity must be disguised in various, often subtle, ways. The Church talks mostly of faith, with perhaps a slight hint that in the future life we may attain the knowledge of God that we seek. Everything the Church does seems designed to hide the essential nature of the Church's life.

For the vast majority of people in all religions are too spiritually immature to understand the gnostic purpose, while those who are more mature may find no more need to abandon the Church than does the eagle its nest; nor could they wish to do so. Through the ancient sacramental structure of the Church they find their own way of obtaining and (if such be their office) of administering her gnostic treasures, even if these treasures must come in curiously heavy wrappings.

The masks of the Church are manifold. For one thing, she must be ever finding fresh wrappings to cover the gnosis that is forever, of course, the same. There are, however, other reasons for the Church's many faces. Not least is the fact that she carries aboard her a very motley crew and a no less extraordinary miscellany of passengers. The Church cannot list her psychic realities on her bill of lading. They must go under some other names. Yet these psychic realities are assuredly what the Church is all about. Apart from them she might as well close her doors, for why would anyone want to enter them?

Every highly developed religion has many faces. Both Hinduism and Buddhism could provide innumerable examples of this fact. Or one might but glance at the difference between the Taoism of the Lao Tzu and the practice of Taoism in most Taoist temples today. The life of a religion certainly does not lie in its institutional organization or the administrative structure of its hierarchy. None but the most crass of literalists would even think of looking for it in the legalistic regulations that all religions sooner or later accumulate. Even the great Christian mystical traditions cannot be said to encompass the life of the Christian Church. Carmelite and Jesuit traditions of spirituality, for example, have been notoriously narrow, because constructed to meet the needs of a particular type of person at a particular time in the world's history. No, the life of the Church (to use Catholic language) lies, rather, in the traffic of the souls of the faithful with God, the "babes in Christ" as well as the mature saints. It lies in the day-to-day prayers and other devotional practices, beliefs and attitudes of mind of the worshipping community. There, if anywhere, we must look for the rhythm of God in the midst of the human plight. Yet what we find is inevitably both an instrument for the attainment of Christian gnosis and an encumbrance.

The Christian Year, with its Easters and its Lents, at once illumines and obscures what it is designed to manifest. The

Church, with its sacraments and sacramentals, its preachings and its processions, its silences and its hymns, its restrictive rules and its proclamations of freedom, its candles and its darknesses, its lamentations and its rejoicings, its asceticisms and its alleluias, its bare walls and its gorgeous vestments, its carbolic spruceness and its rich, warm velvet cosiness, its clouds of incense half-obscuring its blaze of light, symbolizes what it is and must be as the Body of Christ: at once the channel of Christian spirituality and an obstacle to vision. As in a Greek icon, the truth is half revealed, half concealed. Now the worshipper sees a glimmer of light, now a dark cloud overshadowing it. This dappled, sunshine-and-shadow quality gives the Church that mysterious, poignant mixture of winsome beauty and irritating intransigence that some novices in the spiritual way find as irrestible as do some of the more mature among the faithful find it exasperating. Through the most tawdry tinsel shines the ineffable Light of God; yet over the most magnificent religious painting in the world hangs a dreary pall of failure. The grandest pulpit eloquence uttered from the most famous pulpit in the noblest of ancient s͟   ͟s turns into a hollow echo, while the halting words   ͟   ͟allow seminarian or of a broken-down old priest in th͟   ͟age church may turn souls into spiritual volcanoes.

Spiritual immaturity, however, has v͟   ͟le to do with all this. On the contrary, many who have d͟   ͟tly and lovingly pursued their duties as Christians fro͟   ͟e day of their confirmation as little children all dressed ͟   ͟te to the time of their old age with death fast approac͟   ͟em have obviously matured in the interior life; yet͟   ͟urious sense of light and shadow, of joy and sadness, ͟   ͟ination and obfuscation, not only persists but has intensified as they have advanced in age and wisdom. The more they see the riches of their heritage, the more they sense its poverty. The anguish and the joy are inseparable. Those who are most advanced have detected, moreover, that the sense of absence can be more spiritually provocative than is the sense of presence. The deeper they dip into the Church's treasures, the more they are puzzled by the haunting ambivalence that perplexes and fascinates even as it enlightens and obscures, pains and delights. In the moral realm the anguish is notoriously sharp: the complexity of the human situation is labyrinthine, while God's demands are absolute both in their simplicity and in their comprehensiveness. In the realm of grace, the soul, even as it is

being snatched out of the hands of the Enemy, is decimated by the
overwhelming power of the love of God, from which it has fled in
terror, embarrassment and shame. Wherever anyone finds no
such paradox in the Church, he may be certain he is missing
whatever point the Church has to make. He may well fear his
interior life is moribund if it has ever begun. If he finds himself
able to rest content with Freudian or behaviorist interpretations
of his inner state, he can be assured he is a spiritual non-entity.

Many churchgoers, temple worshippers and other religious
devotees have almost no interior life at all, while poets and other
artists who profess not even the slightest interest in religion in any
form have a deep and lively interior life. One need think only of
Proust's *A la recherche du Temps Perdu*, the reconstruction by a
hypersensitive consciousness of the world of a relived past. Joyce,
Irish literary pioneer of *monologue intérieur*, whose first great
masterpiece, *Ulysses*, takes longer to read than to have lived,[1] is
now a classic example in English of the exposition of an interior
reality that commands the attention of every person endowed
with even a spark of creative literary imagination. In reading
Proust and Joyce one knows one has been introduced to a reality
that many churchgoers have not even begun to face. Theirs is a
great creative literature, literature that is great because it deals
with the interior life of human beings sensitive to that dimension
of their existence, and deals with it in such a way as to make it in
some respects infinitely more religious than many of the sermons
in many of the churches of every Christian denomination in the
world; yet Proust had probably less interest in religion than have
most of us in ichthyology, while Joyce, in reaction against his Irish
Jesuit preceptors, supposed himself to be actively hostile to it.

Not only these, but all poets, musicians, painters and other
artists, put "religious people" to shame by the vitality of their
interior life. They are creative. In our universities today the
humanities are often much less creative than are the sciences. In
some cases professors in the humanities, having succumbed to a
positivistic scholasticism taught them by non-creative scientists,
no longer even know what creativity is. Some would value little

---

[1]Containing 260,430 words, with a vocabulary of 29,899 words, it covers
a period of 18 hours 45 minutes of one day, June 16, 1904, in Dublin.
Joyce acknowledged his debt to a novel by Edouard Dujardin, *Les
Lauriers sont coupés*, first published in 1887.

textual exercises on the work of an obscure critic of a critic above Dante's *Commedia* or Shakespeare's *Hamlet*, had they but a courage to match their narrow-minded barrenness. Creative artists, however, are no less lively than they have always been, and they are certainly neither more nor less religious than they were in the past. What then is the difference between the genuinely deep spirituality in such literary pioneers and the spirituality to which learned ascetics and mystics of all religions point as that to which religion, when all is said and done, is about? Is there no difference between Proust and Joyce on the one hand and, on the other, Paul and Augustine? Is not indeed Proust's study of the interior life more exhaustive?

The only difference, and an infinite one, is that the interior life of the artist as such is that of Narcissus looking at his own face in a pool, while that of the religious seeker after gnosis is entirely ruled by the criterion: am I, by these instruments, attaining contact with the divine such as will enable me to justify to myself a claim to know God? In this the Christian (through his or her peculiar recognition of God as supra-personal and therefore at least personal) claims a gnosis that is unique if it be any kind of gnosis at all. For the claim is one of having entered into the kind of interior life in which one is in dialogue with God. The Logos himself, as living act, can fully communicate his presence only as dwelling in, by, and through these words. Without words the Christian could not know the Risen Christ at all; yet even the holiest and most eloquent of words distances the Christian from him of whom he can say: "Closer is he than breathing, and nearer than hands and feet."[2]

What, after all, is the essential difference between Jewish and Christian worship? In Jewish worship there is a deep sense of "waitingness". The Messiah has not yet come. Meanwhile the worshippers assemble in hope and expectation. In Christian worship the Messiah has come and (so the Church repeatedly affirms) is present with us "in his risen glory." Yet faith continues to be the order of the day, as it is in Judaism, for Christian faith affirms that "Christ will come again." In some forms of Christian worship such as that of classical Presbyterianism, in which the Old Testament plays a traditionally conspicuous role both in preaching and in popular imagination, the emphasis on "blind" faith is strident.

---

[2]Tennyson, *The Higher Pantheism*.

Some Protestant worship (not at all reflecting, of course, the central intention of the classical sixteenth-century Reformers) seems almost to be saying "Christ has come and gone." Yet even through such travesties of religion some souls, circumventing all obstacles, contrive to find their way to vision of God.

Catholic worship, however, with its strong insistence on the "Real Presence," gives a poignant sense of something just around the corner yet not to be unveiled lest the glory dazzle human eyes. In the rite of Benediction of the Blessed Sacrament, for instance, which Protestants tend to denigrate as the most nearly "pagan" of Catholic devotions, the traditional words have an anguished note:

> Tantum ergo sacramentum
> veneremur cernui,
> et antiquum documentum
> novo cedat ritui;
> praestet fides supplementum
> sensuum defectui.[3]

"Let ancient custom yield to the new rite, and let faith provide a supplement for the defects of our senses." The ceremony is touching: we acknowledge our human weakness, our incapacity to see the glory of God; yet no provision seems to be made for the progress on this side of the veil of death. The wistfulness remains and is even more acute than in Judaism or Protestantism, because we have been led nearer the brink of gnosis.

No one who knows anything about the nature of religion can dispute the necessity of veiling the paths to gnosis. All teaching, through Word and Sacrament, is parabolic. That which is slightly concealed is, when discovered, all the more brilliant. Yet, how many seem content to let the veil rest forever! Moreover, with bishops and priests afraid to lift it even for their own enlightenment and therefore holding it down with all their might lest others should catch a glimpse, how much progress in gnosis is possible? Only mystics, a rare breed, and a few others valiantly penetrate the veil, attaining through love their own paths to the gnosis of God. There is no other way: even the sacraments (which in Greek are called *mystēria*) necessarily veil God, a veiling so emphatically asserted in another hymn attributed to Saint Thomas, *Adoro te devote, latens deitas*:

---

[3]From the hymn *Pange, lingua*, attributed to Thomas Aquinas.

> Thee we adore, O hidden Deity
> Who in this sacrament dost deign to be.

In the sacraments, especially the Eucharist, to which the whole life of the Church is oriented, the hidden motifs of Christian spirituality come nearest to spilling out. The concept of the Christian sacraments, however, issues from a practice already built into Judaism in the time of Christ. The Jews conceived brief prayers called *berakoth*, blessings and thanksgivings for every action from waking till sleeping. By so pronouncing a *berakah* on each individual thing and action the observant Jew could make them each a dwelling for the *Shekinah*, the mysterious divine presence that dwelt in Israel. Of course these *berakoth* could become mere verbal repetitions, as can the Catholic *Angelus* or rosary; but they open a way for those who know how to turn them to their spiritual advantage. The rosary is a series of fifteen meditations on the mysteries of the Christian faith, each one wrapped and hidden in routine, formal prayers: a *pater noster* and ten *ave marias*. The prayers uttered aloud are but the clothes of the meditations, as every instructed Catholic child is told. Even adults, however, are not told that the meditations themselves are in turn but the clothes of a gnosis that lies behind and beyond them:

> Veil after veil will lift — but there must be
> Veil upon veil behind.[4]

The fact that underneath Catholic worship is a network of hidden psychic motifs can be easily shown to anyone in the least accustomed to psychic phenomena. Sacraments are, we have seen, *mysteria*, and the life of the Church, whatever it is, is thoroughly "mysterious," that is, sacramental. Sacraments conceal and reveal. Sacramentals (holy water, holy oils, and the like) are in the same case. The Church is slightly more timid about them because they are less easy to defend from Scripture, which constitutes the basic, authoritative document for all Christians. The use of holy water, for instance (that is, water that has been blessed by the Church) is in itself a trivial sort of sacramental. It plays no vital role in basic Catholic worship, though it does have a subordinate place. At the *Asperges* before High Mass the priest sprinkles water

---

[4]Edwin Arnold, *The Light of Asia*, Book 8.

on the faithful as a preliminary blessing.* There is nothing essential about such rites. They could go out of style without detriment to the central sacramental system of the Church. Yet the use of holy water is a way of proclaiming that spiritual energy can and is conducted through the simplest and lowliest of physical media. When the Church wishes to communicate God's blessing it may do so by a verbal statement, a proclamation by one of its priests or bishops; yet we are not to suppose that spiritual energy can be communicated only in words. That would be verbal idolatry, more vicious in some ways than are other kinds. In the sacraments, the wedding of words to objects helps to diminish the danger of idolatry.

In everything we do in and through the physical world, psychic energy is being transmitted. These same channels can be used by God and his agents. So, through the use of such simple rites as the *Asperges*, divine energy can be made available to the faithful for their appropriation. The rite is not a mere "aid to devotion" as the more tolerant of Protestants and others like to suppose. It is a real occurrence, as real in the psychic realm as is, in the physical one, the fact that a drop of water may land on my collar and moisten it. There is nothing "magical" about the operation. If I have dropped into church half-drunk and am there merely trying to sober up so as to discuss with my accountant the tax consequences of my latest financial investment, the *Asperges* will do me no more good than would a fragrant breeze on a corpse. Nor is the effect "merely psychological." For whatever good is done me is not something merely concocted by my mind or that of my fellow-worshippers; it is the result of my appropriation of a stream of divine energy that is actually made available to me. Through that silly-looking water-stoup and asperges-stick I can enter into a new dimension of being. It needs but little clairvoyance "to see the flutter of angels' wings" between the drops of water. No Catholic actually puts it this way, except for a few eccentric poets and the like; yet that is what the rite hides behind the clumsy brazen solidity of the instrument and the awkward gestures of the priest.

In some of the more extremely Protestant forms of worship, the Bread and Wine of the Eucharist function somewhat like a woman's wedding ring; that is, one would not wish to dispense

*This practice has been generally abandoned in Roman Catholic Churches though still maintained in some Anglican ones.

with it, since it is a constant reminder of what one hopes is a happy marriage that nevertheless would have been just as much of a reality as if she had never had a ring to wear. In Catholic tradition, that is precisely what the Bread and Wine are *not*. On the contrary, they enter into the loving stream of the Church's life as channels of the Real Presence of Christ, attesting that psychic realities do not come to us in total detachment from the dimension of being in which we have to conduct our daily lives, but pour into us through appointed channels as surely as do we pour coffee out of a coffee-pot or water out of a water pitcher.

The use of relics, which is very ancient, illustrates further psychic implications of Catholic worship. That the family of a Christian during the Neronian persecution should treasure the tattered cloak in which their father or mother, their son or daughter, went forth to meet death in a lion's jaw is at first sight as unremarkable as that a woman should treasure the cap of her soldier-husband fallen in battle or the button of his uniform. The casual sympathizer might deem the practice in both cases harmless if comforting. Gradually, however, and at first no doubt dimly, the inner eye of devotion perceives how psychic forces can and do operate through such relics of holy men and women. True, the fabric of which the cloak is woven is nothing in itself, nothing more than the discarded pants I have sent to the local rummage sale. Nor are the stones of Venice, whatever they were to Ruskin, anything in themselves. Yet such cloaks and such stones are the bearers of mysterious psychic power. No substitute could function in exactly the same way. Of course one could raze all Paris to the ground and erect in its place an entirely new city, cleaner and more streamlined, further up the river, with flats to house the same inhabitants and offices for the same bureaucrats. The physical injury to our planet would be as nothing to what it has already sustained in one way or another. The psychic impoverishment, however, would be incalculably great.

The notion that an icon is more than merely an "aid to devotion" was unequivocally affirmed as early as the eighth century of the Christian era by St. John Damascene, who called it "a channel of divine grace." The Western Church has never entirely understood this. At any rate it has never quite faced up to its implications, so terrified is the West of even the slightest *soupçon* of what is popularly understood as "magic". In Eastern Orthodoxy the blessed icon establishes a mysterious link between it and its prototype, between the image and that which the image represents. The Church, in using the icon, thereby asks confidently that the divine power use this peculiar channel. The West has been character- istically fearful that such notions will discredit the Christian faith by aligning it with what looks too much like primitive magic. Yet the difference between such magic and such sacramentalism is infinite. Moreover, everyone with any sensitivity to psychic realities knows very well the immense power of place: *this* city, *this* church, *this* icon. The site is not only the locus of a particular happening; it has become inseparable from a whole history of happenings. To pray in a church in which a panorama of saints have prayed over the centuries is a special, incomparable experi- ence, as was to Jacob his vision of the ladder between earth and heaven.

Protestants too have recognized, if sometimes more reluctant- ly, what is meant by the sanctification of place. George Whitefield, Wesley's friend, testified that whenever he returned to Oxford he never could help "running to the spot where Jesus Christ first revealed himself to" him and gave him "the new birth." To many, ignorant of the hidden psychic motifs, such attitudes betoken mere sentimentality and are therefore at best foolish and at worst disreputable. These attitudes spring from an unconscious recog- nition of the psychic power that can be channeled through feeble "clay vessels." Many a psyche needs to be exorcized not so much from demons as from fear of the reality of a psychic power that can bring healing and lead to immortality.

The need of such people to sidestep or belittle the psychic motifs in religion is often pressing. Many, unconsciously ap- prehending how religion is saturated with these motifs with which they know they are not equipped to cope, actually associate themselves with a form of religion for the very purpose of using it, its language and its cultic practices, as a cover to disguise what unconsciously they somehow see it to be. Hence, too, the curious combination of suspicion and contempt so typical of the average person on the fringe of the Church. For them the motifs must be hidden, indeed very carefully disguised, because to display them openly for everyone to see would ruin the game the psyche is forced to play on itself and by means of which it hopes, however vainly, to appropriate some of the psychic "goodies" without daring to acknowledge even to itself that they are there. It is a kind of spiritual embezzlement, doomed, however, to failure, like a neurotic theft of clothes of a size one could not possibly wear.

The pattern of sacramental practice that is the channel of so much psychic reality and that has been built into Christian worship over the centuries is intricate. That is why ill-considered attempts to modernize it by bits and pieces are so disastrous, like re-paneling the walls of Versailles in vinyl or adding a high-rise wing to Independence Hall. Not only do they destroy liturgical coherence; they upset psychic equilibrium. To understand Catholic practice one must look at the whole pattern, as one would look at a vast oriental rug. No one understands this better than do the Christian mystics who see the Church as the unique instrument of individual growth. Because the Church is but the soil in which they grow in gnosis, they have no need to oppose it. On the contrary, receiving their nourishment from it, they simply accept it and attend to their growth. They are the true Catholic gnostics, ageless in their spirituality.

Vital to the concept of the sacraments is the principle, established early in the history of the Church during the Donatist controversy in Augustine's time, of *ex opere operato*. The principle is that the sacraments operate irrespective of the spiritual quality of the priest who administers them. In the quaint sixteenth-century English of the Thirty-Nine Articles of the Church of England, "the unworthiness of the ministers . . . hinders not the effect of the Sacraments." Without such a principle, not only would one always be afraid that the officiating priest might be a scoundrel in holy vestments and therefore unable to transmit whatever the sacraments should transmit; one would measure the efficacy of the sacraments by the holiness of the priest administering them, as if one were to value a book by the quality of the librarian from whom one borrowed it. The principle is a safeguard against such subjectivity as would obscure the fact that the Church is but the instrument of divine *dynamis* which, like the power of light, is not affected by impurities through which it may pass, as are, say, water and oil. In other words, the Church is the custodian of a gnostic treasure that is automatically (*ex opere operato*) available to all its members and does not depend on the holiness or learning or any other personal quality of the officiating priest. So the Church itself is called, in Catholic language, the Mystical Body of Christ (*corpus mysticum*). The individual must appropriate the divine grace; he or she does not receive it out of the psychic energy of a particular holy man in whom psychic energy happens to be abundant, but from the Church's store; nor

does the individual learn gnosis from a teacher who happens to be
a capable instructor. Whatever he has to do, he must do it for
himself. A holy or learned person can be at best a mere midwife.
All this implies the notion of the presence of an immense psychic
energy in the Church's spiritual treasury: a very theosophical
notion indeed.

Gnostic traditions such as have been transmitted through
Freemasonry, the Kabbalists, the Rosicrucians and other esoteric
channels, generally represent gnosis as a knowledge to be obtained as a result of secret initiation into ritual and other mysteries; yet he who has been initiated into these secret mysteries
tends to recognize that any knowledge he has really obtained is,
after all, intuitive.[5] Christian mystics from Paul onwards have
seen love (*agapē*) as the only certain way to authentic intuitive
knowledge of God. Paul recognizes its superiority over even faith
and hope, two fundamental theological virtues.[6] It brings its own
illumination and the gnosis it yields is incommunicable. There is
an analogy between the mystical love of God and erotic love
between man and woman. As we have seen, in Hebrew, to know a
woman is to have sexual relations with her. Jephthah's daughter,
being a virgin, is said to have "never known a man."[7] The intimacy
of the relation is such that the partners to it can be said to know
each other in a peculiarly intuitive way. Coition yields a special
form of cognition. If this be so at the erotic level, so at the agapistic
level the unique relationship between God and the soul *is* a
uniquely direct gnosis. Its ineffability springs from its uniqueness. If I have had a genuinely mystical encounter with God, then
no one, not even Francis of Assisi or any other saint of the
Church, could have had precisely *this* encounter of mine; therefore no one else can have *this* knowledge I have of God.

Such a program, in contrast to the highly elaborate systems of
the esoteric schools, sounds at first simple. It is simple, however,
only in the sense in which God is simple. *We* are not simple, and to
attain true gnosis of God is anything other than simple. Those
Christians who think they can perfunctorily hear the Good News

---

[5]*See*, for example, Albert Pike on 28° (Knight of the Sun or Prince
Adept), in *Morals and Dogma of the Ancient and Accepted Scottish Rite of
Freemasonry* (Washington, D.C.: The Roberts Publishing Company,
1966), p. 771.
[6]I Corinthians 13.
[7]Judges 11.39.

and obtain an instant, intuitive grasp of all that Christianity has to offer have ill understood Christianity, which, by its fundamental nature, is a school of gnosis. (In so doing they also, of course, at the same time misunderstand all religions.) Christian *agapē* does indeed bring its unique *gnosis*; but, though the Gospel shows the road to that *agapē*, the *agapē* is by no means instantaneously attained. The attainment is a long and arduous process. Indeed, as we have already seen in various ways, Christian teaching assumes that one has been for long on many an antecedent pilgrimage. He who discovers the Good News is like a scientist who has been trying many highly plausible hypotheses and now believes he has at last found the right one. He may jump for joy; he may even, for a while, scream like a maniac; but he does not change his scientific method. He is not at the end of his experimentation. He has not finished his scientific inquiry. Rather, he is, in a sense, just beginning it. At any rate he thinks he is now making a new and profitable beginning. So when the Christian, having been introduced to *agape*, the secret paths to gnosis, begins his "new life," the first lesson the gnosis on which he enters teaches him is that he has a long way indeed to go to mature in it. In short, like every other gnostic, he must "work at his religion." Otherwise, his claim to gnosis (or whatever it is that he calls it) will be as empty and pretentious as that of the phoniest Valentinian the second century ever saw. Theosophists will readily appreciate the significance of these points.

The habiliments of traditional Catholic worship are well-known: they are visual and auditory, even tactual, olfactory and gustatory. The Church batters at all five doors of the senses. All this sensuous appeal serves as a sort of decoy, disguising what must always be, of course, her central aim: the burrowing of a tunnel to the interior life, to that point (the Catholic mystics have called it "the fine point of the soul") where the awakening to God may take place and the attainment of gnosis be begun.

Subtler still, however, is a much less sensuous camouflage: the emphasis on faith, which is traditionally set in opposition to knowledge. The nature of faith was obscured till the Reformation and the accompanying humanistic and scientific Renaissance. The Alexandrians had seen it as a mere stepping stone to gnosis, a ladder that could be tossed aside once gnosis had been achieved. In medieval thought, faith (*fides*) tended to be identified with belief, the formal belief in revelational propositions. With the dawn of the new age and the more widespread understanding of the value and importance of inductive methods of inquiry, people began to see the concept of faith in a new light. The notion so intoxicated the Reformers that it tended to make them lose sight of the essentially gnostic character of the Christian Way. Nevertheless, the concept of faith as an element in gnosis is of such immense importance for the theosophical understanding of Christianity that I shall devote the next chapter to an investigation of the role of faith in Christian gnosis.

IX

FAITH AS INDUCTIVE GNOSIS

*For myself, it was not logic, then, that carried me
on; as well might one say that the quicksilver
in the barometer changes the weather. It is the
concrete being that reasons; pass a number of
years, and I find my mind in a new place; How?
the whole man moves; paper logic is but the record
of it.*

—J. H. Newman, *Apologia pro Vita Sua*

The notion of faith has been discussed to some extent in earlier
chapters of this book. Probably nothing has been more the subject
of popular misunderstanding than its nature. Too many still
conceive of it as believing what one has no grounds for believing:
as the schoolboy suggested, "believing steadfastly what you know
ain't true." Even the most learned among the ancient Christian
Fathers, however, misrepresented (though of course at a much
higher level) the nature of faith. The Alexandrians tended to
present it as a sort of kindergarten knowledge to be superseded
by a more mature kind of gnosis. Others have treated faith and
knowledge as mutually exclusive. Faith, on their view, is no kind
of knowledge at all.

Hegel (1770–1831) looked on religion as a sort of "baby
philosophy." His system, has been called neo-gnostic, played an
incalculably important role in the development of nineteenth-
century thought, influencing not only his own numerous disciples in Europe and America but also such diverse figures as

Kierkegaard and Marx, Nietzsche and Croce, all of whom were its radical critics. Hegel has been, in recent decades, too little appreciated by contemporary philosophers in the English-speaking world. The reason for Hegel's neglect lies partly in the anti-metaphysical dogmas of the school of logical empiricism that in various forms has dominated the scene in Anglo-American professional philosophy for much of the present century. A less obvious factor should not be overlooked, namely, that some professional philosophers today are unable or reluctant to read Hegel in German (sometimes, indeed, to read anybody in any foreign language), so that untranslatable subtleties in his thought, including his German puns, are lost on them. Yet Hegel certainly did need to be criticized, if only because he, no less than some of his Alexandrian prototypes, inadequately understood the faith–knowledge antinomy, underestimating, therefore, the peculiar significance of faith. The perception of Hegel's failure in this was Kierkegaard's great legacy to modern theological thought. It was a legacy that was not appropriated till at least seventy-five years after Kierkegaard's death in 1855 at the age of forty-two. Even so, the faith–knowledge antinomy continues to plague religious inquiry and to obscure the gnostic concerns of the Christian Way.

Before we go on to the main theme of this chapter (a very important theme) let us look back to the New Testament itself. There and in the Christian literature of the first two centuries generally we find a definite distinction between the terms *pistis* (faith) and *gnōsis* (knowledge). Yet both relate to an act that entails some kind of cognitive response. They sometimes suggest rival *methods* of entering the Christian Way. I shall argue that they are, rather, complementary ingredients. Both call on men and women to recognize Christ as "the Way." Such recognition is, after all, cognition. Why, then, the recurring methodological controversy about the use of the terms "faith" and "knowledge"?

At first sight the dispute seems to reflect a difference of view about how much a Christian needs to know. While sometimes we hear of knowledge of Christ as though it entailed a special insight into divine mysteries such as was expected in other forms of religion, at other times we seem to be asked only to give assent to an astonishingly simple proposal, such as: "Jesus, being the Christ, has risen from the dead and if you believe in him you will be saved." Today, indeed, one hears much in certain theological circles of streamlining the proposal to "Jesus is Lord." At any rate, the underlying injunction is an "Only believe!" The emphasis is sometimes so striking as to suggest conscious opposition to a program making presumptively greater demands. That is to say: "you do not need all that some may say is expected of you as a condition of entrance. In particular, you need not think: thought, indeed, is often an impediment to spiritual progress. Only believe and you are on your way to heaven." This is, of course a parody of New Testament teaching. It cannot be what Jesus, learned rabbi that he was, intended to teach or have his apostles teach.[1]

When we recall that with the creativity that is characteristic of all gnosticism comes the negative aspect, the inevitable tendency to let ideological fancy run riot with pretentious and unwarranted claims to gnosis, we may well be tempted to view faith as a welcome and genuine simplification, one that accords with the requirements of Ockham's famous "razor", a purifying device designed to avoid using more terms when fewer will do. On such a view of the situation, the gnostic approach both claims and demands too much. By following it, not only is one too credulous; one's ego is inflated. Swollen with pride, one gets exaggerated notions of one's importance in the sight of others as well as of one's cosmic status.[2] An ambassador of Christ should be telling his hearers more of God's recognizing *them* than of their recognizing God, and the call to faith rather than knowledge is an expression of just that emphasis on the initiative of God. Apart from such an emphasis, people may come to look somewhat as do those social climbers who boast of being on a first-name basis with the President of the United States till it turns out that he completely denies ever having met them. Christ tells us of some to whom he will say on the Day of Judgment: "I have never known you; away from me, you evil men."[3] Faith does emphasize a dependence on God that gnosis seems to overlook. Gnosis appears to suggest a procedure (so familiar in the descriptions of mystical experience) whereby we are metabolized, so to speak, with God, in the higher cognitive consciousness, rather than one in which, through faith, my personality is intensified in personal encounter with God. On this view, then, faith, whose claims seemed at first sight much more modest, ends by making the prodigious claim to have scraped away all the superfluous knowledge-pretensions that

---

[1]*See,* e.g., Luke 8.50; Acts 16.31.
[2]Romans 12.3.
[3]Matthew 7.23.

seduce the proud and the gullible and to provide instead a purged list of cognitive claims.

Those who in their immaturity espoused the methodology of faith now seem in their maturity to be claiming the virtues of the skeptic. That there is in fact a strong element of agnosticism in all true religion, not least in Christianity, has been widely recognized.[4] Nevertheless, we should also remind ourselves of a notorious fact: one may be more pugnaciously and intolerantly dogmatic over one or two affirmations than over one or two hundred. Our mental hospitals are full of people each of whom is quite sane and even in some cases outstandingly clearheaded on all subjects except one; for instance, that he is Napoleon or a poached egg on toast. This one error, however, is so radical as to vitiate in the long run all his other thoughts. If I urge you not to bother with all the innumerable speculations about the origins of the universe and accept, rather, the solitary proposition that it suddenly appeared in mid-October 4,004 B.C., I can hardly be said to be trying to make you less dogmatic than you were before. On the contrary, if you accepted my counsel, your pretensions would have immeasurably increased. The person who accepts the few "simple propositions" of faith *may* be not less but more audacious than his gnostic counterpart. For what is at issue is the *kind* of knowledge that is being claimed. The kind of knowledge the gnostic has in mind as he surveys the spectrum of his spiritual experience might well entail a less dogmatic and pretentious claim than is expected of him of whom is demanded an "only believe." It is notorious that the spirituality of the votaries of faith can degenerate into a condition of moral collapse and intellectual paralysis. The Roman Church has been accorded much of this notoriety; but no less deserving of it are other branches of the Christian Church in which "new presbyter is but old priest writ large." We must ask, therefore, whether too exclusive an emphasis on faith may not defeat the original purpose of those who enjoined it. What spiritual progress of any kind can be made where *pistis* (faith) makes *nous* (mind) fly out the window?

No one in the early Church taught the idea of Christian gnosis more clearly and categorically than did one of the earliest of the

---

[4]*See,* e. g., an early book of mine: *Christian Doubt* (London: Longmans, 1951).

Fathers, Clement of Alexandria. Like Justin Martyr, he perceived and acknowledged that religious truth is not confined to one tradition but emerges in many cultures. He saw that throughout the history of thought may be discerned common themes, generally ignored by the majority in every society but developed by a minority, though by each in its own way. That does not mean that there is no way better than another any more than it means that heating by an open fire with a hole in the roof of one's earthhouse is as good as the use of solar energy might be. It does mean that the best (that is, the most complete) way does not wholly exclude others that also contain truth. Clement distinguishes stages or levels of faith; yet in the long run they appear to be essentially within the same process. Gnosis *demonstrates* faith.[5] The demonstration is based, at least in part, on a comparison between the Scriptures and history, for the gnosis entails a complete grasp of God's plan for humankind, to use the symbolization favored in the Judaeo-Christian tradition. It is a *mode* of knowing. Moreover, the gnostic tends to become what he knows.[6]

This last notion is an illuminating one. It is not alien to what we see happening in other domains of learning. When one is totally immersed in a field of study, one does sometimes tend to be to some extent so assimilated to it as to look like it. I recall seeing somewhere long ago a series of cartoons caricaturing this fact: an entomologist, for instance, who has become like one of the insects that have been his lifelong study, and an ichthyologist who has come to look rather like a fish. We all know, too, of people who simply love and live so much with horses that after some years they seem to look quite horsey themselves. So the Christian gnostic becomes like Christ, the subject of his devoted study, "in knowledge of whom standeth our eternal life."

Clement also suggests that there is an *akolouthia* (logical sequence or coherence) between one religious truth and another and even between nature and thought.[7] One might suggest, then, not only a fulfilment such as may be seen in Law/Gospel, works/faith, karma-yoga/bhakti-yoga, but a coherence between science and religion: in short the unity of truth that Thomas was much later to champion in opposition to what was commonly taken, in

---

[5]*Stromateis* 7.10. Cf. *Paidagogos* 1.6.
[6]*Stromateis* 4.6.
[7]Cf. the Thomistic doctrine of connaturality.

the Latin world of his time, to be the Averroist doctrine of a double truth. No truths are entirely detachable from other truths. Heresy consists, then, not merely in the *haeresis* (choice) of exaggerating the importance of one truth over the others, which may be a comparatively venial offense, but in cutting one truth off from the others. Clement sees in all things a proportionality, an *analogia*.[8] That gnosis should fulfill or complete faith as the Gospel fulfills and completes the Torah is to him an instance of the ideological connections he sees running through all spiritual values.

I am convinced that underestimating the importance of faith is one of the gravest mistakes intelligent people can make. To do so is to inhibit spiritual progress. Faith is not only the way to gain admission to the spiritual pilgrimage; it is a perpetual ingredient in it, an element in the gnosis that can never be set aside. To set it in sharp contrast to the gnosis, as though separating sheep from goats (whichever be accounted the goats), is like separating enterprise from industry. Both are indispensable and they are of a piece. The traditional antinomy has developed into something artificial and perhaps even one of the rankest red herrings ever drawn across the path of spiritual progress.

The sixteenth-century Reformers' glorification of faith is well-known, its significance not always well-understood. Everyone knows, of course, that the tedium and futility of the late medieval emphasis on penitential works as the way to salvation (at least for the vast majority of people), which was fostered by a kind of crypto-Pelagianism in the medieval Church, led Luther to see that the typical monastic type of program of his day was self-defeating. What was needed, he perceived, was reliance on faith. The Christian must *live by faith*. Faith is not a mere bottom rung of the ladder of gnosis. It is not to be kicked away after one has climbed it. There is no such ladder at all; faith is a perennial ingredient in gnosis.

Theologically, faith had always been seen as the response to revelation. The heirs of the sixteenth-century Reformation went a step further. They developed a posture of glorifying faith as the one disposition above all others needful for a Christian. True, the polemical noise of the age of controversy gradually quietened; but faith remained a sort of watchword of the "Protestant" side,

---

[8]Stromateis 6.10.

which not unnaturally the opposing side took up as a signal for perpetuating the fight, resulting in a Catholic battle-cry on behalf of works. What the Reformers themselves, let alone their adversaries, could not have wholly grasped is that the term "faith" itself was being gradually but decisively transformed by the new attitudes of the age that the humanistic Renaissance was already fostering and that the birth of modern science would soon abundantly sharpen.

Let us see how this change occurred. Why had the men of the Middle Ages so misunderstood the nature of faith? One reason is that they were comparatively unaccustomed to scientific experimentation as we know it today. Intellectually, they were analysts and synthesizers rather than explorers. It is for the magnificent synthesis which the thirteenth-century schoolmen achieved that they are rightly admired by all who understand their great work. Scientific method as we know it today had not made comparable progress. That is not to say that medieval people were lacking in technological skills. On the contrary, their accomplishments in that domain, in terms of their day, are amazing. The development of their thought in the natural sciences was hampered, however, in several ways. For one thing, Aristotle, who had been recovered in the twelfth century, was taken up as the supreme authority in the natural sciences. Aristotle *was* science. His scientific acumen had been remarkable *of its kind* and for his day. Even fifteen hundred years later, when the Christian schoolmen took up his work, it was still an important storehouse of knowledge. True, he was sometimes far wrong and by modern standards occasionally absurd in his conclusions. For instance, not only did he account the female of the species a sort of misbegotten male; he conjectured that the cause of a child's being born female was the prevalence of a south wind at the time of conception!

The inheritance of such errors, however, was not the main hindrance to scientific progress; nor was even the inadequacy of Aristotle's methodology the cause of the trouble. Much more damaging an impediment to scientific progress in the Middle Ages was the tradition of exclusively deductive reasoning, which helped to buttress reliance on ancient authorities. The saying that "the authorities have wax noses" (that is, one can interpret them as one wills) is attributed to several medieval philosophers and seems to have been something of a commonplace. These same philosophers, however, had often to choose one authority over another, and when they did so they appealed to "reason", by which was generally understood, in that context, deductive ratiocination.

Deduction is by its nature and function incapable of yielding any really new knowledge. Deductive logic simply draws forth the implicates of something that is already embedded in given premisses. That does not make it by any means a useless exercise. True one needs no course in logic to learn that if all men are mortal and Socrates is a man, then Socrates must be mortal. The premisses, however, are often much more complex, numerous, and scattered among heaps of irrelevancies, so that the disentanglement of their logical consequences can be a very worthwhile and necessary enterprise indeed. Nevertheless, one does already in some way implicitly know what one formally deduces. By the deductive method, therefore, no new knowledge can ever be attained. No one could discover, for example, a new chemical or a new star or even a new plant or rock by such a method.

Yet devotion to that method did not by any means entirely blind the men of the Middle Ages, for they were extremely observant and made many remarkable discoveries simply by opening their eyes and using such technological tools as they had invented. What hampered them was their lack of development of inductive methods of scientific discovery. Induction was not unknown. Grosseteste (c. 1175–1253) and Roger Bacon (c. 1214–1292), both Franciscans and Oxford men (both probably also studied at Paris; Bacon certainly taught there), were well aware of inductive methods. Their experimentation in the natural sciences was remarkable and far in advance of their day. Grosseteste no doubt inspired Roger Bacon, to whom is generally attributed the invention of the thermometer, gunpowder, and a form of telescope. Such were, however, lonely figures in their day. Not for several centuries were people to begin to see what inductive methods could do for the promotion of human knowledge in all fields. Along with this discovery began to come, among religious people and at first only dimly, an appreciation of the nature of faith.

Faith now began to be seen not as mere assent to a proposition enunciated in the Bible or given out on the authority of Mother Church, but as an independent and indispensable instrument for the attainment of knowledge of religious truth. The principle is this: unless I am willing to make an intellectual venture as does the creative scientist, I can make no headway in Christian gnosis.

Faith is not only an indispensable instrument (along with hope and *agapē*); it *is* inductive gnosis.

Through faith we do not simply turn over knowledge we have already acquired; we put ourselves in the way of new knowledge without which no gnostic progress can be made. Faith involves risk. As Pascal put it in a famous phrase: *il faut parier*. We must indeed bet and go on betting. We engage in a kind of gamble and in the very act of engaging in it we begin to grasp the nature of the gate to gnosis. Gnosis is no mere mulling over truths already revealed or discovered or rationally deduced. It is a going forth into the unknown, a putting of my lone hand into the darkness, a highly informed bet, yet a bet none the less. In short, one cannot get to gnosis in an armchair or even in a gymnasium. One must go on an exploration. Only by ventures of faith, which involve the whole being, moral as well as mental, can one begin to catch a glimmer of what it is to know God. The pure in heart, Jesus affirms, shall *see* God. (I remember how, even as a very small child, I saw instinctively that this was the greatest promise in all the eight beatitudes.) Purity of heart cannot be achieved by any intellectual exercise alone. It is the fruit of many launchings into the ocean. It means being splashed and sometimes almost capsized at each launching by the anguish entailed in the kind of faith that was Abraham's when he went forth "not knowing whither he went." The gnosis of God is not like the multiplication table, which can be learned sitting down by any industrious child. It is more like learning to swim, though that is not, of course, the whole of it. Indeed, "to know how to swim" is knowledge; but it is knowledge acquired in the act of swimming. We have already adumbrated this insight in recalling John Macmurray's experience with skating.

So clear is the discovery of these truths to some beginners that they are apt to think they have found in faith the end of the road to which they have discovered only the gateway. Such a beginner is justified in his jubilation but wrong if he thinks he can rest content with faith. He can no more rest content with faith than can the scientist with the admirable and indeed indispensable disposition with which he approaches what is turning out to be the right hypothesis. Through faith he immediately begins to catch a glimpse of the gnosis to which faith ought to lead; yet it is only a glimpse. Perhaps he shall gain no more in this life. It may take a very long pilgrimage through perhaps thousands of lives before his faith is sufficiently strengthened to deepen his gnosis. No theosophist ever supposed Rome to be built in a day. Gradually, however, he sees the truth that even the Alexandrians could not have fully apprehended: faith is not merely a gateway to gnosis but an indispensable part of the methodology that leads to it. Not even the greatest mystic nor the greatest master of the spiritual life can ever set it aside, for he will need it for the next step in his ladder of ascent to the fullness of gnosis.

How does faith differ from other kinds of knowledge, that is, "ordinary" knowledge such as the knowledge I claim of the existence of my typewriter and of the geraniums in my back yard, on the one hand and, on the other, of my wife or mother? It differs from my knowledge-claim about the geraniums and the typewriter in that my experience of these is indirect and my knowledge of them inferential, while whatever knowledge I attain through faith is infinitely more direct. Something I call my typewriter is available to me as a tool. I am using it now. I know it is not a fiction of my imagination, for it confronts me every time I enter my office. I am confident it would be there if I came into my office to check its presence at midnight or three in the morning. The geraniums are in a similar case. I recognize them as I do my typewriter. Like the typewriter, they are objects of my consciousness. Physicists might describe them very differently from the way in which I see them. I see only whatever it is that comes over to my consciousness through my senses. I do not experience them directly; nor does that matter, since the one serves me well as a tool, however indirectly I apprehend it, and the other pleases me better than the drab weeds that would be there if the colorful geraniums weren't. In the case of my mother or my wife, my experience is much more direct. I know them not as I know typewriters or cans of soup or jasmine or baseball bats but as persons who are judging and valuing me as I am judging and valuing them. They are subjects, not objects. I have been directly confronting them and have been directly confronted by them over and over again through the years. Our spirits have communed so directly that it is as though I had been from time to time melted into them and they into me, though in such a way as to accentuate rather than dim out our respective personalities; for such is the paradox of personal encounter. I never melt into a typewriter or a geranium.

Faith in God, whatever it is, is much more like such a "subject-

subject" relationship than any "subject-object" relationship. Now, of course it should be obvious to any educated person that what I have just been affirming does not in itself do anything toward proving the existence of a Being such as is generally called God or the Creator or the Eternal One. When I say I "walk by faith in" a being whom I encounter, I may be saying that I walk by faith in my super-ego, to use an old Freudian term. The relationship I experience may be the relationship between a "lower" part of my psychic consciousness and a "higher". That, in turn, does not exclude the possibility that God might speak to me through that "higher consciousness" or super-ego. He might use it as an intermediary as, according to biblical and other reports, he uses angels. When I was a very small child my parents "came across" to me in such grandeur and with such authority that they functioned (in terms of my development at that time) much as does God in the reports of devout Christians and others. But then I make a further reflection: they came across to me in this way because they talked to me authoritatively of God and so readily filled the role of divine emissaries. It was *as such* that I accepted their authority. In them I experienced God as surely as one experiences a president or king through his envoy. The man of faith is untroubled by his awareness that he whom he enounters in his "faith-experience" may be but an agent of him whom he acclaims divine. If he claimed more (that is, actual encounter with God), he would be claiming mystical knowledge, not faith. As a man of faith he claims only to have received a signal bearing its own self-authenticating mark. He claims to know the right direction, not to have reached his destination.

Even with the best of directions, however, one may go astray, as all of us know who have tried to follow directions to a friend's house. The left turn he mentions may be obscured by a large tree or even by a truck temporarily stationed there. The notation "fork right" or "bear left" may be ambiguous. Should you meet in fast traffic a sign such as the famous British one, "Do not enter Box 2 unless your exit is clear," you may hesitate and end up losing your way. Yet for all these and other possible misadventures, you are entitled to claim you know the way to your friend's house, though you have never been there. Your entitlement depends, of course, on the trust you have in your friend and his competence in giving you good directions. Faith implies trust.

The fact that faith implies trust brings us to the role of *agapē* in faith. Why do Paul and others insist that agapistic love is the sure way to true gnosis? The answer is that through such love one is led to the kind of trust that is an implicate of faith. Love and trust so nourish each other as to warrant faith, and this faith is not only the way to gnosis but an indispensable ingredient in it. This ingredient can no more be disregarded when we reach gnosis than the two dimensions of plane geometry can be disregarded when we reach an apprehension of the third. Suppose your perception had always been limited to a flat, two-dimensional field, though now and then, perhaps, you had caught a glimpse of another dimension as does one sometimes in a painting in which the artist has treated perspective cleverly. You run your hand over the painting. It is flat; yet it points the way for you to that other dimension. Now suppose that suddenly, or gradually, you do clearly apprehend that third dimension of the physical world. Suppose further that you are so intoxicated by the discovery that you decide to try to dim out the old flat world in which you have always so far lived. You resolve to ignore it as one would properly ignore a page of erroneous calculations one had made in an exercise book. Your new apprehension of the physical world would be even more inadequate than your previously habitual one. For your perception of the third dimension, so separated from the other two, would no longer be a third dimension at all. You would have lost the three-dimensionality you might have grasped. That is an analogy of what happens when one tries to shake off faith to get to gnosis. Such gnosis is less of a gnosis than is faith. It is rightly called false. Gnosis, to be acclaimed as "true", must encompass the faith and agapistic love that are an integral part of the relationship in which the gnosis is attained.

Such a view of the state of affairs presupposes that divine Being is a subject to be encountered, not an object to be apprehended, nor a Greater Self to be realized. The presupposition that God is "The Other" is fundamental to Christian, Jewish and Islamic orthodoxy. In Vedanta, for instance, the situation is radically different. My task is so to hone and to polish what I call my "self" that it shines forth for what it really is: the Great Self, the Ulti-mate. On this view I *am* a manifestation of the divine. Notions of this kind have been popularized in the Western world through the writings of Aldous Huxley and others of his group such as Christopher Isherwood. The latter roundly asserts that man is by nature divine and that the aim of life is to realize one's divinity.[9] Vedantists, Sufis and others in similar mystical traditions generally insist that all religions are essentially one and that in one way or another their purpose is the same: the realization of the self, that is, the realization of the self as a manifestation of the Great Self. This self-realization is gnosis. In nature mysticisms God and Nature are identified.

I would say that such writers who seek to interpret all religions as having the same goal are right in their understanding of that goal as gnosis. That is indeed the purpose and goal of all religions. To say that, however, is by no means to say that all religions are the same. They are different because some of their presuppositions are different and so also, therefore, some of their understandings of what gnosis entails. The confusion here is similar to what would be the confusion in saying that all scientific inquiry is the same. In one sense it is true, since the scientist's aim is always to obtain understanding of the way things are in the universe. In another and more important sense, however, it is false, since the presuppositions of Aristotle and Einstein are so different that of course their methodologies are also different and so, therefore, what they succeed in discovering about the universe is different. Faith is, as we have already seen, an indispensable element in Christian gnosis, as is agapistic love. That is not necessarily the case with all *claims* to gnosis.

A widespread notion prevails that the exaltation of that faith that is especially celebrated in the Reformation heritage excludes claim to knowledge of God. That notion is much mistaken. True, faith is often contrasted with "sight". Nevertheless Calvin writes categorically: "Faith consists in the knowledge of God (*cognitio Dei*) and of Christ."[10] By this Calvin does not mean that we can know the essential Being of God, for on that he is as agnostic as was St. Thomas and such agnosticism is deeply rooted in Christian thought. Yet through faith we do know the divine nature, that is, *qualis sit Deus et quid ejus naturae conveniat*. We know that God is guardian, protector, judge, and so forth. We do not know

---

[9]C. Isherwood, ed., *Vedanta for the Western World* (New York: Viking Press, 1969), p. 1.

[10]Calvin, Institutes III, ii, 5. *Corpus Reformatorum* II, p. 399.

God as he is in himself (*apud se*); but we do know him as he is *erga nos*, in his dealings with us. We know his benevolence toward us. Such knowledge differs, plainly, from what is ordinarily called knowledge, such as knowledge of telephone numbers or even knowledge of the principles of geometry. Faith in God, which "consists in the knowledge of God," is a unique kind of knowledge.

Though there are some technical distinctions to be made between a Thomist and a Calvinist understanding of our knowledge of God, such technical distinctions do not concern us at this point. Both seem to have perceived, each in his own way, though neither could have explicitly so stated it, that faith is an inductive method of attaining gnosis. "For," writes Calvin, "as faith is not content with dubious and versatile opinion, so neither is it with an obscure and perplexed conception, but requires a full and fixed certainty such as is commonly obtained respecting things that have been tried and proved."[11] Our knowledge of God, then, according to Calvin, is real, definite and certain, though not complete, since it consists more in certainty than in comprehension."[12] Calvin, no less than Thomas, could know nothing of Kant's later philosophical doubt on the possibility of certain knowledge of *anything* as it is "in itself." Yet both recognized what was essential for their purposes: the impossibility of knowing God "as he is in himself" (*quid Deus sit*).

The knowledge to which Calvin alludes is not mystical, nor is it what we may expect in the life to come; yet it is indubitably knowledge (*cognitio*). Here then, at the fountainhead of the Reformed Church are clear pronouncements that even in this life, in which we walk *in via* as pilgrims, not as *in patria*, we can have, through the exercise of faith, real knowledge of God. Calvin's understanding of such knowledge differs from both Origen's gnosis and that of the Christian mystics; nevertheless, even as he exalts faith as the supreme category of the Christian life, he proclaims a *method* of Christian gnosis. It is, moreover, a gnosis that can be increased as the exercise of faith is increased. By no reckoning, of course, could Calvin be called a gnostic. He is far too scholastic, not to say legalistic in his methodology. Yet even he

---

[11]*Institutes* III, ii, 15. *Corpus Reformatorum*, II, p. 410.
[12]*Institutes* III, ii, 14. *Corpus Reformatorum*, II, p. 410.

perceives something of the Christian gnosis in his doctrine of the cognitive nature of faith.[13]

The first systematic presentation in the Christian tradition of the soul's struggle against the forces that hold it in thrall is by Evagrius Ponticus (346–399), who closely follows but also christens Stoic patterns of thought. The spiritual fight is against the *pathē*, that is, the impressions that are made on our wills by an exclusive quest of selfish pleasures. In this warfare, faith is the basic weapon. Why? Because it gives us the first glimmer of certitude that our true interest lies not in carnality and self-centeredness but in the higher, spiritual life. Faith awakens in us that awareness of a higher consciousness that our self-centeredness had stifled. From there we begin to see the need for *enkrateia*: the restraint of our natural appetites. We perceive the spiritual advantage of self-discipline, including such ascetic practices as fasting and sexual abstinence. By such means we learn patience and acquire the ability to endure hardships. Our taste for spirituality is enhanced. Once we have this in even the slightest degree we begin to see the fulfilment, infinitesimal though at first it be, of the promises of faith: God's promises to us.

Victory in this warfare (the "battell of the soul" as Zachary Boyd was to call it in his quaint seventeenth-century English) Evagrius names *apatheia*. To us this is misleading, for it does not at all signify, as we might think, apathy or insensibility; nor does it mean that we are rendered incapable of slipping. It means, rather, that when I have achieved *apatheia* my domination over the forces of selfishness and carnality that ruled me has become for me habitual. My higher nature has been established. I may still slide back many a time; but I can never revert to the condition in which I was when I was enslaved by the world, the flesh and the Devil. I have not become impervious to the wiles of the Devil, the allurements of the world, or the lusts of the flesh; but I have been

---

[13]Cf. Hans Urs von Balthasar, "*Pistis* and *Gnosis*" in *Communio: International Catholic Review*, V, 1 (Spring 1978) pp. 86–95. He affirms that the reintegration of *pistis* and *gnosis* is "a vital issue for modern Christendom." His interpretation of the Alexandrian position on this question accords with the view I am taking and his understanding of the cognitive quality of faith has affinities with Calvin's. The article is an English translation by Seán O' hEarchaî of a section from the first chapter of Balthasar's *Herrlichkeit*.

fundamentally liberated from their thraldom. With the attainment of *apatheia* my heart has become capable of the love of God
and gradually the pentecostal fire of his *agapē* is poured into me
and transforms me.

What Evagrius wishes to affirm is clear: through faith I can rise
to a higher plane of existence. Never again can I descend to the
lower level of consciousness as if nothing had happened. A
human being may become very degraded, but he cannot really
become a beast, for he has acquired a consciousness (a conscience)
that precludes that. Under the karmic law a wicked prince may be
reincarnated as a pauper or a serf; but he cannot really reincar-
nate as a caterpillar or a flea. The Stoic motifs behind the teaching
of the Christian Fathers in ascetical and mystical theology are
obvious. What is distinctive is the notion that such processes are
not only completed but transformed by faith. We do not merely
resign ourselves to a constraining power, as a soldier resigns
himself to the orders of his military superior. Faith, the gift of
God, is so vivified by agapistic love that we respond to it with an
element, however feeble, of the divine generosity with which it
has been bestowed, as a beggar, moved by the magnanimity of a
truly kind benefactor, responds with a touch of the latter's graciousness. The *agapē* of God so seizes us that we instinctively echo it
as it transmogrifies us.

The significance of all this for our inquiry is profound. For
when faith is seen both as the key to agapistic love and the subject
of its transforming power, faith becomes inseparable from whatever is the goal of the spiritual life. That this goal is a gnostic one is
abundantly plain. The testimony of the early Fathers, the
medieval schoolmen and the sixteenth-century Reformers is
strikingly unanimous. In medieval language the goal is indubitably the *visio beatifica*, the vision of God in heaven. This vision of
God *constitutes* heaven. It entails, of course, the highest possible
bliss; yet its *essence*, Saint Thomas insists with his usual precision in
such matters, is not the enjoyment but the knowledge of God.
The essence of the Beatific Vision is cognitive. It is gnosis. Nor did
Thomas lack scriptural warrant for his view, since Paul had already written as much to the Corinthians: "Now we are seeing a
dim reflection in a mirror; but then we shall be seeing face to face.
The knowledge that I have now is imperfect (*arti ginoskō ek merous*)
but then shall I know (*epignōsomai*) as fully as I am known."[14]

---

[14]I Corinthians 13.12 (Jerusalem Bible).

Wherever we look in the history of Christian theology, gnosis is the final goal: the *gnōsis* of God.

The more we look at the language, the logic and the dimensions of faith, the more it appears to be a special kind of knowledge. Like all knowledge of God it is a unique *kind* of cognition, since it is directed to One who is unique. Nevertheless, it belongs to the basic epistemological pattern of all our knowing. What makes it so peculiar and so set apart from every other kind of cognitive activity is the method by which it proceeds. It attains its cognitive goal not through mere observation or ratiocination or contemplation or any combination of these, but through action illumined by experience, sustained by hope, and guided by intelligence. The ingredients, needless to say, are not always to be found in their plenitude; but they are sufficiently present in even the humblest act of faith to ensure that the "knight of faith" (as Kierkegaard calls him) is engaged in an act whose outcome is knowledge of some kind or other. Ideally, of course, it is the gnosis of God that is the goal, the *terminus ad quem*, of every Christian, whatsoever the tradition he claims. Through faith he sees not only beyond the senses (that was done long ago, when man first leapt beyond a bestial apprehension) but beyond even the stupendous computer-like activity of his brain. By imagination (a concept that emerges remarkably late in the history of Western thought) he sees ahead of his own situation. Through open-mindedness and responsiveness to what is presented to him from "above" him, he grasps at truths he has not yet fully assimilated.

The struggle is indeed his own, as with any kind of cognitive process; yet he knows enough to know he could not have engaged in it singlehanded. It has come to him from beyond, from a source that he calls God. Its method is indeed inductive. If you want to know its results, you need not look far. As the inscription in St. Paul's Cathedral, London, says of its architect, Christopher Wren, *si monumentum requiris, circumspice*: "if you need a monument, look around you." If you need to be told what faith can accomplish, look at human achievement, scientific, humanistic, and religious. Without faith in something, none of it could have been accomplished or even begun.

Faith in what? In God? In Nature? Are God and Nature the same? If not, how are they different? Of what is our gnosis? To this question we must address ourselves in the next chapter.

X

IS GOD OTHER THAN NATURE?

Nature, the vicar of th'Almighty Lord.
—Chaucer, *The Parlement of Foules*

The notion that God and Nature are to be identified has attracted many people in modern times and is generally taken to have found classic expression in the thought of Spinoza (1632–77), whose celebrated phrase *deus sive natura* (God or Nature) is well-known. Its significance is, however, much subtler than the phrase suggests to modern ears, as we shall presently see. Spinoza is generally called a pantheist, a term also commonly applied to the prevailing world-view of the writers of the Upanishads. The term "pantheism" is a relatively modern one, having been invented (as already noted) by John Toland in 1705. It was a convenient neologism for certain views that seemed to be sharply opposed to Toland's own position, which reflected the fashionable deism of his day, where God was seen as the grand architect of the universe and aloof from his creation. The term gained currency in the theological and philosophical controversies of the eighteenth and nineteenth centuries, in which the term "theism" (probably first used by Richard Cudworth in 1678 in opposition to "atheism") came to be used to signify a position to be distinguished from both that of pantheism and that of deism.

The theist accepted the notion of a personal and transcendent God who, besides having created the world, also preserves and governs it in such a way as to allow for both human freedom and divine intervention by way of "supernatural" miracle. Such a theistic position has been widely taken to be not only compatible with Christianity but even its proper philosophical basis. Yet another position, commonly regarded as deviating from theism without going so far as pantheism is one to which K.C.F. Krause (1781–1832), who expounded such a view of his own, gave the name "panentheism", from the Greek *pan*, *en* and *theos* and suggesting the notion that everything is *in* God though God is more than the universe. This position has had many exponents from Malebranche (1.638–1715) down to our own contemporaries.

The term "pantheism" (to say nothing of the others) is vitiated by an anachronism. Every context in which it is commonly used is likely to be misleading. Since the notion of attaining *gnōsis* through the worship or mystical contemplation of Nature is connected with views commonly dubbed pantheistic and continuing to have devotees, we must explore, in the interest of our inquiry, what the anachronism is.

Genuine belief in traditional Christianity collapsed in Europe in the first half of the eighteenth century. In this, England seems to have led the way. Montesquieu reports that if Christianity, or indeed *religion*, was as much as mentioned in polite society in England, everybody burst into laughter. Bereft of traditional beliefs and forms of worship, people inevitably found other deities. Reason supplanted religion in the minds of many, and just after the French Revolution the Cathedral of Notre Dame de Paris was converted for about a decade into a Temple of Reason. Earlier in the century, however, the worship of Nature was already a vogue. Rousseau (1712–1788) and others deified her and eventually the Romantic poets gave her an almost liturgical devotion, attributing to her the very qualities traditionally reserved for God. Those who less flagrantly flouted tradition tended to modify the cult, representing Nature as, rather, a kind of secondary deity or at least a creature no less exalted than had been Mary in medieval piety. So Longfellow (1807–1882) writes:

> Nature with folded hands seemed there,
> Kneeling at her evening prayer.[1]

Even Lord Byron (1788–1824), who as a polio victim could feel a deep grudge against Nature, could nevertheless call her "the

---

[1] H. W. Longfellow, *Voices of the Night*: Prelude.

kindest mother still."[2] Scientific naturalists, of course, have never
seen such lovely qualities in Nature, at any rate not in their
working hours. To the poets of the Romantic period she did
indeed appear at times, as Matthew Arnold calls her, both cruel
and stubborn; but then the biblical God could appear as a God of
wrath as well as a God of mercy and love. To the scientist Nature
is, of course, neither cruel nor kind. Cats are not cruel to birds as
people are to one another; it is, as we say, simply their nature to
pursue, attack and eat them. Big fish are not cruel to little fish,
though they devour them daily by the billion. Earthquakes and
tornadoes are not cruel, though the human suffering they bring
about is appalling.

What precisely is this Nature that has been seen as beautiful
and kind, vicious and cruel, neutral and indifferent, God's play
dough, God's enemy, God's handmaiden, and even God himself?
The term "nature" is derived from the Latin *natura*, which is
derived in turn from the Latin verb *nasci*, "to be born."[3] The early
Greeks, making no fundamental distinction between matter on
the one hand and life and consciousness on the other, used the
term *physis*, "nature", for everything that is or has ever come into
existence.[4] Later, after Democritus, the Sophists developed a
special interest in man, which led to a distinction between the
"natural" and the "conventional". Language, law, custom, for
instance, being the result of human activities and interests, belong
to the latter category. Later still, through the influence of Plato,
Aristotle and others, a distinction was made between "mind" and
"matter". This led to a tendency to align Nature with the "material" aspect of existence, including, for instance, the human body.

Such was the beginning of an immense confusion about Nature
that continued throughout the Middle Ages and the Renaissance

---

[2] Byron, *Childe Harold*, Canto 2.
[3] Heidegger thinks the Latin translation of *physis* as *natura* obscured the
original meaning. Latin translations of Greek philosophical and theological terms usually did.
[4] The Greek *physis* is a noun corresponding to the Greek verb *phyein*, one
of the words that expresses the idea of being; but it expresses it in such a
way as to include "becoming", so that *physis* is the process of emergence
from the hidden. Nature, so understood, is an aspect of primordial
Being, to which we give the name of God. The distinction between
Nature and God is inescapable; nevertheless, the relation between them
remains controversial.

down to the present day.[5] Scientists still use the term to signify the aggregate of entities that are or can be observed, including, of course, man, and that are susceptible to inspection and study by the empirical methods they employ. They are interested in the order, regularity and (despite Heisenberg's principle) predictability of the universe. The universe is commonly identified with the cosmos, a term that also comes from the Greek: *kosmos*, "order". The universe is *kosmios*, orderly. But what exactly constitutes its orderliness? Twentieth-century science, if it has shown anything at all, has shown that the universe, contrary to what the Newtonian physicists supposed, is certainly not mechanistic. Nor does it behave according to any pattern we should expect if we were applying our notions of rationality. Whatever the universe is, it is not to be described as either rational or a machine. Computers, automobiles and typewriters are indeed singularly unrepresentative of what we know about the universe.

By orderliness, then, can be meant not that the universe conforms to our mechanistic expectations but, rather, that we are able to discern in it patterns that render it intelligible at least to the extent that we can get to understand its workings so as to use our knowledge of them for the enlightenment and profit of humanity. Such is its behavior that we can reasonably expect the orbit of Mars next year to be at least approximately the same as it is this year. In making predictions of that sort, however, we cannot be absolutely certain, as we are, for instance, in mathematics. We cannot be absolutely certain even that the sun will rise tomorrow morning, though most of us would be willing to make a very large bet on its occurrence. Still, it is not a certainty as absolute as, for instance, the fact that the sum of the angles of a rectangle must be 360°, the certainty of which is indeed absolute. In the workings of the universe is a random element, to be found, for example, in quantum physics, in the mutation of genes, and in the operation of natural selection. Scientists can work, nevertheless, with descriptions of the invariancies they abstract from what they find in the universe. These descriptions constitute what are sometimes, though somewhat misleadingly, called scientific "laws".

Christians and others with religious interests continued, with the encouragement they received from ancient traditions they

---

[5]*See* M. - D. Chenu, O.P., *Nature, Man, and Society in the Twelfth Century* (Chicago: Chicago University Press, 1968), ch. 1.

had inherited from pre-Christian thought, to tend to look on the "natural" order as, on the whole "materialistic". To it, they supposed, must belong all natural or physical objects, such as dogs and rivers, and all human artefacts, such as tables and windmills. Any phenomena that did not seem to fit that order of being, such as those accounted miraculous acts of God, had to be relegated to some other order of being, an order called the supernatural, since it appeared to transcend the natural order. Long after the end of the Middle Ages, however, and indeed in the eighteenth century, the Age of Enlightenment in which medieval beliefs were much ridiculed, the old pattern of thought was perpetuated in distinctions such as the Germans made between the *Naturwissenschaften* (natural sciences such as physics and chemistry) and the *Geisteswissenschaften*, such as ethics and metaphysics.

Scientists and humanists alike have generally wished to repudiate that sort of distinction, and the repudiation has usually resulted in a reductionism: the reduction of God to what has been commonly understood as Nature. The term "God", if permitted at all, then comes to be used as an archaic way of saying "Nature". Saying that "God" and "Nature" are synonyms easily becomes a way of saying that, since no purpose can be found in the universe as such, through the methodologies of the sciences, which have been so successful in their study of Nature, no reason can be found for supposing that there is any. Conclusions such as are expressed in the proposition that as the liver secretes bile so the brain secretes thought become at least plausible. No room remains for the discussion of any metaphysical, theological or theosophical question, which have all become meaningless.

That is very far indeed from the position Spinoza upheld. In his view, Nature has a multidimensionality that few if any of his seventeenth-century contemporaries assigned to it. We might say, perhaps, that to Nature Spinoza attributed qualities traditionally attributed to God. It would be better, however, to say that he feels able to dispense with the sharp distinction traditionally made between God as the Supreme Being in a "supernatural" world and Nature as the order of things in the world God has created.

The orthodox Jewish view that was Spinoza's heritage and from which he dissented presupposed, as does the Christian view that has been derived from it, that creation is an act of God and one that, but for the divine will, need not have taken place at all.

In such a view God and the order of existence that he has created are distinctly different orders of being. All that need be said of the created order is that it may in some way reflect the image of God, which according to traditional biblical theology man specifically exhibits. When, because of the developments in the history of ideas that we have just considered, Nature is identified with that created order, the cleavage between God and Nature is not only accounted philosophically sharp, it is invested with a theologically dogmatic sanction, so that any attempt to join them is easily seen as heretical if not blasphemous.

When, however, God is seen as creative *par métier*, so that his creativity is an eternal act, the relation between God and Nature demands further inspection and may be seen to be much closer. A reductionism that makes the term "God" simply a convenient shorthand for the sum total of everything that is in the universe that physicists and other scientists are trying by their proven methods to understand does not at all necessarily follow; nor, of course, could anyone with any sort of theosophical insight find it an acceptable option, since it is grossly inadequate even as an account of our experience. By the same token, attempts to dispose of the "material" world as though it were simply a delusion are similarly unsatisfactory. Some proposals, however, such as would bring God and Nature closer might be plausible.

One such proposal that has found favor among many distinguished thinkers not committed to specific theological orthodoxies is the one Plato offers in his *Timaeus*, which was almost the only work of his that was widely known by medieval Christian scholars.[6] In the *Timaeus*, God is seen as eternally working on an inchoate mass apart from Himself, a sort of cosmic play dough, if you will, to which He gives form. This mass, so worked upon by God, must obviously reflect the imprint of the divine creative act, as the marble of which Michelangelo's *David* is composed reflects the hand of the sculptor. When we look at it and touch it, we do not see Michelangelo, who for all we know (from looking at his work) might have been a dwarfish deaf-mute, a female epileptic cripple, or the handsomest man the world has ever seen. We do

---

[6]William of Conches and others of the School of Chartres favored the *Timaeus* and represented Nature as an animated organism. He even identified it with the Holy Spirit. The medieval Arab thinkers were better acquainted with the text of the Platonic dialogues.

see, however, something of his creative mind. So the psalmist says
about God that "the heavens declare" his glory and "the firma-
ment showeth his handiwork." We might then give the name
"Nature" to the handiwork of God, and seeing in it the divine
traces (the *vestigia* as the thirteenth-century schoolman Bonaventure, a saint and cardinal of the Roman Church, called them),
revere Nature as the locus of the divine disclosure of Him who,
being "the only wise God our Saviour," is to be ascribed "glory and
majesty, dominion and power, both now and ever."[7]

All religions of revelation (Judaism, Christianity and Islam are
obvious examples) insist, however, that even if God does so reveal
himself in Nature, so understood, He also reveals Himself to
human beings in more direct and special ways. This notion becomes somewhat confusing, however, in the sense that it still
preserves something of the generally discarded distinction between a "natural" (material) and supernatural (spiritual) realm.
Man, being the meeting place between the two realms, and having
a foot in both of them, needs to see God as revealing Himself in
both. Indeed, he can see God revealing Himself in "natural"
objects such as tropical sunsets, beech trees in Burgundy, coral
reefs and desert flowers, the ice-fields in Alberta and the aurora
borealis wherever it may be found, only because God has already
enlightened him in more direct ways.

For Nature is not in itself as revelatory as some poets make it
out to be. Pascal (1623–1662), than whom no Christian thinker
has ever been subtler or more penetrating, reminds us that "the
perfections of Nature show that she is the image of God; her
defects show that she is only his image."[8] The Irish Catholic poet,
Joseph Mary Plunkett movingly reports his vision of Christ
throughout the universe:

> I see His blood upon the rose
> And in the stars the glory of His eyes,
> His body gleams amid eternal snows,
> His tears fall from the skies.

---

[7] From a traditional Anglican conclusion to sermons.
[8] B. Pascal, *Pensées*, 580 (New York: Doubleday, Collection Inter-
nationale, 1961), p. 160: "La nature a des perfections pour montrer
qu'elle est l'image de Dieu, et des défauts, pour montrer qu'elle n'en est
que l'image."

> I see His face in every flower;
> The thunder and the singing of the birds
> Are but His voice — and carven by his power
> Rocks are His written words.
>
> All pathways by His feet are worn,
> His strong heart stirs the ever-beating seas,
> His crown of thorns is twined with every thorn,
> His cross is every tree.[9]

Now, of course, nobody could possibly so see natural phenomena who had not already through some other means discerned God in them. Nor could I see beauty in a wizzened old woman in rags, had she not already manifested to me the radiant light of her spirit. Those of us who can see such beauty and kindliness in Mother Nature as poets see in her have brought to her an attitude they have already, however feebly, somehow learned elsewhere. First the ideas are in one way or another proposed to our minds; only then, so interpreting the phenomena, can we construe them as the handiwork of God (or the reflection of that handiwork) in which we see, so to speak, the very print of his hands. The religious consciousness, by so construing natural phenomena, finds a way of taking into account the special kind of experience of God that these phenomena cannot possibly yield when we approach them neutrally with the interest of the chemist or the zoologist.

Once we allow such a construction, however, an important question arises. May not natural phenomena be more than just the artefacts of God? Is the relation between God and Nature even closer, perhaps, than that between divine artist and divine artefact? Indeed, it is not easy to construe natural phenomena as artefacts. Is Mount Everest one artefact and the rainbow over a heather-clad Scottish glen another? Are phenomena such as ice and steam, both of which we know to have emerged from water under certain atmospheric conditions, to be understood as separate creations of God? Plainly not. But then, when we talk of divine creation we must think of the universe as a whole, in all its evolutionary motion and development, including the development of human beings, the highest form of mammals with which we have any empirical acquaintance and to which we belong.

[9]From his *Collected Poems*, 1916, the year in which the author was executed by the British in the Irish Rebellion.

Should we then go a step further? Should we say that what we call
Nature (including of course frogs, mice and roaches as well as the
blue petals of the jacaranda tree that lie strewn outside my window to the delight of passers by) is an *aspect* of God? The German
astronomer Kepler (1571–1630), looking through the telescope,
is said to have exclaimed that he was thinking God's thoughts
after him. Might not we go so far as to say that he was in fact
looking at a special aspect of divine Being?

I am well aware, of course, that such a view looks at first sight
like an emanationism rather than a creationism such as is traditionally taken to be an essential part of biblical orthodoxy. Yet it is
not necessarily incompatible with a form of creationist doctrine in
which God is eternally manifesting himself in a special dimension
of his Being. Such a view is also very far from any reductionist
theory and from any view that makes everything equally
drenched in divinity, so that rocks and Einsteins, sticks of chewing
gum and the Sainte Chapelle, all equally manifest the divine
nature. On the contrary, each does so only in its own restricted
way. Awareness of the nature of God, however, which entails
self-awareness, introduces a new element into the special dimension of divine Being that is here postulated. If this dimension is
evolutionary, as all that we know suggests, then such awareness is
surely a uniquely important stage in the unfolding of Being
within that dimension, as all the great religions, each in its own
way, attest. The "religions of revelation" celebrate its uniqueness
by insisting, as they do, that the creature can never be the Creator.
They insist, indeed, that the creature can fulfill his own nature
and destiny only in always vividly recognizing the relationship in
which he must for ever stand to divinity. He is encouraged to
conduct himself in such a way as to bring himself into tune with
God and so bring out in himself all the various dispositions and
attitudes that will enable him, in the words of the Scottish Catech-
ism, "to glorify God and to enjoy him for ever."

When questions are then posed in forms such as, "Then is not
man after all divine, or at least in process of being divinized?" the
answer must be so constructed as to preclude the misunderstandings that so often ensue when such questions are carelessly
answered. I might say, "No, for you are already divine," which
would be extremely misleading, somewhat like discouraging a
worm from further evolutionary progress on the ground that it
already *has* life. If, however, I reply, "Yes, though you have a long

way to go, possibly through trillions of incarnations, before you are divinized," my answer will be no less productive of misunderstanding. For on the view I am proposing I can never be divine as is he whom we call God. My hope is, rather, that I shall go on reaching point after point at each of which I shall have so realized my own nature and its relationship to God that I shall be able truly to rejoice, time after time, in my self-fulfilment.

In order to understand the import of all this we must consider how we are to see the divine Being to whom such dimensions are attributed. If Western thought has achieved anything at all in the understanding of the divine nature, it is surely the notion that God must be self-limiting. Simone Weil, a great genius of our century, has recognized this, and I have discussed it elsewhere.[10] That is to say, God does not command wherever He might, but lets His creatures be, in freedom to develop and grow as they can. I do not take this to be merely an aspect of the divine nature; it is its very core, the essence of what God is. The significance of it must not be glossed over. To say God is self-limiting does not mean that He occasionally engages in magnanimous acts of generous philanthropy, in the course of which He sometimes goes so far as to abdicate His power. No, it is His habitual way. He so acts for the promotion of the evolution of all things. Such a view does not exclude His providential care or His ample provision of help from angels or other such orders of being whom He may send to attend us. Yet though we are (as theosophists need not be told) constantly the recipients of such help, God does not interfere with our freedom to develop ourselves as we will. By alienating ourselves from Him we make our task more difficult; by attuning ourselves to Him we make it correspondingly easier.

Nature, on the view I am proposing, is certainly to be neither ignored nor denied. It is a divine dimension. Many may find in Nature alone a way to other and greater dimensions of divine Being. It is a comparatively arduous way; but it is a way. It is a way, moreover, that not even the greatest *arahat* may ignore. Genuine science and authentic religion are never fundamentally at loggerheads. How could they be? They are respectively looking, so to speak, at the outside and the inside of God. Some children look only at their mother's face and dress: others see more deeply into her spirit, perhaps not even noticing, let alone remembering,

---

[10]In my *He Who Lets Us Be* (New York: Seabury, 1975).

whether she wears red or yellow or green. Neither wholly ignores, however, either the face or the dress; but how fortunate are they who see behind them to what she is in herself! So with God: no genuine mystic repudiates Nature, seeing in her the vesture of God. God, however, is more than His vesture, and that is what the saints are more apt to discover than are some of the rest of us.

Artists and scientists look at Nature in very different ways. From the standpoint of the ancient *gnōsis*, the perennial theosophical standpoint, both tend to miss the vision of divine Being, though they may come very close to it. The artist, contemplating what he sees in Nature, usually gets little further in the end than Narcissus, beautiful vision though his Narcissus be. The scientist, in his researches, is in a peculiar case. He may touch the hem of divinity and discover how the stitches are made, what needles are used, how the threads are woven. If only he be creative enough, he may probe to the very warp and woof of the lineaments of God. Both are usually better off than are those pseudo-religionists who think they can by-pass both science and art and establish a direct line to God. Wise indeed was the medieval philosopher Saint Thomas (and often little understood) when he observed that *gratia non tollit naturam sed perficit*: grace does not take away Nature but perfects her. He perceived in his thirteenth-century way that Nature cannot be by-passed. It is the gateway to God, though in being the gateway it is also an obstacle. To worship Nature is the worst idolatry, because Nature is so near God, being a dimension of his Being. For the highest idol is the worst, the most dangerous. Few of us could be in danger of worshipping a fetish or a rock; but Nature sometimes does look adorable.

I do not believe that the exponents of the ancient *gnōsis* ever did really confuse Nature with God. When the Upanishads were being written, no one, of course, could have made the distinction as we can and must make it today. Yet the sages always saw a dimensionality of holiness that Nature, as we understand Nature today, could not possibly exhibit. Beyond what we see in the workings of Nature, marvelous as they are, is another and holier dimension of being, another and more overwhelmingly spiritual and personal (or supra-personal) dimension of reality. To all this the ancient sages have always pointed as best they could. Modern inquiries into "psi" and "paranormal" psychology recognize the reality and importance of other dimensions of being which conventional methodologies cannot reach. The dangers are notorious and we need not elaborate upon them here. All important is the growing recognition that while the methods used by the scientists are extremely fruitful, other domains of reality remain to be explored. Theosophists have long known about them. The quantitative methodologies of the traditional sciences, hard or soft, are inadequate for psychical research. They produce some interesting results, but they are inevitably as limited as is arithmetic for mathematics.

It cannot take much scientific imagination to see that the methodologies that fit rocks and trees, rats and cancer viruses, and even those methods dear to sociologists that show us how many Baptists were guilty of shoplifting in November compared with the number of Roman Catholic shoplifters that month are unlikely to carry us very far in any serious inquiry into the domain of whatever lies beyond Nature as conventionally understood. We may talk as much as we please about God; but by means of quantitative methods we are simply never going to be able to analyze the dimension of the One who lies beyond Nature. That anyone should expect to do so is alarmingly and discouragingly jejune. We must find other methods, for here we are dealing with a very different aspect of that reality we call divine Being.

According to traditional Christian revelation, which at this point is by no means entirely alien from that of other religions, we must never neglect the ways of God to man as revealed through what we know scientifically of the nature of the universe. If there is anything that we know by these methods, it is that life is evolutionary. We should consider, then, whether an evolutionary principle may not run through moral and spiritual life as well as biological life. Everything we know points in that direction. Never shall we find any fundamental contradiction between the ways of God in science and the ways of God in religion. The latter ways may take us nearer our gnostic goal, yet they will do so only if we do not attempt to by-pass the ways of science. If only theosophists and exponents of the gnosis in the ancient world could have known about evolutionism as it has been expounded in the last hundred years or so by scientists, they would have jumped for joy. For evolutionism, properly understood, is at the heart of the ancient *gnōsis*.

XI

EVOLUTIONISM AND GNOSIS

Evolution is not a force but a process;
not a cause but a law.
—John Morley

All the sages of antiquity, when they discuss the attainment of *gnōsis*, presuppose moral evolution. This evolution is accomplished under the karmic law and over the course of many incarnations. What we nowadays know about biological evolution, as they did not, broadens our understanding of the evolutionary character of the universe. Evolution is not only a principle of spiritual and moral growth; it is a fundamental principle running through all things. It does not always proceed, however, in exactly the same way.

So to the question how the gnosis of God can be attained, the answer can never be such as one would give if asked how one might learn chemistry or French. Of course one might recommend a great master of the spiritual life, or the reading of this or that book, or a course of monastic discipline; but one could not expect mastery to ensue as one should expect mastery to ensue after a certain number of years of conscientious study of any branch of human learning. Even if one were both intellectually gifted and morally sensitive in the highest degree, one could not simply go to a guru or other teacher and enroll in and diligently pursue a course of brahminical learning or theological study, and then be reasonably assured of attaining one's goal. Presumably all such efforts would help; but such a goal must be pursued over a very long time, much longer than is provided for in one lifetime. Moreover, wisdom does not come through "book learning" alone, but through a wide variety of experiences not merely of different occupations but of different circumstances. The process of attaining the gnosis of God is not so much like that of sculpting a rock as it is like that of the breaking down of rocks into fine sand such as may be worked for diamonds, gold, and other ores. Billions of years passed before the discovery of the art of writing made "book learning" possible, and that discovery was made only a few thousand years ago: very recently indeed in terms of the history of the universe as we know it. The discovery had been even more recent when Jesus discoursed with the doctors in the Temple and when, later, being called upon in the synagogue, he opened the scroll of the Book of Isaiah and found his place in it. In such perspective, writing is a modern invention and reading a modern art. Of course it is an art that has enormously advanced the mental evolution of man and has even provided him with new tools for his moral evolution; but his evolution encompasses far more than can be put into any library. Human development is through a karmic process involving the struggle of living as well as the use of the mind.

When we talk of man and of humanity, what, precisely, do we mean? Man is more than a biological species. Indeed even the concept of fixed biological species cannot be accepted in the way it was before Darwin. Since everything is in the course of development (slowly as do the mills of God and Nature grind), the notion of a biological species is somewhat artificial, though the usage may have convenient practical applications. We can more correctly speak of a species of postage stamp, such as those stamps printed to celebrate the silver jubilee of the reign of George V, or of currencies such as Mexican pesetas and Italian lire. Such species will never change into any other. A Mexican peseta is not in process of becoming a Canadian dollar nor will an Italian lira become a Belgian franc, as are forms of life in process of evolutionary development. That is because they are artificial to begin with, as are kinds of wallpaper and styles of rug. The notion of a human species is peculiarly unsatisfactory, since man, besides being (like all life) in the course of biological development, is also on the way to becoming something that transcends biological development. To the next stage toward which he is so awkwardly moving we may give any convenient name we choose: superman, *beatus*, what you will. In the Sufi tradition of spirituality one may hope to become one of the *wali*, who in an invisible hierarchy keep the world welded together, some even becoming *qutbs*, the pivots on which the inner life of the world turns. At any rate, whether our vision is that of a superman in the manner of Ibsen or Shaw, or else of a more heavenly model, as in the mystical traditions of Buddhism, Christianity and Islam, we must recognize that, in a universe that is fundamentally evolutionary in nature, we who have entered into our curiously decisive condition as human beings are in a peculiar sense (in one way or another) capable of heading for a different *kind* of stage beyond. In this respect we are not like cats or canaries, bats or whales. We are dyophysite, having an animal nature much like that of bulls and cows, yet with a spiritual nature unknown in any other mammal. Huxley saw long ago man's unique destiny as "the sole agent for the future evolution of this planet."

All this makes for a unique poignancy in our human condition, a poignancy that has been a dominant theme in modern existentialism. Our human predicament is unparalleled anywhere else that comes within the range either of our scientific observation or of our poetic imagination. Our insecurity is unique. Cattle graze contentedly in the fields. Angels and any other such celestial grandees that we may postulate seem to dwell securely in their heavens. We alone are at the same time splendid and ludicrous: splendid in our potentiality, ludicrous in our ambivalence. We have learned how to go into orbit in space, a feat that not even our grandfathers could have dared to imagine. We know how to blow the human race to bits, a nightmare they never had to fear. From our heritage in the past we have all sorts of moral codes that have helped mankind to pass far beyond the moral stature of our most primitive human ancestors, and yet we have seen (with help from Nietzsche and others) that as we advance we must no longer rely on mere codes alone but must create, as we proceed, our own morality. The more fully human we are the more we are aware of the absurdity of our situation. How pretentious we are, we gods with genitalia! As we discourse on the loftiests of literary themes, we make ourselves sick by eating too much candy. What can we say of ourselves, cosmic mongrels that we are, half-beast, half-angel, who must stop to urinate even as we leap from earth to heaven? Whatever we are we are no species of anything, certainly no thoroughbreds. Yet we constitute the most extraordinary evolutionary process we have seen anywhere in the universe, more fascinating than even the most imaginative among us can fantasize.

No wonder Pascal called us monsters! What *grandeur* is ours and what *misère*! Tennyson called man a piebald miscellany. Mark Twain remarked that man is the only creature that has a nasty mind. Yet thousands of years ago these words were already written in the *Mahābhārata*: "To you I declare the holy mystery that there is nothing nobler than humanity." Because man is so noble, his baseness looks all the more disgusting; because he is so base, his nobility is all the more awesome. No doubt this is one reason why men and women, who have an opportunity to see, respectively, the other side of the human race, both adore and condemn what they see. For humanity is a stranger monster than was the centaur of ancient mythology, who was merely the body of a horse with the head of a man: an ideal no doubt as much longed for as that of putting an old head on young shoulders. Humanity is stranger still, being a god who is also a dog, a goddess who is also a bitch. Yet our absurdity is the absurdity of everything that is "on the make." We all easily admire whatever is smooth and graceful, as gods and angels are customarily depicted. We can admire, too, the magnificence of the tiger, the sleekness of the porpoise, and the swift, shy elegance of the deer. Angel and beast, prince and peasant, race-horse and cart-horse: each is admirable in his own way. But what of this middle-class monster we call man, this cosmic snob who is neither beast nor god but a ridiculous evolutionary mongrel endlessly trying out high jumps from the swamps to the seventh heaven? He is somewhat like T. S. Eliot's hippopotamus who "rests on his belly in the mud,":

> I saw the 'potamus take wing
> Ascending from the damp savannas,
> And quiring angels round him sing
> The praise of God, in loud hosannas.

> Blood of the Lamb shall wash him clean
> And him shall heavenly arms enfold
> Among the saints he shall be seen
> Performing on a harp of gold.

He shall be washed as white as snow,
By all the martyr'd virgins kist,
While the True Church remains below
Wrapt in the old miasmal mist.[1]

Of course we all know what Eliot was poking fun at; but he was
also providing us with a parable of our human condition. Man is a
clumsy hippo who can nevertheless take off, however awkwardly,
on angelic wings. The more he is in process of salvation the more
ludicrous he looks. His awkwardness stems from his being in
soteriological adolescence. An adolescent youth, being neither
man nor boy, looks awkward, as though all arms and legs. Human
beings in their struggle toward salvation and advancement to the
next stage in the evolutionary process look more absurd still: they
are like flying hippopotamuses.

The concept of salvation is inevitably bound up with gnosis, for
the knowledge of God can never be in any sense merely informative. It is through knowledge that man is saved from his human
predicament: what Christian theologians traditionally call his
fallen condition. Such a process takes many embodiments. As a
sculptor (who has to understand his subject well both before he
begins work and while he is working on it) takes up several
stances, now from this angle, now from that, now in front, now
behind, till he knows his subject "inside out", so we must be
re-embodied in many ways to gain the experience that is an
essential part of the process of our attainment of gnosis. Not all
religions officially teach reincarnation as a standard doctrine.
The Christian Church, for instance, has not done so, though the
doctrine was held by some, possibly many, in the first century or
so after the death of Jesus. All the great religions, however,
including of course Christianity, are about salvation.

In the Christian Way, salvation is offered through Jesus Christ.
The very name "Jesus" represents the late Hebrew and Aramaic
"Yeshua", signifying "Yahweh is my salvation." That Jesus saves
has been the watchword, the battle-cry of all evangelical Christians. Through Jesus salvation is made available as never before;
yet it must be appropriated. The Church, as the unique instrument of God, witnesses to the saving power of Christ; but the
individual must appropriate the salvation that is offered, and that

---

[1]The Oxford Book of Modern Verse, 1892-1935 (Oxford: The Clarendon
Press, 1936), No. 254, p. 280.

appropriation entails the acquisition of the saving gnosis of God. It is that same God, writes Paul, who "said, 'Let there be light shining out of darkness,' who has shone in our minds to radiate the light of the knowledge (*tēs gnōseōs*) of God's glory, the glory on the face of Christ."[2] According to Christian teaching, the individual, inflamed by the *agapē* that is infused into the Church by the power of the Holy Spirit of God, is put directly in the way of such knowledge of God as earthbound men and women can hope to attain in this present life.

The ancient gnosis made much of intermediaries: beings of an order much higher than ourselves, some of whom counsel and help humankind, others of whom even "superintend" or govern spheres of the universe. Christianity, through its Semitic background, certainly inherits such a tradition, both in its angelological and in its hagiographic lore. True, in popular Catholic devotion the saints sometimes seem to crowd out the angels; nevertheless, the angelic hierarchy is an inalienable part of Christian tradition from New Testament times. Prominent in the Wisdom literature dating some centuries before the Christian era (a literature with which the New Testament writers were familiar and which they quoted as Holy Writ), the tradition of angels was an integral part of the religious outlook of all the first Christians. The angel Gabriel brought the good news of the birth of Christ to the Virgin Mary. Michael, prince of the heavenly hosts, is especially venerated in Christian lore. As in Roman mythology every man had his "Genius" to guide him and every woman her "Juno", so the notion of a guardian angel, assigned to every Christian, has played a considerable part in popular devotion. This angel protects one and guides one over the thornier paths of life. As, in the mosque, the Muslim worshippers bow to the recording angels present at prayer, so Christians, when the Mass or Eucharist is offered by the priest, affirm that it is offered "with angels and archangels" and all the other orders in the celestial hierarchy, such as the seraphim, who join in the solemn act of giving praise and thanks to God. Finally, as the faithful soul finishes this life's pilgrimage, the officiating priest asks in one of the loveliest prayers of the Church that angels may carry him to his destination.

---

[2]II Corinthians 4.6.

This notion is plainly connected to notions familiar to
theosophists from time immemorial and appears also in innumerable forms in "secular" Western literature. It has been illumined by the accounts in our own time of death-life experiences such as those described by Dr. Kübler-Ross and others.
True, for orthodox Christians of every tradition, Jesus alone is
Saviour. Nevertheless, intermediaries such as angels and "the
saints of heaven" do minister within the process he initiates. This
tradition of intermediaries is of crucial importance in our consideration of the gnostic aspect of Christian thought, especially in
the evolutionary understanding of the universe with which we are
now concerned.

What we are to call beings superior to ourselves does not matter
very much for our present purpose. More important is that they
must exist and that we humans, who have taken so long to reach
our present transient condition in the "many mansions" of God,
may be presumed to have further to go on the evolutionary path.
The notion that we could be the lords of creation, the ultimate
triumph of development, is surely a peculiarly outrageous piece
of arrogance. It is nevertheless one that people seem prone to
perpetrate at certain stages of human development.

According to a story in the *Qur'ān*, God, having finished his
creation, commanded the angels to bow down in reverence before Adam, the first man. Lucifer refused.[3] It is a very strange
story. Since angels are so much venerated in Islamic tradition, the
command seems, even for Allah, curiously arbitrary and unexpected. That generals and other major officers in the celestial
army should be flung from heaven for not saluting a newly-
created sergeant such as man does seem rather a primitive fan-
tasy. Be that as it may, the notion that this chimera, this flying
hippopotamus we call man, should be the *terminus ad quem* of the
creativity of God is surely the most unbelievable doctrine ever
proposed in the history of religions, which is not a negligible
affirmation. It might have seemed less unbelievable before Darwin; but it certainly does seem so to any intelligent person today.
Either man is just a biological accident in a purposeless universe
or else he is at a stage at which, if he is making any progress at all,
he must be acutely aware both that his race is transient and that, as
there are many orders of being below him, so there must surely be

---

[3]*Qur'an, sura* XX, 116.

some above him. That I should have been a monkey or even a frog at an earlier stage of my development does not at all disconcert me; but that I should either continue to be or end up as a human being seems to me intolerable.

Medieval thought, deprived though it was of the knowledge of the evolutionary character of the universe, was too enlightened for any such conclusion. The marvelous genius of Thomas Aquinas perceived as clearly as could anyone have perceived in the thirteenth century that there must be beings higher than man. He explains, indeed, why even on philosophical (*i.e.*, rational) grounds it must be so. Adopting the terminology of the Bible and the tradition of mystical theology that has come down to the later Middle Ages through the Pseudo-Dionysius, who flourished about the year 500, Thomas sees that in the hierarchy of being there must be entities superior to man. He could not possibly have given the reasons that would have seemed so obvious to him had he lived today; but he sees in his own way the absolute necessity for it, if there be any purpose in the universe at all. His insight on this particular point is extraordinarily acute, because he does labor under the difficulty of a now archaic, non-evolutionary type of science. Yet he boldly proposes, for instance, that angels must transcend our human condition in at least one important respect: they must be "pure intelligences"; that is, they can have no bodies. Having no bodies, they cannot belong to a class, as do we, because for technical reasons Thomas thinks it is through the possession of a particular type of body that creatures belong to a species: dog, cat, sheep, man. Each angel is a species of his own: in Thomist language he is a "separate substance." Thomas's angels, moreover, being non-spatial, take no time to move from one place to another. They constitute, in his system, what he takes to be a necessary order of entities in the hierarchy of being.[4] At least they put man in his place! Thomas is able to borrow some of his ideas from the somewhat elaborate hierarchical system of angels that the Pseudo-Dionysius had provided: three choirs, to be precise, with three orders apiece, making nine orders of angels in all, with seraphim in the top rank and ordinary angels in the bottom.

---

[4]Thomas discusses the question of angels in *Summa Theologiae*, I, qq. 50-64, and elsewhere. All the medieval schoolmen, from Bonaventure to Scotus accept in principle the schema of angelology handed down by the Pseudo-Dionysius.

What is important for us in this great medieval tradition is that we have a clear enunciation of the principle: man is neither the lord of creation nor the end of a process. He is on the way to somewhere. The saints and the blessed (*sancti et beati*) in heaven constitute yet another mode of existence; one into which we humans may hope to enter but have not yet approached. Neither the children of the Middle Ages nor those of the Renaissance had much interest in animals, because animals, on their view, had no future. In the medieval bestiaries one finds a great curiosity about beasts and they must indeed have been a puzzling order of being, having no future and so no real theological or theosophical interest. (Dogs and cats are still notoriously maltreated, not least in the Latin countries, in ways that shock even the least religious people in other parts of the world.) Man, on the contrary, being destined for heaven or hell, had a future. It entailed a fearsome alternative, of course; nevertheless, it was a future.

Today we can see the future of the human race in other terms. Provided that we do not completely destroy ourselves in a nuclear war or other such planetary suicide, we must evolve, for we cannot stand still. Yet we cannot say precisely how individuals shall evolve, for that depends on how they think and act. Modern scientific knowledge teaches us to expect evolution only because it is the law of being. In the expectation, however, is a paradox. *Biological* evolution such as interested Darwin seems to have reached its goal in man. That is to say, on the biological level man has nowhere to go. Perhaps there was a time when he might have developed wings; but if so that time is past, since he has now found other means of doing what wings would have done for him. Winged humans would now merely add to our traffic problems. Man does have large undeveloped areas in his brain; but the development of these would presumably make little or no difference to him biologically, greatly though it might affect his future evolution on other lines. If our biological evolution be virtually completed, our future evolution must take some other form. We cannot predict, however, what form it is to take for human beings in general. The reason for this is so important that we should give some attention to it here.

Some evolutionists have suggested that man will eventually so control the future course of his evolution as to become completely self-determining.[5] Such confidence in the human race is surely unwarranted, if only because what we call the human race is, as we have seen, a process, not a species. Those nineteenth-century evolutionists who saw some of the religious implications of the evolutionary principle saw also that for the human race at large evolution could not possibly proceed steadily as one expects childhood to go on to adulthood as a matter of course. Individual differences are too great. One such writer puts the situation with commendable candor: "The gulf that separates the highest animals from the lowest men is as nothing compared with the wider differences that lie between those lowest men and the Dantes, the Shakespeares, and the Newtons of the race."[6]

All that we know of spirituality and moral development points to an elitist principle. Evolution in the spiritual dimension must proceed differently from the way in which biological evolution unfolds. If there is anything at all that we can say about humanity, it is that the individual differences in spiritual development are incalculably great. All religion, indeed, presupposes a moral and spiritual elitism. According to the author of the Apocalypse, the number of the redeemed is remarkably small.[7] The 144,000 constitute a very select club indeed, even for Israel, and however allegorically the number be interpreted. Many religions recognize in one way or another that the mass of humanity will perish and that only some will gain the palm of victory.[8] The Hebrews recorded an instance of the principle in the Book of Genesis. Abraham, pleading to the Lord for Sodom and Gomorrah, was reduced in the course of his bargaining to ask that he be expected to find only as few as ten righteous people. The Lord agreed to stay his hand if even ten could be found. In the long run, how-

---

[5]*See,* for example, T. Dobzhansky, *Mankind Evolving* (New Haven: Yale University Press, 1962).

[6]M. J. Savage, *The Religion of Evolution* (Boston: Lockwood, Brooks and Co., 1876), p. 51. *See also,* for a satirical approach, in fictional form, to the question of the difficulty of defining man, a novel by Vercors [pseudonym for Jean Bruller], *You Shall Know Them* (Boston. Little, Brown and Co., 1953).

[7]Revelation 7.4.

[8]Origen's universalism deviates from the central Christian tradition that failure is possible, not to say common.

ever, only Lot and his wife and two daughters escaped, and Lot's wife perished through hesitation on the way. The story provides a paradigm for the principle of election that governs all religious thought, however variously the principle may be expressed. Only a minority even feebly turn in any direction that could lead them to the gnosis, and of that minority far fewer still succeed.

The notion that certain people are arbitrarily favored by God is a recurrent theme, not least in Christianity. Mary is greeted by the angel as "highly favored". The elect are "snatched like brands from the burning." Augustine saw himself as the most undeserving man to receive the grace that came to him. Yet is such selectivity as arbitrary as the reports suggest? Augustine, like Paul and many others, feeling deeply their unworthiness to be enlisted among those selected for redemption, are overwhelmed by the magnanimity of God who has so graciously favored them. Their gratitude springs from a loving heart. Such loving gratitude should make one humble: too humble perhaps to recognize how far one has already advanced in the evolutionary process. Such conversion experience is a turning point in which one recognizes for the first time that the old mechanistic forms of evolution have to give way to a new form in which evolution proceeds through personal relationship in which love supersedes law. Augustine was well aware that one does not become a Christian out of a moral vacuum. He sometimes even hints that one must be a good pagan first, in order to be ready for the turnabout which conversion is. Such awareness distinguishes an authentic evolutionary leap in spirituality from spurious claims.

The nature of evolutionary development changes all along, as the process unfolds. In the unfolding of the biological process, a kind of individuation is achieved; nevertheless, the organism cannot yet dispense with the ant-like gregariousness that is necessary for survival. Even at the human level the individual needs personal relationships in order to overcome the self-centeredness that would otherwise fatally impede his moral growth. Yet he finds he also needs that solitude that hermits and other holy men and women have chosen as the way to saving knowledge of God. In biological evolution those animals survive who most skilfully adapt to their environment in such a way as to avoid destruction; but they must also learn to organize themselves to the best advantage. Survival of the fittest is not merely, as has often been popularly supposed, a tooth-and-claw affair. Time comes when the ability to co-operate is more important than brute strength, as agility proves superior to mere brawn. But then, as the human level is reached, some individuals find that they must make a leap beyond the old methods that served well in the past. Certainly they must learn a new one to make any progress in the attainment of gnosis. Awareness of the nature and power of agapistic love is the first step toward the attainment of that gnosis of God that Paul and others so clearly hold out as the goal of the new life whose joys they proclaim as the fruit of being *en Christō*: in Christ.

Our human situation today is nevertheless peculiarly fraught with danger. That our scientific progress has resulted in our capacity for nuclear self-destruction is obvious and well-known. So let us turn instead to another example that may more effectively bring home to us the nature of our peril.

One of the paradoxes in the progress we have achieved in medicine (a progress perhaps even more spectacular than in any other field of human knowledge) is this: having enormously decreased hospital mortality in the last sixty years or so we have also brought about an alarming deterioration in the quality of the genetic pool. Such is the progress in genetics that it has become medically feasible to predict accurately the chances of a couple's having a defective offspring. For example, the probability is 50% that a person who has any dominant trait will pass it on to his or her offspring. Some traits are recessive, so that one must get the undesirable gene through both parents. Cystic fibrosis would be an example. Suppose both parents are free of muscular dystrophy and have one child equally free of the defective gene, yet their second child has the disease. The chances are 25% that any further child will have two good genes; 50% that it will have a good and a bad gene and so be a potential carrier; and 25% that it will have two defective genes and so personally inherit the crippling disease. There are other cases with more complicated probabilities. Moreover there is now the possibility of checking out, sometimes with almost 100% accuracy, sometimes much less, the presence of recessive genes.

Such knowledge presents us with a problem in medical ethics that was never before there in its present form. Sixty years ago there was really very little to be said for sterilization of the biologically unfit, for one could never have been sure at that time that even the most unpromising couple might not produce a normal child, perhaps even a Leonardo or a Mozart. (Incidentally,

Leonardo, being of illegitimate birth, would have been a likely candidate for abortion, as indeed also would many of the greatest figures in history, including, for instance, Jesus.) It is still possible that, in many an unpromising case, a genius might be born; yet with our knowledge of the statistical probabilities, the risk we assume is far more terrifying than it seemed in the past. The fearsome probability is that in a century or a century and a half from now one child out of ten will be born with a genetic defect. We are now so clever at the biological salvation of mankind that we are headed for a colossal genetic catastrophe. When nature was allowed to take its course we had a tolerably healthy prognosis for mankind. Now we have so far advanced in medical skill that our geneticists can promise us that the deterioration of the human race is assured unless some action is taken. Though sixty years ago there was little to be said for mandatory sterilization, the choice is less simple today, to say the least. Yet today, no less than yesterday, one could point out the obvious dangers of legislation that would put so formidable a weapon in the hands of a potentially dictatorial government. When we find, however, as we do, two parents with IQs of 50 having ten or fifteen children all with IQs of 60 or 70 at most, can we still be content to leave the whole question in the lap of God? Yet what is the alternative? At least one country (Denmark) has introduced legislation requiring, in the case of prospective marriage partners having one of an official list of genetic defects, sterilization before a marriage certificate may be issued. One obvious effect of such legislation is that the children of the biologically unfit shall be predominantly illegitimate.

I mention this quandary to dramatize not so much our human plight as the nature of our human situation. Biologically we are mammals and at the end of our evolutionary pilgrimage. We have learned, somewhat belatedly, the genetic laws of the propagation of our race. The evolutionary path we are now called upon to take will be very different; yet it is still an evolutionary path. It is likely to be not for the many but for the few. The way has been plotted for us for some thousands of years (which in terms of the history of our planet might be listed under "current events"); but it entails such new modes of thinking and acting that few are even now aware of the revolution that has taken place at the cosmic crossroads where humanity now is. Like Dante and his guide Virgil in the depths of hell, at the center of gravity in Satan's belly, we find ourselves turned upside down, called upon to do every-thing in reverse, to go in the opposite direction from that to which all our instinct has for so long pointed us, and yet not to repudiate the biological laws under which we were born.

Yet is it so new for us? We were born, every one of us, dangling from a placenta, yet with an infinite capacity for the attainment of freedom. The exponents of the ancient gnosis saw in that capacity the true destiny of man. Contrary to what is popularly supposed, Christianity, no more than any other religion, is not for every-man. It is for the few. According to the liturgy, the chalice is not poured out *pro omnibus* but only *pro multis*: not for all but for many, a very unspecific number. The Blood of Christ is given for those who desire more than anything else to be saved *to see God*. That gnosis is indeed salvation, which is what religion is about.

XII

KARMA, REINCARNATION
AND THE ANCIENT GNOSIS

> *The Books say well, my Brothers! each man's life*
> *The outcome of his former living is;*
> *The bygone wrongs bring forth sorrows and woes,*
> *The bygone right breeds bliss.*
> —Sir Edwin Arnold, *The Light of Asia*

> *Someone may ask, "How are the dead raised,*
> *and what sort of body do they have when they*
> *come back?" They are stupid questions. . .*
> *each sort of seed gets its own sort of body.*
> —I Corinthians 15.35.

We have seen to what a remarkable extent the motifs of modern existentialism parallel those of the ancient gnosis. Prominent among these common motifs is the triadic concept of individuality, alienation, and freedom. The karmic law, which presupposes that triad, can be seen to be its implicate. For if, alienated from my environment, I am free to evolve into an ever more individualized self, my evolution must proceed according to a predetermined principle. All exercise of freedom implies such a framework. If it were otherwise, the freedom would be the ability to do whatever my caprice dictated. Such freedom, even were it imaginable, would lack all purpose, and purpose is clearly implied in the kind of evolution by means of which a self can be more and more individualized. The cosmic law under which my moral evolution can proceed is called in Sanskrit *karma*. It is the inexorable principle under which I act. In terms of karma I evolve my individuality and "rise" to "higher" dimensions of being or "planes" of consciousness.

Connected with this karmic principle is the doctrine of reincarnation. Reincarnationism, though it has an ancestry in primitive magical notions of metamorphosis, emerges as a thoroughly ethical principle, bound to the karmic law and entailing the presupposition of spiritual evolution that is so characteristic of the ancient gnosis. That it is part of the basic ideological furniture of the entire sub-continent of India is well-known; but it has arisen also and, so far as can be seen, independently in other cultures, including that of our own Western and predominantly Christian society. Its influence in the West, astonishing misunderstandings and oppositions notwithstanding, has been immense. Today it is giving rise to a new, profound, and widespread interest.[1] The opposition against it, expressed by some earlier Christian writers such as Tertullian, attest its existence, to say nothing of its importance, in early Christian thought.

A seventh-century Church council, after affirming the doctrine of the resurrection of the body, expressly denounces those who have suggested that we shall "rise in a body of air or in any different sort of body as some have foolishly thought; but we shall rise in this very body in which we now live and are and move."[2] The bishops, after having proclaimed this excessively specific interpretation of the doctrine of the resurrection, went on to cite the example of Christ. Christ, they affirmed, has ascended into heaven where "he sits at the Father's right hand" and whence he shall return to judge the conduct of each person *while he was in the body*. This is a good example of the way in which spiritual doctrines that could illumine the understanding of an imaginative and receptive mind become ludicrously and materialistically

---

[1]*See* my *Reincarnation in Christianity* (Wheaton: Theosophical Publishing House, Quest Books, 1978).

[2]The Eleventh Council of Toledo, whose creed was presented to it by the Metropolitan Quiricus and adopted by the seventeen bishops present, November 9, A.D. 675. Since it is by no reckoning a general council of the Church it is *not* binding on either Roman Catholics, Eastern Orthodox, or any other Christians.

cheapened by the carnally-minded, who as often as not are to be found among ecclesiastical leaders.

Even in such a cheap, vulgar travesty of the beautiful and ancient doctrine of the resurrection of the body, which has deep affinities with the ancient gnosis, there is of course still a surviving element of truth. The embodiment to which one shall next be called need not be radically different from the one we now have, thought it may be in some cases healthier. Eventually we may attain a kind of body grander than our wildest imaginings, perhaps on some other planet in some distant galaxy. Speculation about the kind of body we shall inherit or attain is really too trivial a preoccupation for those of us who acknowledge the fundamental principle of the venerable law of karma.[3] It is rather too much as though, having discovered the cause of and cure for cancer, we were to spend time wondering whether the pills would come coated in blue or in pink. The fundamental principle of karma is that what we sow we reap, whether within an hour, as in the case of our swallowing hydrochloric acid, or a somewhat longer time, as in the case of a thoughtless injury to a friend, awareness of which injury we have consigned to the subconscious psyche. In the case of a really deep-seated sullenness of spirit and culpable destruction of one's spiritual vision, it might take many lifetimes.

That karmic principle, part of the ancient gnosis, appears in many guises wherever the notion of "divine judgment" emerges. This notion of a "judgment", closely associated with doctrines of immortality and resurrection, is often understood in Christian theology in an allegorical fashion as a do-it-yourself-job. Traditionally, however, it has been generally represented, after the manner of Michelangelo's splendid painting, very much as a criminal court of law, with Satan as Public Prosecutor, Christ as Chief Justice, and oneself as a very untrained, inexpert, and unqualified counsel in one's own defense. Yet the truth behind the somewhat primitive idea of a "day of reckoning," a "day of wrath," a "judgment day," is profoundly important, even though the day be not one measurable into twenty-four hours or specifiable as a Saturday or a Monday, since it is every day and forever. Some contemporary theologians who style themselves "liberal" soft-pedal such traditional notions out of existence, because, knowing nothing of psychic realities, they fail to understand the

---

[3]*See* I Corinthians 15.35.

basically gnostic character of the Christian faith, which they very mistakenly dilute, bowdlerize, and de-gnosticize into a program of inexpert social welfare.

Then those who still, if dimly, see such psychic realities, wonder why the average churchgoer can see no point to ideas such as salvation and redemption, and why preachers often draw a blank when they preach the mercy of the Lord to those who understand nothing of his judgment. They may wonder how, when preachers occasionally speak beautifully of helpers, of how angels are ever hovering near us to guide our feet across those treacherous pitfalls and away from those fearsome precipices lurking on all sides of the dangerous road of life, people gape. But how could people understand the meaning of divine mercy if they had never first understood the inexorable law of God's wrath, so simply and beautifully expressed in the karmic principle? After several generations of sermons on the need for rummage sales to help parishes to contribute to programs for teaching the poor Third World children to understand that thrift and industry are outmoded ideas, capitalist inventions for the exploitation of whoever may or may not be listening, while all the time the preacher is giving the general impression that "God" is a funny way of talking reverently about a non-reality that is for some inexplicable reason socially important, is it even mildly astonishing that the hearers no longer understand any religious truth at all? Is it remarkable that if the preacher began to use the term "Superstar" for "God", people would just assume it to be another expression of some new liturgical fashion, like "Holy Spirit" for "Holy Ghost"? Is it surprising, indeed, that some actually suppose these fads and nervous changes are just ways of keeping people on their toes, like the drill instructor's shouting "left" when everybody expected him to yell "right"? One Episcopalian lady, when I asked her whether she might not like to join her husband in his churchgoing, replied that her exercise-bicycle gives her all the exercise she needs to keep her trim. I know she was not being smart-alecky or flip. Can she be blamed for supposing, since Christianity is represented as being about social welfare, that the standing and the kneeling, the bobbing and the bowing, traditional in Anglican and other Catholic worship, is just an old-fashioned way of taking exercise before modern fitness equipment had been invented? When people see that church assemblies are willing to take venerable doctrines inherited from Christian antiquity and change them almost literally overnight as voters vote district supervisors in and out of office, would anyone really expect us to be surprised by their going on to vote religion out of existence as one might vote to break up a discarded battleship or bulldoze a slum area in the Bronx? For when the kind of religion purveyed becomes an opiate (as Marx so ignorantly called all religion) how could we expect that there should be anybody left to protect but the users of the drug? Since they are presumably under its influence, their protest, if any, would be unlikely to be heard very far away.

Yet the notion of karma poses a very pertinent question. Do we really need to tell people about it? Here is a man, a decent fellow: more than a decent fellow, for he goes to church regularly and is genuinely interested in religious ideas, though rather too busy with his work, hoping to make enough money to keep his family well and happy and to get a good education for his children. Why need one bother him with such an esoteric notion as karma? Would it really matter if he were to die, having passed through life in complete ignorance of the term? No, it would not matter in the sense that not knowing of it would not fundamentally change anything in his circumstances. In this sense it does not matter if I do not know whether my liver is in my thorax or in my big toe or whether, indeed, I have ever heard of the organ. It will work for me, as will my kidneys and my fingers, my stomach and my lungs, so long as all goes well. If things go amiss, no doubt I can always go to a hospital and have an operation. Taking a medical course would not radically change the situation. If I have ulcers, it will not remove them; if I do not, it is unlikely to give them to me. So the karmic principle will work whether I know about it or not. Knowing about it, however, is likely to make things easier for me, perhaps infinitely easier. Instead of a karmic work-out that may take a thousand lifetimes, I may be able to sidetrack much of the labor and sorrow attending such a string of rather boring lifetimes by a better understanding of my possible destiny and my need for its fulfilment, enabling me to cry out for salvation, and to work it out far more expeditiously than would have been possible in my ignorance. Knowledge of cosmic laws, which in the last resort are psychic and moral principles, is a tremendous time-saver and an infinitely valuable saver of energy.

We rightly deplore the thoughtless waste of physical energy, of the resources that sustain biological life on our planet. It is due largely to ignorance. But what of the far more staggering reflection: the stupendous waste of psychic energy caused by ignorance of the most elementary principles of the ancient gnosis? Imagine a man or woman spending a million lifetimes working out a comparatively simple karmic problem that he or she could have worked out in one lifetime or even less and thus have gone on so much more quickly to a more interesting and profitable development in spiritual evolution. We deplore our waste of energy through poor organization of our desk, or bad arrangement of our studies, or mishandling of our family life. We say we give ourselves (to say nothing of others) a hundred headaches we could have avoided in such a way as to bring us comfort, convenience, and the promise of a richer future; but surely knowledge of the karmic principle could save us more headaches than could any mere course in filing or seminar in office management.

One should respect, however, the view held by many Christians who sincerely feel that since they are in the Lord's hands they need not, perhaps even should not, inquire further. With Christ as the ground of their hope, why should they ask for more? Is not the whole point of the Christian faith the joy of knowing one is in the right hands? For those who can rest content with an attitude of such childlike simplicity, the attitude may be commendable, especially when it betokens that genuine humility that is so vital to deep religious insight. In fact, however, intelligent Christians cannot and should not long remain so immature in their faith. The question then is: on what lines do they seek to develop their maturation in the faith? Theologians, biblical scholars, and other professionals do in fact leave such an attitude far behind, while others who have not the time and sometimes not the capacity to mature must flit from one idea to another, many of them trying not to stray too far from what they take to be official doctrine yet ill at ease with such pseudo-explanations as they can make within such confines. Others, of course (and who can tell how many others?) simply abandon belief in and respect for Christianity, while bawling the hymns and creeds that they take to be the ritual price of admission to the club. Sociologically, such attitudes play a very large part in promoting the recruitment at all levels of the worst leadership the Church could possibly obtain within its membership. For the childlike disposition that can be admirable at one stage of religious development can degenerate into petrified immaturity and a chronic distaste for spiritual enterprise, which is plainly the antithesis of faith as we have seen the nature of faith to be. Worse still, the more learned the victims of this petrifaction the sadder the results, since they can be used by unscrupulous church leaders to give the illusion of buttressing what all honest and intelligent inquirers know cannot be upheld by such means.

Yet important spiritual insights do find their way into the Church. The insights of Jungian psychology, for example, and other forms of psychoanalytical therapy, have been already welcomed by many into the everyday pastoral work of the Church, and no twentieth-century writer can be more aptly described as gnostic. Jung, however, does not radically affect metaphysical presuppositions and so can be admitted without too much difficulty into even the most theologically conservative circles, on the ground that his work touches only the psychological aspect of religion. True, this is a questionable opinion, but it is also sufficiently plausible for the pragmatic purposes of the Church. Yet for those whose attitudes toward religion are not too fatally constricted, the concept of karma could open the way to an immense enrichment, showing people how to make more economical use of their spiritual energies instead of being sidetracked into years of wearisome work they could so happily and profitably avoid. More will be said on this in our concluding chapter.

Reincarnation is a corollary of the karmic principle. Moreover, apart from the karmic principle, reincarnation becomes a merely magical and rather silly notion, being entirely bereft of moral foundation. The karmic principle also presupposes a spiritual and moral evolutionism in the universe that extends from our primitive sub-human animal ancestors to whatever superhuman development lies ahead. It provides an infinitely more intelligible theory of our destiny and of cosmic purpose than is available in traditionalist Christian theologies. The practical need for such a theory of purpose and destiny among people who enjoy religious experience of any kind is obvious in face of the nihilism that prevails in intellectual circles. Moreover, though karma sounds alien to Christian and other Western ears, the principle appears in other guises in Western literature. Kant, as I have shown elsewhere, is an illustrious example.[4]

The notion that the karmic principle is mechanistic has discouraged many Westerners from accepting it. Of course it may be

[4]*Reincarnation in Christianity*, Chapter XI.

so interpreted; but in the ancient gnosis it is part of a larger scheme that excludes the relevance of that particular objection. Where divine Being is understood in wholly impersonal terms, then so of course is the karmic principle, which naturally reflects the mechanistic undergirding of such a view. Such an artificial restriction of our understanding of the nature of divinity, however, is by no means necessary or desirable. If, as we have seen, the motifs of modern religious existentialism have striking affinity with those of the ancient gnosis, the personal and suprapersonal nature of divine Being cannot be by any means alien from gnostic tradition. In fact, they are indigenous to it, as the strong emphasis on "invisible helpers," on "masters", and on "Lords of Karma" (who, as Felix Layton puts it, may "defer payment" till the individual is strong enough to meet the consequences of his actions) clearly suggests.[5]

Above all, the principle of self-sacrifice that is writ so deeply into the ancient gnosis would be unintelligible if the karmic principles were as mechanistic as its antagonists suppose. In a mechanistic universe, love can have no place, and self-sacrifice is the most complete expression of love. When the late A. C. Ewing objected to what he considered the "mercantile flavour about the conception" of the karmic principle, the impossibility of self-sacrifice was what he had in mind.[6] To think of karma in such terms is to ignore its other face, the graciousness that emanates from the psychic world. As we rise to higher and higher planes of consciousness we feel "the winds of God" and learn how "the Spirit bloweth where it listeth." The karmic principle is not thereby demolished any more than plane geometry is abolished by awareness of solid geometry. "Grace," remarks St. Thomas, "presupposes nature and perfection the perfectible."[7] We work laboriously on the treadmills of our karma till at last, suddenly, we get what might be called, in a popular way, a moral windfall, a godsend. In Christian language "God takes over" and "I am overwhelmed by irresistible grace." There are moments in our life when everything we touch seems suddenly to turn to gold,

---

[5]Felix Layton, "Karma in Motion", in Virginia Hanson, ed., *Karma* (Wheaton: Theosophical Publishing House, Quest Books, 1975), p. 87.
[6]A. C. Ewing, "The Philosophy of McTaggart, with Special Reference to the Doctrine of Reincarnation," in *Aryan Path*, February, 1957.
[7]*Summa Theologiae*, I, 2, 2 ad 1.

quite unexpectedly, quite inexplicably by any ordinary method of
explanation. It is like getting a "second wind." Having come to
what I thought was the end of my tether, I suddenly find myself
able not only to go on but to go on far better than I had been
doing. It is somewhat like the phenomenon of a preacher who,
having stuck closely to his admirably prepared notes, suddenly
loses them, or his place in them, and no less suddenly talks
extempore like an angel from heaven with mighty power. His
audience may thoughtlessly wish he never prepared a script, so
that he could talk like that always; but of course if he never
prepared a script he would talk even in his "inspired" moments
more like an idiot than an angel. So karma is the ground of grace,
the moral law that makes grace possible.

I go on following the old and tried methods, laboriously working out what I seem to have to do in life, when suddenly there
comes to me an inner questioning, a new idea that turns me
upside down. In the language of religion, I am "converted". My
foundations have been shaken. I ask myself, in effect, what was all
that dreary labor for? What trouble I could have saved myself had
I but known what I know now! It was as if, having a washing
machine at my disposal, I put the clothes in it and then rubbed
them and rinsed them by hand when I could have pushed a
button. Or it may seem as though, never having learned to smile, I
wasted years of effort trying to win friends with scant success till
suddenly I learned the secret, which immediately opened a
thousand doors. Grace and salvation are not alien to karma; they
are its working out on another dimension. Karma has many
dimensions.

The discovery of these other dimensions may take millions of
re-embodiments. So integral to the karmic principle is the notion
of spiritual evolution that we are not to suppose that any poor
struggling soul is "to win them all" or "to lose them all" in one little
life and so be condemned forever to the consequences of his
decisions, of the feeble successes and pathetic little failures of that
one little piece of striving, bound within the confines of anything
from a few weeks to a few decades of life. How can a poor
industrious little bank teller or factory worker be expected to
enter into such higher planes of consciousness all in one life?
Sometime he or she may indeed do precisely that; but if not, is
there no hope? Or else are we to suppose that everything is
magically made all right at death, making all the striving in any

case vain? The concept of re-embodiment makes not only life and death more intelligible; it makes grace more beautiful than ever, being a dimension of the very nature of all things. Nothing is wasted; but we cannot expect "our ship to come in," if we have never sent it out.

The notion of the perfectibility of man is bound up with the ancient gnosis.[8] By "perfectibility" is meant here his perfectibility into a being who is harmonious, orderly, free of moral defect, and metaphysically all that ideally he can be. That means, however, that man must be able sooner or later to transcend his present condition. It means perfectibility into the superman, into a state that lies beyond the human condition as we know it. That is an implicate of the concept of moral and spiritual evolution. The perfectibility of man *is* his capacity to transcend the human condition. That is not done in a day or a lifetime. It takes many lifetimes, possibly trillions. Scientific, medical and sociological progress in human well-being and human society, important and welcome though certainly they are, are at best but tokens or symbols of human perfectibility. They can sometimes even be tragic impediments to our real progress. Better communications have notoriously too often resulted in our not only saying less and less to more and more people but saying more unimportant things more inelegantly to more unreceptive people. We have seen in an earlier chapter that improved medical knowledge can put in jeopardy the future health of the race by exposing it to an increased incidence of grave genetic defects. Surely no one need be reminded that scientific progress has made possible the neutron bomb. Advance in any branch of human knowledge can never be evil *per se*; yet when knowledge of the spiritual verities and moral realities is so ludicrously outstripped by knowledge of chemistry and physics, of mathematics and linguistics, the results for humanity are likely to be catastrophic. Only through the spiritual progress of the individual in his lone pilgrimage through the ages can I eventually complete my liberation and transcend my humanity. By the transcendence of my humanity I no more mean discarding it than I would claim now to have discarded my

---

[8]On the history of the notion of human perfectibility, *see* John Passmore, *The Perfectibility of Man* (New York: Charles Scribner's Sons, 1970) and Martin Foss, *The Idea of Perfection in the Western World* (Princeton: Princeton University Press, 1946).

animality. For already I am, though an animal, not merely an animal, and I hope I am on my way to being more than a mere man.

Such notions may seem to some so obviously congenial to the heart and indisputable to the mind that they may ask once again whether gnosticism be not merely a name for all that humanity has agreed upon. The point is well-taken, in the sense that the ancient gnosis is, like existentialism, humanism *of a kind*. Did not Sartre himself entitle one of his more popular treatments of the subject *L'Existentialisme est un humanisme*? The question is: what *kind* of humanism? In a later chapter we shall take the opportunity of exploring that question. Here we need show only that, contrary to what has just been suggested, the ancient gnosis is not by any means a vapid affirmation of incontestable truths. It is a firm stance. It stands far more definitely and to the point against very seriously held philosophical positions than do most religious creeds. One example here should suffice.

Among currently pervasive doctrines, none is more assiduously and often uncritically taught than the notion that each person is the product of his or her environment, principally (following Freud) the environment of his very early childhood but also his environment in the larger sense of "what has been done to him." This view is really a wider application of Feuerbach's neat epigram that I am what I eat. I am what is fed to me by my heredity, my genes, my parents, my relatives, my friends, my teachers, and not least, my life-situation. Yet when, adhering to this view, I seem to blame my parents or society or my childhood poverty or other circumstance for my vices and failures and non-achievements, I am not really blaming them as if they were responsible agents, since of course, on the behaviorist view I have taken, there *are* no responsible agents, only circumstances and their victims. Still, my view enables me to treat the highest human achievements and the noblest human deeds as though they had come about by a fortuitous concurrence of circumstances. Since I am what I am by chance I can tell the Buddha how lucky he was to have been enlightened and Dante how fortunate he was to have hit on the theme of the *Commedia* at just the right time to gain him literary immortality. I might even tell Michelangelo that he must have been born with a silver spoon in his mouth to have done all these splendid paintings that millions claim to admire because so many experts have done so. Reading Freud's *Leonardo da Vinci and a Memory of his Childhood*, from which I learn that a bird brushed the lips of Leonardo as he lay in his cradle, I may rejoice, with some assistance from Freud, that this circumstance sublimated Leonardo's libido in such a way as to make him into the genius he became! For once I have acquiesced in the basic premisses I will go to any lengths to avoid countenancing the possibility that genius may be, as Edison affirmed it is, one per cent inspiration and ninety-nine per cent perspiration. The fundamental presuppositions underlying such behaviorist dogmas are indeed most clearly antithetical to the ancient gnosis and the perennial theosophy. Those who subscribe to them, since they see no moral or spiritual purpose in the universe, could learn nothing from reincarnationism or the principle of karma. This principle, however, stands far more firmly and explicitly against the view I have been pillorying than does, for instance, the Nicene Creed, which was devised for another, more specialized purpose.

The ancient gnosis indeed provides a bulwark against reductionism of every kind. The karmic principle, with its reincarnationist corollary, takes care in advance of all reductionist theories, including, for example, the now outmoded mechanistic reductionism of Newtonian physics. For in the ancient gnosis a correlative of the thrust of the past that is *karma* is the pull toward the future that the ancient Indian sages called *swadharma*. Expressed in the simplest Western terms, the twin principle means this: I cannot escape my history and must recognize and face it; but I can create my future. The better I learn how long my history is, the harder I shall work for the future that I know can be no shorter.

XIII

PRAYER AS THE EXERCISE OF PSYCHIC ENERGY

God answers sharp and sudden on some prayers,
And thrusts the thing we've prayed for in our face,
A gauntlet with a gift in't.
—Elizabeth Barrett Browning, *Aurora Leigh*

Prayer is probably the most puzzling of all religious practices. It is very general, if not universal, in the religions of the world; yet few persons could give a cogent account of what they take it to be or to do. On no practice in religion does a gnostic understanding shed more explanatory light.

Nor is any religious concept more cherished by the devout or more ridiculed by unbelievers. Prayer, especially petitionary prayer, in which the petitioner asks for a specific grace or favor or occurrence, does seem at first sight a ludicrous practice. On the German side the Lutheran chaplain is invoking divine aid to kill the British on what he calls the enemy lines at the very moment that the Anglican chaplain on the British side is supplicating no less resolutely, though in a different language, for the defeat of the Germans. Whom is God to answer favorably? On what basis is he to choose between the petitioners? My business competitor, being as it happens a practicing Christian, prays God for his success that may ruin me, while I, being similarly devoted to the Lord, pray for the business success that means so much to me and to my family but may ruin him. Even intercessory prayer presents

164

difficulties. Perhaps I, hearing of your grandfather's illness, dutifully and lovingly pray for his recovery, while you, knowing the situation better, pray even more vehemently for his death, which you believe to be best for him. Many people, not least those unaccustomed to a life of prayer, see the whole process as both silly and futile.[1]

True, much petitionary prayer is of such a character that some have questioned whether it is a proper form of prayer at all, not a mere relic of primitive superstition. Had not we better confine ourselves to contemplative, meditative forms of devotion? After all, in petitionary prayer the well-instructed faithful know they should always add, even if with a sigh, "But Thy will be done!" This seemingly self-effacing addition not only cancels most of what they have taken the trouble to say, but also calls attention to the fact that they have been nevertheless telling God what he is presumed to know better than can any of us. We are all familiar with satirizations such as: "O God, as thou knowest, we are going to have a little rummage sale on Saturday and we pray that thou wilt not forget our need for a big turn-out to make money for the new candlesticks which, as thou knowest, we need so badly." Such prayers make God look like a semi-programmed computer. If God knows about my grandfather's gout, as may be safely presumed from my affirmation of belief in his omniscience, what point is there in telling him and invoking his help? Are we to suppose he has been withholding healing till my prayer is offered? Is God like a senator or congressman waiting until he sees a large enough number of letters from his constituents before he takes action?

Behind the practice of prayer, however, lies a much deeper purpose. Prayer is a direction of psychic energy. It can be the most powerful energy a human being is capable of generating. Of course, the less selfishly petitionary the prayer, the more powerful it is; but even the feeblest prayer can have a beneficial effect on the human psyche. It can engage it in an operation in the realm of psychic reality whose significance may far exceed any other action we might perform. Occasionally prayer brings about events that people may call miraculous, such as the sudden shriveling up of a

---

[1]For a conventional treatment of the problem of petitionary prayer, *see* George Buttrick, *Prayer* (New York: Abingdon-Cokesbury, 1942), Chapters V and VI.

malignant tumor. Alexis Carrel, M.D., a French Nobel laureate, reports having seen with his own eyes such an occurrence at Lourdes.

Even that, however, is not what is most remarkable about the power of prayer. Carrel points out that all prayer, from the meanest and lowliest kind to the greatest mystical ecstasy, has one thing in common: it links the supplicant with the infinite psychic power that spins the universe. The supplicant, seeking to augment his very limited psychic energy from that inexhaustible source, is so enriched that his whole being is strengthened and renewed in the very act of prayer. Though our requests be overlaid with selfishness or vanity or even deceit, the slightest degree of love or gratitude within the meager syllables of our prayers can make these reach their target. Prayer is the basic exercise of the spirit. It is even more necessary for the psyche than is walking for the body.

To recognize the power of prayer and its significance in human life is to go far toward understanding what the evolution of man really means. Cicero noticed long ago that we are distinguished from the other mammals by two faculties, which he punningly designated *ratio et oratio,* reason and speech; but *oratio* is also the Latin word for prayer. Human dignity consists of man's capacity for prayer, for hooking himself up to the source of cosmic power. Prayer is an instrument of the moral growth of human beings, whatever else it may be besides. At no level, however, does evolution occur with the inevitability of the freezing or vaporization of water at certain temperatures. One cannot predict it as one might predict a riot from an observation of the temper of a crowd. We have every reason to expect benzine to boil at 80.4° Celsius, but no reason to suppose that any external state of affairs will bring about a sense of ethical obligation or moral duty, for moral evolution is an individual achievement. That spiritual advancement does not necessarily occur is surely one of the easiest propositions to demonstrate, since many people pass a whole lifetime without the slightest indication of any improvement that might suggest the possibility of their doing better in a trillion lifetimes. So far as the evidence goes, they might still be talking, at the end of the trillionth, of bridge-scores and new hats and the fiddle-faddle of ecclesiastical politics. Spiritual evolution is by no means inevitable. The dinosaur and the sabre-toothed tiger did not succeed even at the biological level: why, at the spiritual level, should I? Whether I do or do not depends on me, not on anyone or anything else. This principle appears to hold true even at the lowest stages of evolution; but the higher I develop, the more existentially crucial the truth becomes for me, on whom at every stage my leap beyond depends. Paradoxically, the man or woman who most clearly perceives this truth is the one who feels most acutely the need for help from beyond, from the source of energy apart from which no advancement in the evolutionary spiral can take place. To be hooked up to even the lowliest helper in that stream of psychic energy can produce incalculably great results. That God helps humankind through his angels and his saints is a more profound insight of Catholic tradition than many exponents of that tradition have generally understood.

Prayer takes a multiplicity of forms: the spontaneous shout of joy; the measured ceremonial liturgy of synagogue and church; the mechanical repetition of trusted old formulas; even the prayer-wheel and the mechanical rosary for the automobile dash; the quiet communion with God in a little nook; the timid request of a hesitant and fearful soul; the simple, trustful, mother-prompted phrases of a little child kneeling by a cot at bedtime; the anguished supplication of a distraught wife for her dying husband; the flight of a mystic toward divine union; the stiff, calm silence of an old-fashioned Quaker meeting-house; the scream of a tormented and deranged mind battering at the gates of heaven; the over-elegant diction of a prim priest at his personal devotions; the robust whisper of the noontide *Angelus* in field or farmyard; the sobbing of a penitent drunk; even the silly, selfish prayer of a spoiled child: all activate and, in varying ways, appropriate the energy that is at our disposal, the psychic energy that enhances our gnosis of God.

Many are the stories of earnest people who have worked themselves to such a state of exhaustion that they were ready to collapse, mentally and physically, and who then suddenly, as a result of one simple prayer, have found themselves renewed, invigorated and transformed. In desperation, at the end of their tether, they have at last opened the sluice-gates of their spirit to the unbounded psychic energies beyond that are at the divine disposal. It was to them as if, choking for breath, they had at least opened their lungs and taken in the oxygen they needed. I remember visiting a Vedanta temple in which, as I sat meditating for some minutes, I became aware of the presence of another person (there was only one) about twenty feet behind me. I felt a tremendous surge of psychic energy radiating from this person whom I had not even noticed as I entered. It was joyous presence, emanating immense psychic energy. As I turned to leave, I glanced at its source, a somewhat nondescript woman probably in her late thirties, whose face shone so brightly with a psychic glow that the entire area for several yards in front of her seemed to be bathed in light. *That* is prayer. I have often wondered, too, at the psychic power generated in a crowded little church in which many people are really engaged in prayer. Compared to such a flood of psychic energy, the roar of a 100,000-spectator crowd in a football stadium is inaudible. The energy released by even the most pedestrian of prayers can be stupendous. What, then, of the prayer of a Teresa or a Schweitzer?

The secret of the power of prayer is love. The prayers of the self-centered and of unbelievers have usually little effect. The prayer of an archbishop, if it be loveless, can be entirely futile, locking the gates of God against him as effectively as if he had turned the keys of a medieval keep. All genuine prayer implies some kind of genuine knowledge of the existence of the psychic power needed for the occasion and of its divine source. Friederich Heiler, in a classic study on prayer wrote long ago: "Belief in the personality of God is the necessary presupposition, the fundamental condition of all prayer." Prayer is not a mere talking to oneself, and if one so thinks of prayer it will be singularly ineffective. It is "a turning of man to another Being to whom he inwardly opens his heart; it is the speech of an 'I' to a 'Thou'."[2] That does not mean that God is to be conceived in crudely personal terms, for indeed He must be as supra-personal as He is supra-impersonal; nevertheless, in prayer He deigns to stoop to let us relate to Him as to a father or a friend.

The crudity of the prayers of simple, primitive people may make us smile. Savages, anthropologists tell us, have been known

---

[2]F. Heiler, *Prayer*, tr. S. McComb (New York: Oxford University Press, Galaxy Books, 1958), p. 356. The original, *Das Gebet* was published in 1918, four years before the original German edition of Martin Buber's *Ich und Du*, which has become the classic treatment of the concept of the I-Thou relationship between man and man and between man and God. The notion had already been adumbrated in the writings of Thomas Erskine (1788-1870).

to threaten and cajole their gods. Sometimes they will even try to appeal to their competitive spirit with suggestive hints such as: "Other ancestral spirits bless their people: why not thou?" The singer of the Rig-Veda reminds Agni: "If I were thou and thou wert I, thy wishes would be realized." George MacDonald, in his novel *David Elginbrod*, cites an epitaph:

> Here lie I, Martin Elginbrodde.
> Have mercy o' my soul, Lord God,
> As I would do, were I Lord God,
> And ye were Martin Elginbrodde.

Yet even such prayers, though far from what they might be, are prayers of a kind and can make contact with the cosmic energy, if only the supplicants can open themselves wide enough to receive it. At least one of the functions of prayer, if not the chief one, is to expand our souls in such a way as to eventually make possible for us a leap into a higher state of consciousness. The prayer at the lower end of the leap is likely to sound crude at the end at which the higher consciousness is achieved. Our today's prayer will assuredly seem crude when we have achieved our next evolutionary leap. Yet it is only those who have gone to school who can look back on the awkwardness of their kindergarten handwriting.

What difference does a gnostic outlook make to one's life of prayer? Briefly, one understands better what one is trying to do. One is not simply going to plead with a cosmic senile grandfather noted for his occasional generosity. One is, rather, trying to engage the healthy psychic energy that is available and to make oneself, in one way or another, impervious to the unhealthy psychic energy that abounds. For the gnostic's life of prayer makes him more and more aware of the presence and destructive power of the demonic as well as of the benevolence of the energy that flows from divine Being. That is why the gnostic mind is ready to enlist whatever help may be available. He knows what dangers lurk round about him. Christian faith was from the first conceived as the supreme weapon against them.

In Catholic and Eastern Orthodox Christian practice, much of the prayer of the faithful is addressed to the saints and angels, especially to Mary, the Theotokos (God-bearer) and Virgin Mother. These are not mediators between God and humankind; they are, rather, God's emissaries and our helpers. The notion of helpers, to which I have already so much alluded in the course of the present book is a standard one in the ancient gnosis and in theosophical literature throughout the ages. In a Mandaean creation myth, for example, the divine creative act is accomplished with the aid of angelic helpers. When Ptahil-Uthra receives a commission to create Adam, he is given various names, including that of Gabriel the Messenger. He, too, in turn has helpers, men who have been set in charge of souls. Such notions belong, of course, to the polytheistic climate that is antecedent to the development of monotheism. Yet when monotheism is eventually achieved, the helpers, though uncompromisingly subordinated to the One God as a matter of metaphysical principle, are not dispensed with. The angels and other helpers, whoever they may be, are recognized as real beings, beings whose mode of consciousness is greater than ours.

The notion that there might be no beings of a higher order than ourselves other than God is radically alien to the gnostic mind, the mind to which (often unwittingly) Catholic tradition is hospitable. Theoretically, we may be said not to need them, since we can go directly to God, who is available and open to receive the prayers of all his creatures. Nevertheless, so handicapped are we by the limitations of our mode of consciousness that helpers are provided to draw us upward. If ever a creature should have been able to receive directly the message God wished to communicate, surely Mary, according to Catholic presuppositions, must have been that most privileged of creatures. Yet even she receives the annunciation through the angel Gabriel. If, then, God speaks to us through such helpers, can it be improper for us to speak to Him through them? Such, at any rate, is the ancient Catholic view, which is extended to the heroes of the Church, saints and martyrs who have triumphed over the forces of evil and have been raised to a new life with God. To them we pray, not offering them worship (*latria*), which belongs to God alone, but asking them to help us to direct our psychic energy so that it may be deployed in the most fruitful manner.

This typically Catholic attitude has deep roots in the ancient gnosis. It implies what theosophists and gnostics have always recognized, that the universe is peopled by many orders of beings, among whom we humans, though varying among ourselves very much in spiritual advancement, are even at the best mere beginners compared with "the heavenly hosts." How can we, who at best shuffle along like spastics in the Kingdom of God, hope to shoot straight in the realm of psychic marksmanship? Our being able to shoot at all is due, according to traditional Christian doctrine, to our redemption by Christ; but in appropriating the grace that is so made available to me I have to use every help I can get. Were I to ignore the helpers who surround me, I should be properly called not only spastic but blind. So, in traditional Catholic language, I "invoke the prayers of the saints." In so doing I seek the help of those less handicapped than I to guide my hand while I shoot the psychic arrows I call my prayers. If I am aware of special helpers in the psychic dimension of being in which I have attained such capacity as I may have, I lean especially on them.

These special helpers need not be in any official calendar of saints. They may include, for example, a revered teacher or parent or friend who has gone ahead to "the fuller life" beyond. Traditional Roman Catholic discipline, which tends to seek to control everything the faithful do, limits authorized reception of such supplications to those who have been approved by the Church and designated as qualified to receive them.[3] Such control may be useful for those whose psychic awareness is at a minimal level, as is unfortunately the case with the majority of people. It is a safeguard against their seduction by demonic agencies. Plainly, however, the Church cannot so limit those of the faithful who are in fact aware of the presence of helpers not on the official list. The mere existence of such an official list, however, attests what many of us claim we already very well know: that the Church is a school of gnosis, a school of psychic training that must provide for kindergarten as well as college. Woe to those who thwart or discourage or belittle the feeble steps of toddlers in the gnosis of God!

Origen, after discoursing on the importance of choosing a suitable place for prayer, suggests that "it may be, angelic powers also stand by the gatherings of believers, and the power of the Lord and Saviour himself, and holy spirits as well, those who have fallen asleep before us. . . ."[4] He goes on to suggest that at such

---

[3]These are persons who have been beatified or canonized or at least under consideration for beatification. The latter are traditionally designated "Venerable", a title not to be confused with the one assigned in the Anglican Communion to certain functionaries called archdeacons.
[4]Cf. Psalm 34.7.

assemblies of the faithful, each person's guardian angel is present too, indeed that there is, as he quaintly puts it, "a double church, the one of men, the other of angels."[5] The same notion of "angelic helpers" is preserved in the Mass, where the priest, before entering upon the holiest part of the eucharistic celebration, joins himself and the assembled faithful with the angelic hosts. Muslims also recognize the presence of recording angels during their prayers in the mosque.

The notion of invisible helpers across the veil of death has an obverse side, since the practice of prayers *for* the dead is ancient and was virtually universal till Reformation times. Calvin's extreme antipathy to it was due to its association with the debased form of the doctrine of purgatory that he knew in the late medieval Church. His distaste was transmitted to generations of those in the Reformed Church down to the present century and has waned only to the extent that the violence of anti-Roman prejudice has abated. World War I, which raised so many questions about the afterlife with such poignancy in the minds of many who had been so suddenly and so tragically bereaved, fostered re-assessment of the traditional Protestant antipathy to prayers for the dead, even in those circles in which such prayers had been for so long forbidden as "popish".[6] Yet if prayer cannot function through the veil that separates this life from the life beyond, it is difficult to see how it could be supposed to function at all, since prayer, if it be taken seriously, must somehow be supposed to transcend time and space as we know them. The notion that a New Englander's prayer might reach as far as Virginia but not stretch to the Pacific very well and not at all to other planets would be surely a paradigm of absurdity. So in Catholic tradition we pray both *for* and *to* the departed, confident that we can function towards those we love both as helpers and as helped. All this is implied in the doctrine of the Communion of the Saints, celebrated as a major feast of the Christian calendar, though sometimes sadly neglected or ill-understood.

---

[5]Origen, *On Prayer,* in J. E. L. Oulton and H. Chadwick, *Alexandrian Christianity* (Philadelphia: Westminster, Library of Christian Classics, 1954), p. 325.
[6]*See,* e.g., the anonymous concluding essay on the subject in a collection entitled *Concerning Prayer* (London: Macmillan, 1917), pp. 479 ff.

All prayer, from the crudest petitioning to the loftiest mystical contemplation, is an engagement of psychic energy. It presupposes, however unconscious be the presupposition, awareness of a psychic realm. As surely as our dropping a letter in the mail box presupposes our belief in the existence of a postal system of mail delivery, engagement in any kind of prayer presupposes awareness of a psychic channel of communication. Such a presupposition is as much a part of the ancient gnosis and the *theosophia perennis* as is the recognition of the presence and activity of invisible helpers. It has also another side: the recognition of demonic forces, of the truth that "your adversary the devil, as a roaring lion, goeth about, seeking whom he may devour." Prayer lifts the individual above the immediate, empirically observable situation and carries it beyond the accustomed temporal and spatial limitations of our work-a-day world. By taking us out of the so-called "now" it engages our memory in such a way as to carry us, however minimally, into that psychic realm in which our own memory provides us with an intimation of our immortal destiny. In short, the life of prayer is the life of awareness of those higher levels of consciousness that has always been so much the subject-matter of the ancient gnosis. Because prayer is engagement in the gnosis of God we can see the significance of the apostolic command to pray without ceasing, which would otherwise seem impossible to obey.[7] Prayers offered with little awareness of the reality of the psychic realm must inevitably be as fumbling as one's attempts to follow conversation in a language one does not understand.

In the history of the literature on prayer can be found a well-established calculus of values. No one who knows anything about prayer would rate the mere use of formulas of vocal prayer over contemplation or mystical union, though opinion on the relative value of such vocal prayer would vary considerably. The rosary is an example of an ingenious attempt to try to get simple people to meditate on the great mysteries of the Christian faith against a backdrop of easily remembered and recited vocal prayers. Promoted by St. Dominic in a campaign to revive a traditional Catholic outlook among those who in the twelfth had been captured by what the Church accounted the dangerous heresy of

---

[7] I Thessalonians 5.17.

the Albigenses, it proved very popular. The psychological reasons for this popularity are interesting. Prominent among them is the fact that one can, in theory at any rate, engage in such prayer at a wide variety of levels, so that it has had some of the appeal that some forms of twentieth-century dancing have enjoyed: anyone can do them in a way, by merely walking round the room, though to do them properly demands more training, practice and aptitude. In dealing with people at all sorts of levels both of literacy and of psychic insights, as is the case in any society that purports to function as a Church, such elasticity is necessary. Notoriously, however, the rosary tends to degenerate into the mere mumbling of the vocal prayers with little or no thought of the mysteries of the faith, joyful, sorrowful or glorious, on which the worshipper is supposed to be meditating. It seems that Gresham's Law in economics, according to which bad money drives out good, applied not only also to education (as is well-known in academic circles that have witnessed the ousting of good programs by bad) but not least to the Church's prayer-life: the noblest prayers, liturgical or personal, tend to be expelled in favor of those that are the cheapest, dullest and most conducive to non-think. Yet in the tradition of the great religions of the world, Buddhism no less than Christianity, is a recognition of the fact that not all kinds of prayer are of equal value or efficacy.

In the Benedictine tradition, the most venerable monastic heritage of Christian spirituality in the West, the recitation of a lengthy cycle of vocal prayers and other devotions was established in the early days of the Order that Benedict founded in the sixth century. The routine of prayer in choir occupies about five hours of the day. The whole psalter of one hundred and fifty psalms is recited or sung in the course of a week. This daily routine, called "God's work" (*opus Dei*), is traditionally the fundamental duty and work of the choir monk. Whatever other work, intellectual or manual, he may do, he must never neglect this *opus Dei* without good reason. Yet a mere recitation of the words will not carry a monk or nun very far in the way of the spiritual life to which he or she has been called. The success of a monk's vocation is to be judged, rather, by his attainment in contemplative prayer, which obviously must always be a private transaction between God and the monk. In short, his "real" life of prayer must rise as a descant above the melody of his verbal plainsong.[8] This descant sym-

---

[8] I say "melody" advisedly, since plainsong is not polyphonous.

bolizes, moreover, the descant of faith over doubt, of hope over fear, of love over mere learning. The aim is a mystical union with God achieved, however, in the characteristically sober Benedictine tradition of careful attention to the external words. The theory is that the mystical flight is most securely attained by those who know how to plant their feet firmly on earth. It is noteworthy that the Cistercians, who represent the most notable reform of the ancient Benedictine Order, insisted even more strongly on manual labor in the fields, though their contemplative aim, classically expressed in the devotional spirit of Bernard of Clairvaux, is not really distinguishable from that of the earlier luminaries of the Benedictine Order. It is the mystical union with God, the consummation of which lies at the heart of all authentic prayer. In this mystical union the soul is caught up into and *knows* God as intimately as is possible within human life.

The variety of Christian traditions of prayer is astonishing; yet all seem to move on the fringe of the gnosis of God, which must be, of course, in theory, their common aim, despite the Church's theological protest that it should never be a conscious one; that is, one should never set out to attain the mystical union with God in which true gnosis lies but, rather, go about one's business in hope that it may come about.

The Spanish mystics constitute a very different and special school in which a distinctive ethos is noticeable to even the most superficial student; nevertheless, for all the vivid imagery they use in their attempt to communicate what is, after all, fundamentally incommunicable in human language, their method is designed to lead to the same result, which is once again the gnosis of God. The German and English mystics, no less than those of the Salesian tradition of France, have all that same basic aim. Henri Bremond calls that tradition *humanisme dévot*, the method of pure love (*pur amour*), that is, the union of the soul with God in the pure love that attains a gnosis of God beyond but not necessarily opposed to such more limited knowledge as may be attained through learning.

Pascal, whose Jansenist sympathies would seem to place him at the opposite pole from that of the "humane" Salesian tradition, was indubitably also a mystic, as his striking account of his experience (a note of which he carried for many years, sewn into his doublet) attests. He, too, original mathematician and literary satirist that he was, in the great French tradition of humanistic and scientific inquiry, and classic exponent of the peculiar nature

of faith, is very much in the way of the Christian gnosis as it was
expounded by Paul. Neither the humane learning nor the scientific inquiry that are tremendous forces in the history of Western
culture is at all necessarily antagonistic to either Christian experience or the Christian gnosis that is its outcome.

The dangers attending the mystical path of the *humaniste dévot*
are notorious. For that path may easily lead to that false gnosis
against which Paul and others so vehemently warn us. If it does
so, however, it does so because of the evil dispositions of arrogance and pride that vitiate all worthwhile human enterprises.
The pursuit of truth in any guise can never be wrong or bereft of
value, except to the extent that it is undertaken with the blinders
of human vice, among which pride is, according to all classical
Christian doctrine, the most pernicious. The love of God that is
the indispensable ingredient in Christian gnosis is not achieved in
a vacuum, any more than the Gospel can come without an
antecedent Torah. When the love of God is truly attained it
removes such obstacles to gnosis, freeing us from the limitations
of our human condition and removing us from the perils that
beset every merely human attempt at enlightenment.

For this reason, the genuine mystic grasps the nature of the
psychic realm and understands the workings of psychic energy as
can no other human being. He has become aware of the nature of
the warfare symbolized in Christian literature as the battle between Lucifer and Michael, between the demonic and the divine.
For him the major preoccupations of even a comparatively un-
corrupt Church tend to recede into the background, pertaining,
as they must seem to him to pertain, to the country of the blind
where seeing-eye dogs are necessarily the best guardians of tradition. Seeing-eye dogs are indispensable to the blind; but to the
sighted they can seem but picturesque appurtenances to be loved
and admired for their patience and fidelity, constant reminders
of the glorious joy of possessing sight.

XIV

HUMANISM AND THE GNOSIS

> *To you alone is given a growth and a
> development that depends on your own
> free will. You bear in yourself the
> seeds of a universal life.*
>
> —God, addressing Adam in
> Pico della Mirandola's
> *Speech on the Dignity of Man*

The term "humanism" is comparatively a newcomer to the English language. Invented or naturalized in 1834 from the German *Humanismus* by Coleridge (1772–1834), a lover of neologisms, it made its way slowly into nineteenth-century English despite a prejudice against its German sound. Coleridge used it to designate a special theological opinion of his day, the main thrust of which was a denial of the orthodox Christian doctrine of the uniqueness of the divinity of Jesus Christ. A little later in the century, Sir William Hamilton spoke, in relation to "the learned schools" (*die gelehrten Schulen*), of "the principles of a genuine humanism." Later still we find John Addington Symonds (1840–1893) alluding to the "German sound" of the term. It seems to have been used in German for the first time, however, by the Bavarian scholar F. J. Niethammer, in a work published in 1808.[1]

---

[1] *Der Streit des Philanthropismus und des Humanismus in der Theorie des Erziehungsunterrichts unserer Zeit.*

The term "humanist" had made an easier passage into English long before Coleridge's time, being, as Symonds also notes, "pure Italian" (*umanista*) and the designation of a professor of the humanities. *Umanità* was the generic name in Italian for humane culture, a term fraught with every kind of graciousness and respectability the Renaissance could bestow upon it. In some academic circles today, influenced as they are by contemporary forms of scholasticism as infertile as any in the fifteenth century, the term "humanities" has become almost as opprobrious as the term "divinity." Toward the end of the Middle Ages, however, it had acquired singularly positive connotations. The use of the term "humane" occurs in English at least as early as 1500 in the sense of "kindly in demeanor." It is in this sense that the word was used when the Royal Humane Society was founded in England in 1774, a society that still gives awards for services to humanitarian causes. The term "humane" is also used in English in another sense, from at least as early as the seventeenth century, in the phrase translating the Latin *litterae humaniores,* the literary, historical and philosophical studies still known to Oxford men and women as "Greats" and relating to classical Greek and Latin literature. This respectable lineage goes back in Italian to at least the Quattrocento, the name given in Italian to the fifteenth century.

The ambiguities in the meaning of "humanism" and "humanist" have enormously proliferated in our own day. Yet despite the baffling variety of their connotations, probably most people, on hearing either of these terms, think of something that, or someone who, is opposed to all religious conceptualizations, theological or theosophical. They think of an outlook that reposes confidence in man alone as the master of his destiny, which often turns out to be a meager one for the individual, though perhaps a fairly substantial one for the race, provided that the race does not annihilate itself with its own nuclear or other scientific discoveries. On this understanding, these terms acquire negative connotations that are definitely and clearly hostile to all theosophical speculations and theological interpretations. Many people, indeed, in our day, take the term "humanism" to be the proper designation for all that is antithetical to religion and "humanist" as the suitable designation for any antagonist of a religious outlook of any kind. Such an understanding not only grievously restricts but disastrously distorts the rich and venerable concept of the study of the humanities, which are the proper study, as we noted in an earlier chapter, of free men contradistinguished from slaves. This study pertains to all that is human. It celebrates the glory of man in all the dimensions of which he is capable, including, obviously, his religious aspirations. For historically the concept of humanism certainly did not exclude, or in any way seek to diminish, the aspirations of man to a destiny beyond his present state or to confine him in any way that would limit his spiritual capacity or his vision of divine Being. Indeed, the dignity of man that the humanist tradition so lauded depended absolutely, in the last resort, on his divine origin, apart from which he would have been accounted not much different from a biologically enlivened piece of mud.

In Italy in the Quattrocento, the humanists constituted a kind of priesthood of the domain of arts and letters. Though these Quattrocento humanists wore no cassock or other insignia of a clerical state, nor clothed themselves in the habit of a monastic or other religious order, they were not infrequently dedicated to what was, (not least from a modern perspective) a distinctly religious purpose. For they expounded a spirituality at once more creative, more purifying, and more liberating than could have been found in the decadent scholasticism of their day, at a time when the sun had long set on the golden age of thirteenth-century scholasticism, and degeneration of the scholastic method into a tedious infertility had brought its impending collapse into sight. Marsiglio Ficino (1433–1499), for instance, claimed for himself in a letter to Lorenzo de' Medici the proud title of *sacerdos musarum*: priest of the Muses. Far from accounting himself a rebel against either religion in general or Christianity in particular, he saw himself as representative of a Christian brotherhood of literature and the creative arts.

Nor was the Quattrocento humanist the ethically irresponsible dilettante that fanatics in the Church would have liked to paint him. He was, however, certainly an individualist. Indeed he was often more devoutly consecrated to his individualism than were his monastic and other counterparts devoted to their vows of poverty, chastity and obedience. Yet he could often feel a deep sense of moral duty toward his own brotherhood, an obligation not to let it down by giving its enemies grounds for scorn. Some humanists led lives of greater simplicity than was common in many a convent. They felt the brotherhood should foster a mood of self-sacrifice such as would exhibit the spiritual nature of their calling. For theirs was a deep respect for the spiritual empire of *humanitas* that they saw resurrected out of the ashes of imperial Rome. So remote were they from the "secular humanism" of today that Pico read his classics as a Benedictine read his Office. *Humanitas* was the celebration of God's supreme creative act: the creation of man. How could there be a radical distinction between "sacred" and "secular" studies, since all genuine study is sanctified work, whatever the label society chooses to give it? Wisdom is indivisible and philosophy is, according to the etymology of the word, "the love of wisdom."

Such attitudes brought the Italian and German humanists of that age very close to a gnostic frame of mind. True, not all were favorably disposed to the natural sciences. Nor is that entirely remarkable, in view of the widespread association of science with magic in the Middle Ages. Yet some were in the vanguard of the scientific as well as the humanistic revolution. Giordano Bruno, captured at Venice in 1592 and burnt at the stake at Rome on the Campo dei Fiori on February 17, 1600, is an excellent example of such a humanist of the following century, one who was plainly disposed to a reincarnationist view and to other opinions characteristic of the ancient gnosis.[2] Pico della Mirandola (1463–1494) and others had also been deeply interested in hermetic and other occult literature.

Nor was the *pietas* toward the religion of their fathers that was generally typical of the humanists a merely sentimental affection or a nostalgic hankering such as Santayana's who, after he had completely renounced the Church's creeds, loved the haunting smell of her incense, the peal of her bells, the muffled whisper of her prayers, and the mysteriously celestial echoes in the floating properties of her plainsong. In the fourteenth century Petrarch (1304–1374) had written admiringly of the contemplative life and on the contempt one ought to have of the world (*De contemptu mundi*), recalling Augustine's method of introspection from the transitory things of earth to the eternal joys of the spirit. His contemporary, Boccaccio (1313–1375), to whom is attributed the celebrated but now somewhat threadbare witticism that the

---

[2] For an illuminating note on a possible reason for the timing of Bruno's execution, *see* Appendix C to Antoinette Mann Eaterson, *The Infinite Worlds of Giordano Bruno* (Springfield, Illinois: Charles C. Thomas, 1970), pp. 196ff.

Christian Church must be divine to have survived so much corruption, hailed Petrarch with the salutation: *spes unica nostri*,
seeing in him the only hope of their age. The phrase had specific
overtones, for the Cross of Christ was traditionally hailed in the
phrase *ave crux, spes unica*, and the motto of the semi-eremitical
Carthusians, to whom Petrarch had dedicated one of his works, is
stat crux, dum volvitur orbis: while the world turns, the cross stands.
No doubt Boccaccio's point was that he saw in Petrarch a free
spirit far more Christ-like than that of the avaricious bishops and
crafty popes who gave themselves out as Christ's ambassadors on
earth yet only too plainly guarded the Church only as a vast
holding of real estate and other mercantile property.

So closely was the thought of the Quattrocento humanists generally tied to its traditional religious moorings that Pico, for
instance, was clothed on his deathbed by Savonarola in the habit
of a Dominican friar. Pico took the humanist scholar or poet to be
called to a life of greater sacrifice than that of the cloister. Naturally there were humanists who lacked the *docta pietas*, the learned
devotion, that was the spirit of the best of their brotherhood; but
since there has certainly never been any dearth of unworthy
representatives of the official hierarchy of the Church, we may
regard that circumstance as historically insignificant.

The meaning of humanism depends, of course, on the doctrine
of man that underlies it. If one sees no more in man than an
unusually well-organized mammalian biped with less strength
than some other more handsome mammals but an endowment of
exceptional cunning that has enabled him so far to survive, if
nowadays somewhat precariously, then one's humanism will be
limited accordingly. It will be little more than a popularized
version of a scientific anthropology. If with Jewish and Christian
humanists and some others with similar visions of the nature of
man, one sees man as a special creature of God, made in the
divine image, one's humanism will be obviously very different. If
one's doctrine of man, being in the Socratic tradition, envisions a
divine origin and glorious destiny for humanity that transcends
this brief earthly life, leading one to see the human plight and
salvation from it in existentialist terms, then one's humanism may
be so closely related to the ancient gnosis as to be virtually identi-
fiable with gnosticism in its most general sense. In short, with a
gnostic outlook on the nature of man, the humanist has the same
basic concerns as has the gnostic. What Sartre predicated of exist-

entialism (that it is a humanism), if it be true of even his nihilistic type, can be confidently asserted of gnosticism, whose foci, as we have abundantly seen, are: (1) man's plight, (2) the means of his salvation, and (3) the destiny beyond this life for which he may strive.

For that tradition of humanism stands through history as an outlook which, though profoundly religious, is a loud and clear and ongoing protest against the obscurantism of literalistic and legalistic misunderstandings of the nature of religion. Christianity, having been born and cradled in a gnostic climate, and being a subtle and learned answer to the gnostic quests of the Graeco-Roman world, is nothing if not a humanism. As it purports to be the true gnosis, the agapistic gnosis, so it consequently claims to teach the true humanism.

That this is no platitude may be easily shown. Christianity, no less than other religions, has an infinite capacity for oversimplification and literalization. We are only too familiar with such phenomena in the contemporary scene. They have been present, however, in one form or another, from the earliest times. A full demonstration of the facts would demand a detailed account of the entire history of Christian thought; nevertheless, some salient examples should suffice. Most people in all ages are literalistic and legalistic in their understanding of religious ideas. That is no more remarkable than the fact that most bankers are more likely to have the mind of bank tellers than of members of the Federal Reserve Board. The fact that many in the early Church were attracted to the Christian Way who did not understand and who could not possibly have understood its full implications is inevitable and obvious. One of the problems confronting them was what to do about their old religious and cultural heritage from the great Graeco-Roman civilization whence they had sprung. When they were intelligent enough to see much good in their old heritage, which might well have encompassed, for instance, the nobler aspects of Stoicism that we see reflected, for example, in the *Meditations* of the Emperor Marcus Aurelius, they would ask themselves precisely what it was that they were rejecting. That is never an easy matter to explain to an illiterate person who happens to be also unimaginative. In the dying (as also in the ashes of the deceased) Roman Empire, the old pagan culture often showed remarkable signs of moral vigor. How does one explain to such a convert what ought to be his attitude to it, now that he has embraced a Christianity that has inherited the uncompromising biblical insistence on a total devotion to the One True God?

The simplest, though also a very misleading, way to deal with such misgivings is to tell the "babe in Christ" that the Old Way is the Devil's and the New Way Christ's. That is indeed pretty much what Theodore of Mopsuestia (c. 350-428), for instance, did say to candidates for Christian baptism. The old pagan way, with everything associated with it, including the circus, the racecourse and the theater, are all specifically in the service of Satan. Now of course many gnostic teachers have also fallen into this trap. We find it in the Manichees and in the Albigenses. It is a hazard of the preacher's vocation. When converts are numerous and many of them uneducated, catechists have to draw their pictures in a very sharp black and white. Yet converts cannot but run into trouble as a result of such oversimplifications, and the more intelligent they are the faster they run into it, as they try to mature in their new life. When Gentile converts to Christianity in the ancient world were chided by their friends for their devotion to this strange god Christos and were questioned about the sincerity of their new belief, what could they say? In their perplexity they might well find themselves retorting: "By Zeus, yes I do believe in the Lord Christ." How confusing to their psyches! Yet how natural and how inevitable.

Many early Christian preachers did sound anti-humanistic. Even the golden-mouthed John Chrysostom (c. 337-407), for instance, berates Christian parents for not bringing up their children properly, citing practices that might not seem either to us or to his contemporaries to be as vicious as he sometimes makes them sound. He asks how a Christian parent can allow his or her son to grow his hair long in the effeminate pagan way. Girls, he says, should not be allowed earrings and other such adornments that will make them a greater burden to their future husbands than even the tax collector. If parents so pamper their children they will have only themselves to blame when their children turn out vicious. They should seek rather to make their children athletes for Christ, inculcating them constantly with the ideals of humility and chastity, vividly aware of the vanity of this world. Yet for all this severity, Chrystostom recognizes that what he is really trying to get across is that if only children be taught what were, after all, the sober virtues known to the pagan world, they will grow up to display not only these virtues but new Christian ones that will transform all their moral qualities. He urges that boys be taught to be courteous to everybody so that, being courteous to slaves and other inferiors, they will be the more respectful to their peers. In all these exhortations a Christian humanism shines through; yet the average convert could hardly be expected to discern it.

Jerome (c. 342-420), one of the most acrimonious controversialists in the history of Christianity as well as the learned translator of the Bible into the Latin version that was to be used as the basis of the version officially adopted by the Roman Catholic Church, loved, in his youth, the good things of pagan life, not the least of which were classics such as Cicero, whose literary style he admired and sought to emulate. About the year 374 he believed himself to have been greeted in a dream by an angelic or other visitant who chided him: "You are a Ciceronian, not a Christian." This vision led Jerome to renounce for a long time all pagan learning and culture as unworthy of a convert to the Christian faith. At last, however, he perceived that he could not have been such an effective ambassador of the Christian cause had not he been so steeped in the great pagan classics and nurtured on the grandeurs of Ciceronian style. In his later years, therefore, he soft-pedalled the importance of that vision. Centuries afterwards, however, medieval and Renaissance artists seized on his vision as a convenient symbol of his conversion to the Christian Way. In so doing they helped to obscure its nature and oversimplify the distinction between humanism and Christianity.

Many in the early Church, such as Tertullian, took a more decided stand against humanistic elements in Christianity and so promoted the ambivalent attitude that prevailed through the Middle Ages and whose effects are visible in the obscurantism of so much of the religious climate of our own time. Certainly a Christian humanism could never be taken for granted at any time in the Church's history. There was never any dearth of fanatics who affected to disparage everything pertaining to what today we call "secular" culture, whether it came under the guise of the Graeco-Roman or of some other tradition. We know this from the diligence with which medieval humanists like Coluccio Salutati had to plead the cause of Christian humanism to his generation. Dante's debt to Virgil is well-known; but his choice of that literary symbol of the humanism of the Graeco-Roman world to conduct him through the infernal regions and the seven-storeyed mountain of purgatory was a deliberate one: a device to uphold him and to promulgate the vision of Christian humanism that Dante so clearly beheld. The artificiality of much medieval scholasticism had obscured the humanistic and therefore the gnostic understanding of Christian truth.

The humane traditon we have been considering has had striking counterparts in non-Western cultures, notably that of China, where humanism in its Confucian form played an enormous role in molding a civilization that enjoyed incomparable splendor at a time when Europe, after the fall of Rome, was little more than a barbaric wilderness. At that time of China's glory, Europeans lived mostly in mud huts. The face of the land, dangerous to the traveler, was punctuated by an occasional hospitable haven, an outpost of Benedict's monastic system that portended to some visionaries the dawn of a new Christian age and marked to others the persistence of the lingering lamps of the humane heritage of a decaying *romanitas*. We have seen that that humane tradition is eminently compatible with Judaism and Christianity, though distorted forms of both of these can and do exist in opposition to them. The forms of religion most hostile to living spiritual realities are the intolerant legalisms and literalisms which, besides suffocating spirituality, encourage sacerdotal arrogance and corruption that destroy the humane element in religion. That humane element is, like the mystical aspect of religion, an expression of the ancient gnosis. It has a definite goal for humanity. Its vision is of a human destiny not bounded either by this planet or by this life. It is an optimistic humanism, a humanism *par excellence*.

In the nature of the case, the humane element, no less than the gnostic one, tends to be hidden. For while the face of religion needs, if it does not totally depend on, publicity, and therefore thrives on the mass media of the present-day, the occult character of its inmost life is almost always ill-served by publicity. It generally avoids it. It has no need of it, since it relies on the psychic world for the much more thoroughgoing and effective means of communication it has always had at its disposal, to which even modern technology cannot add anything very important and certainly not anything indispensable. The history of the Church, therefore, tends to be a history of its face, inventories of its stones and mortar, its slabs of porphyry and its pots of gold. It consists largely of chronicles of the events connected with its political

maneuvers, its corporate structure, and its administrative organization. The spirituality of the Church, theosophical and
humane, is necessarily unobtrusive, often more so than even the
most secret military or naval operation in human history. A
history of the inner life of the Church would be as difficult to
write as a history of the inner thoughts of great men and women
throughout the ages. We can hear only the echoes. We see but the
traces. Yet in these echoes and in these traces are the very vestiges
of God.

In the medieval world, intellectual attention was focused on
divine Being as the chief *locus* of scholastic dialectic. That did not
mean that everybody took the existence of God as axiomatic. Had
the divine existence been a universally accepted axiom,
Maimonides and Thomas need never have discussed it at all. It
did mean, however, that the medieval schoolmen made God the
center of philosophical disputation. With the Renaissance, man
became the new focus of attention. That, in turn, did not mean
that everybody became suddenly anthropocentric or that people
ceased to believe in God or engaged in a general disparagement
of religion. Far from it. Movements of that kind since the Renaissance have been sporadic and limited. It did mean, however, that
people now saw the discussion of the nature of man to be a more
profitable way of discussing *all* questions, literary, scientific and
even theological. For in man was seen a microcosm of the universe. Knowledge of his nature would provide a clue to the
knowledge of all things, because all things are reflected in man.
If, as the theologians had always taught, man is made in the image
of God, then God could be seen in man. If, as the naturalists
generally preferred to say, man is a part of nature, then by
looking at him we could see all nature. Whatever the truth about
the mystery of God and the universe, it could be found in the
mystery of man.

That mood, ushered in by the Renaissance, has never since
substantially changed. The immense interest in psychology that
was developed early in the present century is but an example of its
results. The humane spirit, fostered by a combination of that
mood with a basically religious outlook, can grow and has indeed
grown quietly and unobtrusively within the highly institutionalized and often hierarchical organizations that constitute the shell of the Christian Church. Plainly, however, it can
never be at home with the intolerant literalisms and legalisms that

such institutionalized religion inevitably promotes. Its obvious allies are the mystical, gnostic and theosophical movements that spiritually leaven every institutional religion, be it Hinduism or Judaism, Christianity or Islam. Religious humanism and the gnosis are natural allies.

Not all periods in history are equally propitious for either the humanistic or the gnostic elements in the Church. In some periods they tend to go almost entirely underground, being heard of, if at all, only in mysterious little whispers. Their effects, in such times, are observable very privately, as unexpected, momentary, scent-laden gusts of the spirit, wafted to us from an alien and exotic clime. At other times, as in the nineteenth century, for example, the claims of humanism are so openly enunciated that they pervade the thinking and outlook of all people, religious and otherwise. In our own time, now that the importance of man has come to be generally accounted axiomatic, the passage from religious humanism to gnosticism and theosophy looks more promising. Christian humanists, meanwhile, are beginning to appreciate where their best friends are to be found. Some of them are already becoming aware of the affinities between the ancient Christian gnosis and the life of the Church as it flourishes today amid the inhumanities and obscurantism of institutional religion. The future is, of course, as always, unpredictable; yet there are certainly portents. To an assessment of their significance our last chapter is to be devoted.

XV

A RENAISSANCE IN
CHRISTIAN THOUGHT?

The first thing is to acquire wisdom;
gain understanding though it cost you all you have.
Do not forsake her and she will keep you safe;
love her, and she will guard you;
cherish her, and she will lift you high;
if only you embrace her, she will bring you to honour.
She will set a garland of grace on your head
and bestow on you a crown of glory.

—Proverbs 4.7-9 (N.E.B.)

No unusual powers of discernment are needed to see that we are
witnessing a period of deep unrest in the Christian Church. The
malaise reminds one in some ways of the distress of the Church in
the late Middle Ages, during the century and a half before
Luther's final break with Rome in 1521. The learned among
churchmen had done everything they could during that period,
by seeking to reform the Church from within, so as to avoid such
an outcome. The need for a twentieth-century reformation of the
Church has for long been felt in our own time, and various
writers, including myself, have exhibited, each in his own way, the
need for it. The need, as I saw it twenty years ago, entailed three
forms of revival: revival of discipline, revival of the interior life,

revival of liturgy, *in that order of importance*.[1] Since then a pattern uncannily reminiscent of the eve of the sixteenth-century Reformation has been gradually unfolding: a pattern of corruption leading to widespread contempt for "the Church", despite deep sentimental attachment to it on the part of many. That a reformation must come to correct these ills is well-known to all who know anything at all of the inner workings and power structure of the Church. What is disputable is only the form the Coming Reformation is to take.

Not only is the form of the Coming Reformation unpredictable; so also is the nature of the process and the time it will take. Where institutions control and administer immense wealth, as is certainly the case with the Christian Church, not least in America, those who control and administer it do not readily yield their power, and the more corruptly they have acquired it the less willingly they give it up. A hundred and fifty years before Luther's break with Rome, John Wyclif was attacking in England the concept of the *dominium* (lordship, ownership) by bishops and rectors of their ecclesiastical benefices, as though Christ's vineyard were a piece of real estate to be subdivided for lease or sale. This part of his teaching naturally incurred the special wrath of those whom he pilloried, for when churchmen have lost their spiritual influence they are more than ordinarily jealous of their temporal power. The Church today, having dramatically lost its influence during the past few decades, has retained control of billions, together with unique privileges in tax exemption. These circumstances do not augur well for an easy reform of the Church. The corruption is likely to become worse. The struggle is likely to be prolonged. Yet one cannot tell, nor is the timing very important.

What is more important is the form the reformation is to take. While no one who believes in the freedom of the human will would be so rash as to venture a prediction, we can usefully note some observations and perhaps even estimate some probabilities. First we should note that the Church is by any reckoning a unique institution. Though the principles that sociologists, psychologists and political scientists follow in respect to the dynamics of institutions apply in some measure to the Church, there are peculiar

---

[1] *The Coming Reformation* (Philadelphia: Westminster, 1960).

elements in the Church that make it partly insusceptible to the
kind of analysis one would apply to, say, Dupont or General
Motors, or to a nation such as Venezuela or France.

Because of the Church's vocation as the unique instrument of a
divine activity, it is also the ideal hide-out of humanity's worst
foes: those who seek to kill the soul of humanity and feed off the
carcass that is left behind. Business corporations, being devoted
to an exclusively profit-making aim, have some built-in correctives against corruption, correctives that the Church lacks.
Everyone in General Electric has the same goal and everyone
knows it. Some are better than others at pursuing it and therefore
have an advantage; but all play the same game. Some are cleverer
at getting around the rules; but such deviancies cannot go for
very long undetected. Some at the top may exploit others, or at
any rate are likely to be accused of doing so; but if they exploit
them they do so in a common enterprise. Though labor calls
management an enemy, everyone knows there are no enemies of
the common goal, only bitter rivals.

In the Church the situation is radically different, since the
exploiters have an entirely different aim from the only one that
justifies the Church's existence. These exploiters, therefore, are
indeed enemies. They are not enemies merely as burglars and
arsonists are enemies of homeowners and their insurance com-
panies, or even as spies are enemies of the nation that unwillingly
harbors them. Burglars, hoping for an easy livelihood, are willing
to risk for it the possible loss of their liberty. Arsonists usually
want only to destroy out of spite or pique or to cover up a crime.
Spies, despicable though they be, seek only to be mercenaries for
a pay usually well-earned in view of the high risk their work
entails and the courage and stamina it demands. None compares
in turpitude with those who exploit the Church. These are uniquely despicable, because they are not mere thieves with a thief's
code of honor, or arsonists with a distorted craving for perverted
excitement, or spies with a willingness to sell even their own
motherland for profit. They have been called parasites, vampires, cannibals, but unworthily, for parasites flatter their host by
selecting him, and vampires their prey, while cannibals, after all,
are but following a dietary instinct, cruel and disgusting though it
generally seems to the rest of us. The Church's internal enemies
are infinitely more depraved, for they take no risk, can plead no
inherited dietary or culinary propensity, and their conduct cer-

tainly does not disguise any unuttered flattering respect. Too unadventurous to rob or to rape, too timid to murder, too phlegmatic to burn anything, too cowardly to spy, they ferret their way into the Household of Faith they so vehemently hate and despise. There they spend all their working lives, sucking the material by-products of the pilgrims' loving hearts, feeding their own bellies on the Body of Christ.

Once many years ago I dropped into St. Patrick's Cathedral, New York City. I had knelt only a few moments in meditation in a rear pew when I noticed a man get into the one in front of me where a girl was kneeling at prayer. Suddenly he leapt out of the pew, having snatched her purse as she prayed, and fled like a whippet to a waiting car. She was a Colombian, on her first visit to New York, almost entirely without English, and carrying all her money in her purse as well as both her own and her mother's passports. Another worshipper who accompanied me to call the police remarked that it was the filthiest act he had ever seen, stealing a little foreign girl's purse while she was saying her prayers; but as I thought of what it symbolized I wondered about that. What the enemies of the Church, some in the hierarchy, perpetrate on the faithful for no less ignoble ends (taking advantage of their masochistic weaknesses and encouraging the nonthink that serves evildoers so well, and with no need of even the qualities of daring or fleetness of foot such as this robber displayed) make his vicious act seem, by comparison, almost benign. The turpitude of a corrupt senator or bank president is tawdry; the turpitude of a wicked bishop is the vilest of all.

Only a few decades ago America's propensity for churchgoing was the wonder of all Christendom. At a time when churchgoing had so declined in England that only ten per cent of the population of London, then still very homogeneous, was estimated to attend any place of worship with anything resembling regularity (such as even every few weeks) and that of Scotland about twenty-five per cent, churchgoing in the United States could still be called a normal pattern of behavior. Today Americans are deserting the Church in droves. In one recent decade the Episcopal Church lost a million members out of an estimated four million. Toward the end of that period a bishop of that Church, against the advice of many, including some highly influential persons, lay people and clergy, purported to ordain to the priesthood on the Feast of the Circumcision of Jesus, a priestess known

to be and proud of being not only a lesbian but the co-president of
a national American homosexual society. She was later licensed to
officiate in another diocese by a bishop who was shortly afterwards unavailable for comment, because he was undergoing
treatment for alcoholism. Roman Catholics are usually more dis-
creet about their difficulties; nevertheless, they cannot easily
disguise the fact that their seminaries, often magnificently fur-
nished with all that money can buy, are in many cases all but
empty. The old monastic orders and the newer congregations of
priests and brothers and sisters generally account themselves
blessed by God if they have even little handfuls of postulants.
Though Protestant meetings, evocative of the old "sawdust trail"
that was the staple diet of America in the old frontier days, still
have a market, with "drive-in" and other such modern gimmicks
and enticements, their effect on intelligent Christians is always
negligible and usually negative, to put it politely. The "mainline
Protestant" churches, though often surviving through dogged
efforts by the faithful few, are generally well-pleased if they
succeed in not shutting their doors.

What has happened? Why the antipathy to the Church, especially on the part of the more intelligent of inquirers? It is certainly not the old ill-repute the Church once acquired for wrongs
and cruelties such as the Inquisition. These practices have been so
long ago renounced that even the old breast-beating repentance
for them is outmoded. In matters of social justice, too, the
Church's voice is loud. If sometimes it seems a little too nervously
emphatic, few notice because few care, and those who do are not
much convinced by anything the Church says on any kind of
justice, since her record on justice within her own organization is
embarrassingly notorious. Intellectual dishonesty in the crasser
forms that have brought the Church into such obloquy has not
entirely disappeared; but educated churchpeople are generally
better alerted to it. They are therefore less disposed to swallowing
it, preferring, rather, to wave it aside as part of an antique scenery
and archaic charm. Even the diminishment in numbers is accounted by many an improvement: they claim it as a sign of
purification!

Numbers are not so important as some think. The reason for
the decline in quantity is in any case sociologically complex. The
reason for the decline in quality is, by contrast, painfully simple.
The Church has come to be regarded by intelligent people, as

never before, the Citadel of Non-Think. The anti-intellectualism that afflicts it is all the more striking for its being so stunningly unconscious. It takes many forms. Each denomination expresses the stultification in its own distinctive way. It matters little whether poisons are prepared in powdered or liquid form, under a green or a yellow label. The result is always the same in the end. It arises not merely from the human tendency to sloth that affects all of us. It is a mental laziness, distinctive (not to say peculiar) to the Church, a device to anaesthetize churchpeople into total insensitivity to spiritual values, making them blind to even what constitutes a religious question and deaf to every spiritual proclamation. I have yet to find any experienced Protestant pastor willing to deny the fact that most churchpeople would raise less objection to diminishing or adding to the number of Persons in the Holy and Undivided Trinity than to changing an accustomed hymn tune, despite a very general reluctance on the part of many to sing with any enthusiasm any hymn at all. In many cases sermons have absolutely nothing to do with anything that even the most easygoing churchpeople or the most statistic-hungry sociologist could possibly have the effrontery to call related to either Christianity or any other religion in the world. A friend of mine, an experienced American rector, reports that on a recent visit to Scotland he found himself in Pitlochry, a lovely and tourist-frequented village in Perthshire. He decided to worship at the local kirk. Knowing that the Presbyterian Church of Scotland once enjoyed world-wide attention for its theological preaching, he not unnaturally expected to hear at least echoes of that homiletic tradition. He found, however, that in fact the entire half-hour sermon made no mention of God, morality or religion, even in the most obscure or furtive way, being exclusively and uncompromisingly devoted to the subject of North Sea Oil. Can one wonder then at the reluctance of intelligent inquirers to take seriously the hypothesis that the Church might have something to do with religion?

The considerable scholarship, some of it of the highest quality, that exists in the Church exists almost in a vacuum. Yet since such scholarship depends on the Church, after all, as its principal and usually its only patron, seminary scholarship is not always as independent or as liberated as it is often given out to be. Its effect on the average man or woman in the pew is minimal. More often than not the tendency of the pew is toward the "fundamentalist" factions who symbolize the natural fright caused by the current situation we are considering and who laudably, however ignorantly, try to preserve the values they dimly see in the only way they know how. Others engage in that feverish activity that they think will make a parish look alive, appearances notwithstanding: the parish office bustle, the rummage sales, the bazaars, the little Lenten Talks, the picnics and other paraphernalia of non-think. As morticians know, the only way to make a corpse look like a living person is to deck it out in finery and apply somewhat dramatic cosmetics to its face. Even then it does not deceive many onlookers, of course; but perhaps children might be taken in, and most churchgoers are nowadays pretty juvenile in all matters relating to the spiritual life, even though they may be highly intelligent in other affairs.

The labels churchpeople adopt reflect the simple-mindedness and juvenility of any religious attitudes they might be supposed (by the charitable) to have. They dub themselves "conservative" or "liberal", though what they are conserving usually turns out to be their accustomed way of life and what they are liberal about is generally anything that they think will not affect that pattern. The well-to-do, who include guilt-ridden bishops, feeling themselves comparatively unaffected by welfare programs and the like, are often inclined to adopt the "liberal" label because they think it gives them an aura of generosity and compassion. The poor, when they have time to give the matter any thought at all, no less unnaturally follow suit. (Kings are usually royalist, popes papist, and the poor in favor of welfare.) The middle-classes tend on the whole to adopt the "conservative" label for no less obvious reasons. Rarely do any seem to notice that the labels have almost nothing to do with religion at all.

Shortly after the death of Pope Benedict XV on January 22, 1922, Monsignor Giuseppe Pizzardo called a young seminarian into his office.

"You belong in diplomacy," e said. "You have the mind for it. I am recommending you to the Accademia dei Nobili Ecclesiastici."

The academy to which he referred is the training school for diplomats and leaders of the Roman Catholic Church. The young seminarian he had called in was Giovanni Battista Montini, the future Pope Paul VI. No doubt like any other seminarian he must have felt gratified to be proposed for such training. He was still, however, sufficiently innocent of the Church's ways to object that he had not yet finished either his literary studies at the University of Rome or his studies in canon law at the Gregorian. Monsignor Pizzardo pooh-poohed the objections as one would wave aside the objections of a child who sought an extra half-hour of play before being called into the house.

"A degree or two!" exclaimed the monsignor. "What difference do they make, degrees? Let them go. The Church needs qualities in certain places. God provides these qualities in certain people. You have the mind of a diplomat."[2]

Presumably that conversation could not have been pursued further. In a way it sounds natural and indeed amiable. Yet in it may be discerned a paradigm of the attitude of the hierarchy to the intellect. It is by no means an entirely negative one. The intellect is to be exercised as should be also the body. As one should be encouraged to walk and swim and play football, so one ought to be encouraged to exercise the mind by certain approved studies. Nevertheless, as one should be prepared to mortify the body by fasting and other such physical austerities, so one must be prepared to sacrifice the intellect whenever that should seem desirable in the institutional interests of the Church. The Jesuits have traditionally spoken of the *sacrifizio dell'intelletto*, as though one could sacrifice one's intellect as one might have to sacrifice one's taste for football or the opera. An American cardinal archbishop was encouraged, if not ordered, in his seminary days to have his studies curtailed or kaleidoscoped so that he might all the sooner give his remarkable talents as a financier to the service of the Church. The learned in the Church obviously do not share that estimate of the role of the human intellect; but in the eyes of the hierarchy the learned have no important function. In the eyes of some members of the hierarchy their work is even dangerous *per se*. Nor is the Roman Catholic Church by any means alone in such attitudes; Anglicans, Lutherans and Presbyterians all favorably compete in securing the triumph of Non-Think.

Scholarship is by no means, however, the only qualification necessary for religious leadership. Diplomacy is extremely important, indeed vital, in all institutions, not only in international affairs. A talent for it is a gift that is rare, though not so rare as, for example, creative thought or musical genius or philosophical

---

[2]William E. Barrett, *Shepherd of Mankind: a Biography of Pope Paul VI* (New York: Doubleday, 1964), pp. 84 f.

acumen. The monsignor was perceptive in his choice of candidate for the Accademia. Some nine months later the Fascisti were to march on Rome and in November Mussolini was to assume full dictatorial powers over Italy at a time when the Pope was still a voluntary prisoner in the Vatican.[3] Plainly the Church needed diplomats. What the learned in all Churches question is whether any Church needs them at such a price. The attitude of the hierarchy and other leaders is that it is not a price at all. That attitude is perhaps more than any other factor what inhibits the Church's hospitality to the very different kind of wisdom available in the ancient gnosis.

No reform in the Church, no purificatory movement, can do any good till churchpeople face the realities of the situation. They are naturally reluctant to do so, for no one likes to admit to being the victim of fraud. That is why so many impostors and confidence tricksters go free. There is, however, no other way. The attempts at reform, many of them sincere, that we are seeing on all sides in the Church, far from getting to the root of the disease, merely aggravate it. Rome, to which the reign of John XXIII had seemed to many to bring in so much fresh air, has tragically impoverished her liturgy, which for all its shortcomings had a dignity and beauty that commanded the admiration of educated people all over the world. Altars are abandoned; little tables are thrust out among the worshippers to reduce the ancient mysteries to the level of social get-togethers to which few come save those who feel compelled by deep-rooted instinct to endure the new rites in obedience to a legislative order. Many Roman Catholics find themselves saddled with old legalisms while they are left with only a de-religionized religion. Anglicans have wantonly thrown away so much of a priceless liturgical heritage and have condoned—or at best, tolerated—such unmentionable outrages in the Church that many seriously wonder whether hideously sinister evil forces may not have been at work to bring about so much ruin in so short a time. After centuries of devotion to a Prayer Book tradition of exceptional beauty and some theological

---

[3]The voluntary imprisonment of the popes ended with the Treaty of the Lateran in 1929, as a result of conversations between Mussolini and Cardinal Gasparri. This treaty gave the papacy sovereignty over the territory now known as Vatican City. For a good brief account of the background and proceedings, *see* Benedict Williamson, *The Treaty of the Lateran.* (London: Burns Oates, 1929).

felicity, worship has been cheapened and distorted as if to match the "progress" from the patine of fine Sheraton tables and Hepplewhite chairs to the dull glaze of varnished sawdust-and-plastic furniture.

All this is done partly in the name of simplification; yet services are interrupted by explanatory commentaries read by often ignorant young people whose inner life is vacuous enough to make what they say sound as convincing as a love song sung by a boy of ten. The agony on the face of many of their hearers, terrible though it be, cannot match the anguish in the hearts of those too sad to attend any more. Thousands of priests and ministers would leave the Church tomorrow but are prevented by financial considerations. The purse strings of the Church are in hands other than theirs, a circumstance that may recall to some the apostolic practice according to which they were in the custody of Judas. The Church today, unwilling to face the awful reality of the situation with the terrible consequences it must bring about, is still listening to and taking counsel from her enemies and ignoring her friends.

Meanwhile, interest in genuinely religious questions outside the Church is not only unabated but notably vivacious. Many, if not most, students in universities and colleges with a "secular" or "public" label, while they have often little or no church connection, are hardly less often extremely inquisitive about profoundly religious concerns. Yet they have real difficulty in understanding the notion that the Church might be supposed to have anything specifically to do with what interests them. They recognize the Church as a societal institution. They take varying attitudes toward it, ranging from slight hostility to (much oftener) the sort of indifference with which the average person would view a pension fund for the widows of unsuccessful Arctic explorers. When forced to think about churches at all they generally get only far enough to recognize that they have some special functions, mostly connected with marriage and death. They may notice that churches are often, and nowadays often feverishly, engaged in social-activist enterprises, some of which they may approve and others of which they disapprove, so that they are confirmed in their opinion that churches merely echo the preoccupations of the society in which they appear but do so in such a curious way as to make their efforts quite negligible. Churches, therefore, look more and more irrelevant to people's religious quests. In their political activities they seem at once slightly sinister and somewhat naive, both of which they usually are. Above all they seem neurotic and quite irrelevant to anything that could interest any normal person, stupid or clever, American or foreign, serious or flip, scientific or humanistic. Those students who have read Russell's *Why I am not a Christian* have been usually much impressed by it, especially by the suggestion that the Church in all its forms seems to foster untruthfulness, promote dishonesty, and perpetrate deceit.

The magnets that attract these young people, some of which they sometimes try to bring into the Church, are varied. Vedanta, Krishna Consciousness, Scientology, Baha'i, TM, ESP, are but well-known examples. Yet the magnets have something in common: they seem to deal with questions that have always interested seekers after religious truth. Whether they do so well or ill is beside the point. Young people tend to think, however mistakenly, that they are 'occultist', for any religious idea to which one is unaccustomed looks hidden, mysterious, 'occult', when one encounters it for the first time.

Does all this betoken, then, a theosophical renaissance in our time among those brought up, however tenuously, in or alongside a Christian rather than, say, a Hindu or a Buddhist culture? Does it even augur a theosophical renaissance in the Church itself? These questions are not easy. They may prove unanswerable; nevertheless, they are questions we must try, at least, to explore, since even an incomplete answer could have immense value for the awakening of spirituality in our time through the appropriation of the ancient gnosis.

The impediments against a gnostic or theosophical renaissance in the Church are formidable. Perhaps the most obvious is that the Church has already lost, in some cases irretrievably, many of the very people who would have helped to foster it. Among those who remain, a considerable group, perceiving so much amiss in the Church, and attributing it to a stiffnecked lack of heartiness, fancy that what is needed is a new pentecostalism, a movement of the Spirit that will sweep away the cobwebs and revitalize the Body of Christ. Such movements have certainly refreshed the Church many times and in many ways in the Church's history, and new ones may well do so again. Yet while they can clean and brush up the Household of Faith, making it more sanitary and infusing into it a most welcome and pulsating new life, they do not nourish the minds of the faithful or improve their vision.

Moreover, most churchpeople, indoctrinated with a travesty of the concept of faith, show a remarkable readiness to shelter behind it as an excuse for avoiding all religious questions except those that are of no fundamental importance in releasing men and women from their prisons and setting them on a path of spiritual evolution. They use the concept of faith to exonerate them from the consideration of the most profound questions, such as the nature of the afterlife. Such matters are simply thrown into God's hands, much as the typical small investor does not feel the need to inquire into the nature of the world's monetary and banking systems, being content to trust his few hundred dollars to his bank on the ground that his friends have for long done so and he hasn't heard of anyone's losing a penny yet. For many, faith means little more than that and certainly not anything such as, by any reckoning, the New Testament writers could have intended. Nor are such attitudes confined to the uninstructed; they are not only found among the more educated and thoughtful but are actively promoted by their leaders. The very pretensions to thoughtfulness in the Church, where they exist, serve too often as a device to avoid probing deep enough to approach basic issues at all. Jesus plainly had something in mind comparable to this when he charged the Pharisees with preoccupation with trivia while neglecting "the weightier matters."[4]

I doubt, therefore, if we ought to expect a widespread change on the part of the majority of church folk in this matter in the near future. What we might expect, however, is a considerable renaissance of theosophical interest on the part of some who might influence Christian thought in such a direction. That such an expectation is reasonable is attested by the fact that large numbers of people are indubitably tired of the religious presuppositions and churchy chit-chat and more weary still of the mish-mash of social issues that so many churches are providing in desperate attempts to keep people inside.

The extraordinary neglect within the Church of the inner life suggests that we might be on the verge of a genuine renaissance of interest in the questions that properly interest all authentic pil-

---

[4]Matthew 23.23.

grims. Can history teach us how and in what circumstances one
might expect such movements to occur? If so, a scholarly collection of recent studies of various renaissances in Christian history
may help us.[5] These papers range from one on the Christian
humanism of Augustine to one by Alec Vidler on an abortive
renaissance in the early years of the present century: that of the
group of priests and others (e.g., Loisy, Bremond, Tyrrell) associated with the movement technically called Modernism, who
used the Premonstratensian priory in Sussex, England, as their
focal center. This miscellany shows that such intellectual rebirths
generally take place in an atmosphere in which some important
aspect of religious truth has been conspicuously neglected.
Eamon Duffy, for instance, reminds us that the widespread im-
morality prevalent in England after the Restoration of the
Monarchy under Charles II and the lack of effective discipline in
the Church led many to hanker after a supposed pristine purity in
Primitive Christianity. Two studies of Alan of Lille treat the
renaissance in the twelfth century that brought about a renewal of
respect for both nature and humanity in the wake of an age that
had dwarfed man and belittled nature. John Barkley's study of
two movements in nineteenth-century Scotland tells once again
an oft-told wistful tale. Extraordinarily fanatical and obstinate
antipathy to all forms of art, visual or otherwise, inevitably led to
attempts at liturgical and doctrinal revival.[6] Stupendous opposition greeted all such attempts to fulfill the extremely modest aims
of these societies whose members cried out for water in a land of
liturgical drought where only very brackish streams had been
allowed to trickle into the Church's pastures.

Of course there are other factors that must be present to bring
about an important renaissance; but not the least essential is a
special neglect such as we find behind these and other rebirths in
Christian history. That a truly astounding neglect of the gnostic

---

[5]Ecclesiastical History, *Renaissance and Renewal in Christian History*, ed.
Derek Baker (Oxford: Basil Blackwell, 1977).

[6]Expressed respectively in the foundation of the Church Service Society
in 1865 and the Scottish Church Society in 1892. The former aimed at
liturgical reform, the latter at the recovery of ancient Catholic doctrine.
That both were struggling, if unwittingly, after a discovery of the ancient
gnosis, as was also Edward Irving's movement earlier in that century,
would not be a difficult thesis to sustain.

and theosophical elements in Christian tradition has charac-
terized most kinds of churchmanship needs no demonstration.
Even while highly sophisticated theological developments were
taking place, comparatively little interest was taken by churchmen in gnostic or theosophical concerns till the fairly recent
discoveries of manuscripts (such as the Nag Hammadi library)
having indisputably gnostic features. Even the extremely important constituent in early Christian thought that was provided by
the Alexandrian tradition received scant attention from the
learned, while few ordinary churchgoers had ever heard of its
existence till gnostic ideas came into prominence through such
manuscript discoveries.

The revival of interest in the mystical aspects of religion and the
readiness of many to see in mysticism an essentially good element
is noteworthy and, I think, salutary. True, the mystic's way is
fraught with danger; but so is everything that demands solitary
courage. What is promising about the mystical revival is that it
underlines the extreme disenchantment of people, especially
young people, with not only the diet the Church has fed them but
the calculus of values it upholds and cannot disguise. They are
coming to see that it upholds such a calculus of values because of
the bankruptcy of its own spiritual life. The old saying that good
actors make fiction sound like truth while preachers make truth
sound like fiction no longer adequately meets the case when so
many preachers, having nothing to say and compelled by their
office to say something, obviously cannot conceivably make what
they do say sound like even good fiction, let alone the truth. It
usually sounds, not unexpectedly, just like themselves, a fitting
expression of the state of their inner life. Yet they go on talking
and talking and talking. They are deeply distrusted, often even by
their own flocks; but what can people do? Even the worst of folk
usually come to church with at least a vague notion that it is for
their spiritual enlightenment and health. What can they do when
they find that the "experts" (as they take priests and pastors to be)
not only know less than many of their people about God but are
willing to stand up regularly week after week publicly displaying
their ignorance? What could we do if we suddenly found the
medical profession in such a parlous state? Not much at first; but
before long we would do whatever we could. Within my parents'
memory some doctors were still prescribing leeches for most of
their patients' ills. Some patients were so satisfied with the results

that they kept the leeches as pets. But most patients learned in time to expect better of their medical advisers.

That the leaders of the Church have been alarmed for some time is plain. Unfortunately, the very lack of spiritual perception among these leaders inevitably led them to misread the signs. Concluding that the trouble lay in matters such as the somewhat Byzantine pomp of the Church's liturgy and her archaic language, they thought to remedy the situation by cheapening these through an extensive de-beautification program. A greater respect for the human intellect is the last thing such leaders would ever conceive as a remedy for anything. Since they usually owe their position of leadership to a widespread estimate of it as a dangerous poison, they cannot imagine that it could ever have a salutary effect on the Church, despite the considerable success they formerly achieved by lip service to it. The old façade of theological paraphernalia designed to give the impression of the possession of religious truth, as though religious truth were a bundle of General Obligation Bonds bought at a discount and redeemable at par, has crumbled very much. Though many in the Church are still at the counterpart of the leech-medicine stage, I am convinced that the demand for something better is on the increase and that the people making it tend to be those statistically most likely to outlive the others. Those who have known or can recapture the joy of the Church in its beauty, the wonder of its *agapē*, its infinite capactiy for authentic humanization, and its inward concern (however obscured) for progress to a fuller life, will one day hanker after it and come back to infuse it with that *sophia* and that *gnōsis* that are its birthright. For as Jesus never renounced Moses, neither did Paul abjure Solomon. Wisdom shall return to her ancient habitation, be it synagogue or church, Solomon's Temple or Chartres Cathedral, Hagia Sophia or the village chapel. When people find in the synagogue or church the holy Widsom they are seeking, they will flock to it so fast that no one need ring a bell, for indeed they will be there before the bells can be rung. Yet meanwhile, despite the loss of her ancient beauty, let the Church keep at least her bells, for in the coming theosophical renaissance, bells will be much needed to celebrate the re-enthronement of Wisdom in her ancient dwelling.

In every church with a Lady altar is mystically symbolized the Holy Wisdom, the Lady Philosophy, awaiting those who desire her.For

Wisdom is bright, and does not grow dim.
By those who love her she is readily seen,
and found by those who look for her.
Quick to anticipate those who desire her, she makes herself
                                        known to them.
Watch for her early and you will have no trouble;
you will find her sitting at your gates.
Even to think about her is understanding fully grown;
be on the alert for her and anxiety will quickly leave you.
She herself walks about looking for those who are worthy of
her
and graciously shows herself to them as they go,
in every thought of theirs coming to meet them.[7]

So let us keep the bells. We shall need them to ring in Wisdom. Wisdom brings the only freedom through the exercise of which men and women can leap forward to the new life. Wisdom, the ancient gnosis, carries the key.

---

[7]Wisdom 6.12-16 (J.B.). Christian theologians will see here an adumbration of the doctrine of prevenient grace.

BIBLIOGRAPHY

Adam, Alfred. *Die Psalmen des Thomas und das Perlenlied als zeugnisse vorchristlicher Gnosis.* Berlin: A. Töpelmann, 1959.

Ambelain, Robert. *La notion gnostique du demiurge dans les Écritures et les Traditions judéo-chrétiennes.* Paris: Éditions Adyar, 1959.

Amélineau, M.E. *Essai sur le gnosticisme égyptien.* (Annales du Musée Guimet, tome 14ième.) Paris: Ernest Leroux, 1887.

Arseniev, Nicholas. *We Beheld His Glory.* New York: Morehouse Publishing Company, 1936.
> An Eastern Orthodox theologian's view of the experiential character of primitive Christianity and of the mystery of the Church. Has comments on Anglican faith and life as seen through the eyes of an Eastern Orthodox. Is of some relevance to studies of gnosticism.

Baaren, T. P. van. "Towards a Definition of Gnosticism". In *Le Origini dello gnosticismo.* Edited by U. Bianchi.

Baker, Augustine, O.S.B. *Holy Wisdom.* (Originally published in 1657 as *Sancta Sophia.*) Wheathampstead, Herts., England: Anthony Clarke Books, 1972.

Balthasar, Hans Urs von. "Pistis and Gnosis". In *Communio: International Catholic Review*, V, 1, (Spring 1978), pp. 86-95.
> A perceptive study by a distinguished contemporary Swiss Catholic theologian.

Bartsch, Hans Werner. *Gnostisches Gut und Gemeindetradition bei Ignatius von Antiochien.* Gütersloh: C. Bertelsmann, 1940.

Benz, Ernst. *Les Sources mystiques de la philosophie romantique allemande.* Paris: Vrin, 1968.
> Has some interesting sections on Böhme, Swedenborg et al., and the influence of theosophical and mystical ideas on German philosophy.

Betz, Hans Dieter. *Paul's Apology II Corinthians 10-13 and the Socratic Tradition.* Berkeley: Center for Hermeneutical Studies, 1970. 30 pages. LC 75-35038.

_____. *Paul's Concept of Freedom in the Context of Hellenistic Discussions about the Possibility of Human Freedom.* Berkeley: Center for Hermeneutical Studies, 1977. 51 pages. LC 77-22596.

Beyschlag, Karlmann. *Simon Magus und die christliche Gnosis.* Tübingen: Mohr, 1974.

Bianchi, U., ed. *Le Origini dello Gnosticismo.* (Proceedings of the Coloquium at Messina, 1966.) Leiden, 1967. *See* especially papers by H. Ringgren, M. Mansoor and M. Simon.

Böhlig, Alexander. *Zum Hellenismus in den Schriften von Nag Hammadi.* Wiesbaden: Harrassowitz, 1975.

Bokser, Baruch. *Philo's Description of Jewish Practices.* Berkeley: Center for Hermeneutical Studies, 1977. 41 pages. LC 77-14931.

Bolgiani, Franco. *Forme di gnosticismo nella tradizione ebraica e cristiana dall' antichità al secolo XX.* Torino: G. Giappichelli, 1975.

Bornkamm, Günther. *Mythos und Legende in den apokryphen Thomasakten.* Göttingen: Vandenhoeck und Ruprecht, 1933.

Borsch, F. H. *The Christian and Gnostic Son of Man.* Naperville, Illinois: Allenson, 1970.

Bouyer, L. "Saint Paul et les origines de la Gnose". In *Revue des sciences Religieuses*, 25 (1951), pp. 69-74.

Bruns, J. E. *The Forbidden Gospel.* New York: Harper and Row, 1976.

Bultmann, Rudolf. *Primitive Christianity in its Contemporary Setting.* London: World Publishing Company, 1956.

_____. "Gnosis". In *Bible Key Words.* New York: Fernhill, 1963.

_____. *Theology of the New Testament.* Translated by K. Grobel. New York: Charles Scribner's Sons, 2 vols., 1951, 1955. *See* especially Vol. I, sect. 15: "Gnostic Motifs".

_____. "Zur Geschichte der Lichtsymbolik in Altertum". In *Philologie*, 97 (1948), pp. 1-36.

Burkitt, F. C. *Church and Gnosis.* Cambridge: Cambridge University Press, 1932.

Burrows, Millar. *The Dead Sea Scrolls.* New York: The Viking Press, 1955.

Cerfaux, L. "Gnose préchrétienne et biblique". In *Dictionaire de la Bible*, Supplément III (1938), cols. 659-701.

Colpe, C. "New Testament and Gnostic Christology". In *Studies in the History of Religions*, XIV, 1968. Edited by J. Neusner. *See* pp. 227-243.

Corbin, Henry. *Terre céleste et corps de résurrection*. Paris: Buchet-Chastel, 1960.

Cornélis, Humbert and Léonard, A. *La Gnose éternelle*. Paris: A Fayard, 1959.

Cross, F. L. *The Jung Codex*. New York: Morehouse-Gorham Company, 1955.

Cullmann, Oscar. *Le Problème littéraire et historique du roman pseudo-Clémentin*. Paris: Félix Alcan, 1930.

Daniélou, Jean, S.J. (Cardinal). *The Theology of Jewish Christianity*. Translated by J. H. Baker. London: Darton, Longman and Todd, 1964.

———. "Akolouthia chez Grégoire de Nysse". In *Revue des Sciences Religieuses*, 27 (1953), pp. 219-249.

D'Arcy, Martin C., S.J. *The Meeting of Love and Knowledge*. New York: Harper and Bros., 1957.
The reply of the distinguished Jesuit to objections offered by Dr. Ananda K. Coomaraswamy to his use of terms, such as "gnostic" and "wisdom".

Davies, W. D. "Knowledge in the Dead Sea Scrolls and Matthew 11.25-30". In *Harvard Theological Review*, 46 (1953), pp. 113-139.

———, and Daube, David, eds. *The Background of the New Testament and its Eschatology*. Cambridge: Cambridge University Press, 1954. *See* especially pp. 52-80.

Déchanet, J.-M., O.S.B., *Christian Yoga*. New York: Harper and Row, Perennial Library, 1972. (Original French ed. 1956.)

Dodds, E. R. *The Greeks and the Irrational*. Berkeley: University of California Press, 1951.

Doresse, Jean. *Les livres secrets des gnostiques d'Égypte*. Paris: Plon, 1958.

Dörrie, H. "L'Âme dans le Néoplatonisme". In *Revue de Théologie et de Philosophie*, 11 (1973), pp. 116-134.

Drijvers, H.J.W. "Edessa und das jüdische Christentum". In *Vigiliae Christianae*, 24 (1970), pp. 4-33.

Drummond, Henry. *Natural Law in the Spiritual World* (14th. ed.). London: Hodder and Stroughton, 1884. A classic in religious evolutionism.

Drummond, J. *Philo Judaeus*. London: Williams and Norgate, 1888.

Dupont, Jacques. *Gnosis: la connaissance religieuse dans les Épitres de S. Paul* (2nd. ed.). Louvain: E. Nauwelaerts, 1960. A Louvain dissertation.

Dupont-Somner, André. *La doctrine gnostique de la lettre "Waw", d'après une lamelle araméenne inédite.* Paris: P. Geuthner, 1946.

Eberz, Johann. *Sophia und Logos.* München: Basel, Reinhardt, 1967.

Enslin, Morton Scott. *Christian Beginnings.* New York: Harper and Bros., 1938.

Elsas, Christoph. *Neuplatonische und gnostische Weltablehung in der Schule Plotins.* Berlin: de Gruyter, 1975.

Eltester, Walther. *Christentum und Gnosis.* Berlin: Töpelmann, 1969.

Evola, Jules. *Métaphysique du sexe.* Paris: Payot, 1959.

Farrer, Austin. "Gnosticism". In *Interpretation and Belief.* Edited by Charles C. Conti. London: SPCK, 1976.
    A remarkable paper by an exceptionally brilliant and creative English theologian whose prolific writings reflect his profound sympathy with the traditions of the Alexandrian school.

Faye, Eugène de. *Gnostiques et gnosticisme*, (2nd. ed.). Paris: Geuthner, 1925.

Festugière, André M.J. *La révelation d'Hermès Trismégiste.* Paris: Librairie Lecoffre, J. Gabbalda et cie., 1944.

Fletcher, Frank T.H. *Pascal and the Mystical Tradition.* Oxford: Basil Blackwell, 1954.

Foerster, Werner. *Die Gnosis.* Zürich: Artemis Verlag, 1969-71.

_____. *Gnosis: a Selection of Gnostic Texts.* 2 vols. English translation by R. McL. Wilson. Oxford: Clarendon Press, 1972.

Frei, Walter. *Geschichte und Idee der Gnosis.* Zürich: Juris, 1958.

Frenkian, A.M. "Les origines de la théologie négative de Parménide à Plotin". In *Rivista Clasica,* 15 (1943), 11-50.

Friedländer, Moriz. *Der vorchristliche jüdische Gnosticismus.* Göttingen: Vandenhoeck und Ruprecht, 1898.

Furse, Margaret Lewis. *Mysticism: Window on a World View.* Nashville, Tennessee: Abingdon, 1977.
    Treats mysticism as recovery of immediacy.

Fürst, W. *Kirche oder Gnosis.* München: Kaiser, 1961.

Grant, R.M. *Gnosticism: a Source Book of Heretical Writings from the Early Christian Period,* 2nd. ed. New York: Harper, 1961.

————. *Gnosticism and Early Christianity*. New York: Columbia University Press, 1966.

————. "The Earliest Christian Gnosticism". In *Church History*, 22 (1953), pp. 81-98.

Grant, R.M. and Freedman, D.N. *The Secret Sayings of Jesus*. New York: Doubleday, 1960. Contains maps of the "gnostic world".

Graves, Robert and Patai, Raphael. *Hebrew Myths: The Book of Genesis*. New York: McGraw Hill Book Company, 1966.

Groningen, G. van. *First Century Gnosticism: Its Origins and Motifs*. Leiden: E.J. Brill, 1967.

Guillaumont, A. et al. *The Gospel according to Thomas*. Leiden: E.J. Brill, 1959. The Coptic text with English translation.

Guitton, J. *Great Heresies and Church Councils*. London: Harwell Press, 1965.

Guttman, J. *Philosophies of Judaism*. New York: Holt, Rinehart and Winston, 1964.

Haardt, Robert. *Die Gnosis*. Salzburg: O. Müller, 1967.

————. "Gnosticism". In *Sacramentum Mundi*, II (1968), pp. 379-381.

Haenchen, E. "Gab es eine vorchristliche Gnosis?" In *Zeitschrift für Theologie und Kirche*, 49 (1952), pp. 316-349.

Herman, E. *The Meaning and Value of Mysticism*. Boston: The Pilgrim Press, 1915.
Has some interesting observations on gnosticism and the Christian mystical traditions, e.g., that gnosticism "crumbled to decay before it had reached maturity," lacking "an opposing force strong enough to mold it."

Hofius, Otfried. *Katapausis*. Tübingen: Mohr, 1970. Revision of a Göttingen dissertation.

John of the Cross. *Ascent of Mount Carmel*. Translated by E. A. Peers. New York: Doubleday, Image Books, 1958.

Jonas, Hans. *The Bible in Modern Scholarship*. Nashville, Tennessee: Abingdon, 1965.

————. *The Gnostic Religion*. Boston: Beacon, 1963. Originally published 1958. Includes translations of source materials.

————. *Gnosis und Spätantiker Geist*. Göttingen: Vandenhoeck und Ruprecht, 1954.

Jung, Carl. *Memories, Dreams, Reflections*. New York: Pantheon, 1961.
Gnostic interest runs through almost all Jung's prolific writings.

Kadloubovsky, E. and Palmer, G. E. H. *Writings from the Philokalia*.
London: Faber and Faber, 1951.
Expounds the Hesychastic methods, claiming that the practice has
"nothing to do" with pagan mysticism, with which he identifies
gnosticism of the first and second centuries of the Christian era.
The Philokalia purports to contain "an interpretation of the secret
life of our Lord Jesus Christ."

Kemmler, D.W. *Faith and Human Reason*. Leiden: Brill, 1975.

King, Charles W. *The Gnostics and Their Remains, Ancient and Medieval*.
Minneapolis: Wizards Bookshelf, 1973.

Kingsland, William. *The Gnosis or Ancient Wisdom in the Christian Scriptures*.
London: G. Allen and Unwin, 1937.

Köhler, W. *Die Gnosis*. Tübingen: Mohr, 1911.

Kübel, Paul. *Schuld und Schicksal bei Origenes, Gnostikern und Platonikern*.
Stuttgart: Calwer Verlag, 1973.

Kuhn, A.B. *A Rebirth for Christianity*. Wheaton: Theosophical Publishing
House, 1970.
A theosophical interpretation of Christianity.

Lacarrière, Jacques. *Les Gnostiques*. Paris: Gallimard, 1973.

Laeuchli, Samuel. *The Language of Faith*. Nashville, Abingdon, 1962.
Discusses semantic differences between gnostic and non-gnostic
Christian language. The first chapter includes a discussion of the
creative element in gnostic language.

Lamplaugh, F. *The Gnosis of the Light*. London: J.M. Watkins, 1918.

Langerbeck, Hermann. *Aufsätze zur Gnosis*. Göttingen: Vandenhoeck
und Ruprecht, 1967.

Lavelle, Louis. *La Présence totale*. Paris: Aubier, 1934.
The thought of this profound French thinker, which has some
affinities with that of Spinoza and even more with that of Malebranche, often reflects a neo-gnostic outlook.

Lea, Thomas S. *Materials for the Study of the Apostolic Gnosis*. Oxford:
Blackwell, 1919-22.

Leisegang, Hans. *Die Gnosis*. Stuttgart: A. Kroner, 1955.

MacRae, George, S.J. *The Thunder: Perfect Mind* (Nag Hammadi Codex
VI, Tractate 2) Berkeley: Center for Hermeneutical Studies, 1973. 36
pages. LC75-44028.

———. "Gnosticism and New Testament Studies". In *Bible Today*, 38 (1968), pp. 2623-2630.

———. "The Coptic-Gnostic Apocalypse of Adam". In *Heythrop Journal*, 6 (1965), pp. 27-35.

Mansel, H.L. *The Gnostic Heresies of the First and Second Centuries*. London: John Murray, 1875.
    Historically of some interest as showing the attitudes and outlook of a scholarly conservative churchman on the gnostic problem as it was seen 100 years ago.

Marcus, Ralph. "Pharisees, Essenes and Gnostics". In *Journal of Biblical Literature*, 73 (1954).

Maxwell, L. LeRoy. *Doctrine and Parenesis in the Epistle to the Hebrews with Special Reference to Pre-Christian Gnosticism*. (Microfilm) Ann Arbor, Michigan: University Microfilms, 1970. A Yale dissertation.

Mead, G.R.S. *Fragments of a Faith Forgotten*. London and Benares: Theosophical Publishing Society, 1900.

———. *The Gnostic John the Baptizer*. London: J. M. Watkins, 1924.

Ménard, J.-É. "Le chant de la perle". In *Revue des Sciences Religieuses*, 41 (1968), pp. 289-325.

Metzger, Bruce. *An Introduction to the Apocrypha*. New York: Oxford University Press, 1957.

Miegge, G. *Gospel and Myth*. Translated by Stephen Neill. Richmond, Va.: John Knox Press, 1960.

Mortley, Raoul. *The Problem of Knowledge in Late Antiquity*. Berkeley, California: Center for Hermeneutical Studies, 1978. 56 pages. LC 78-15918.

Mouravieff, Boris. *Gnosis*, 3 vols. Paris: La Colombe, 1961-65.

Mowry, Lucetta. *The Dead Sea Scrolls and the Early Church*. Notre Dame University Press, 1966.

Nag Hammadi Codices. Leiden: Brill, 1972. *See also* Robinson, J. M.

Neumann, Erich. *The Great Mother: An Analysis of Archetypes*. New York: Bollingen Series, XLVII, 1955.

Nock, A.D. "Gnosticism". In *Harvard Theological Review*, 57 (1964). Posthumously published article. Many of this distinguished Anglo-American scholar's writings are of special interest to students of gnosticism.

Oden, T.C. "From Event to Language: the Church's Use of Gnostic Mythology". In *Religion in Life*, 36 (1967), pp. 92-99.

Osborn, E.F. *The Philosophy of Clement of Alexandria*. Cambridge: Cambridge University Press, 1957. A balanced account. *See* especially p. 14 and pp. 176.

Oulton, J.E.L. and Chadwick, H. *Alexandrian Christianity*. Philadelphia: Westminster (Library of Christian Classics), 1954.

Pagels, Elaine. *The Gnostic Paul: Exegesis of the Pauline Letters*. Philadelphia: Fortress Press, 1975.
　　The author follows H. Conzelmann in supposing the gnostic terminology of Paul to be accounted for by the view that certain terms were subsequently developed by the second-century gnostics into a technical vocabulary.

——. *The Johannine Gospel in Gnostic Exegesis*. Nashville, Tennessee: Abingdon, 1973. Based on her Harvard dissertation.

Pearson, Birger A. *Philo and the Gnostics on Man and Salvation*. Berkeley: Center for Hermeneutical Studies, 1977. 60 pages. LC 77-14930.

Peers, E. Allison. *Studies of the Spanish Mystics*, 2 Vols. London: Sheldon Press, 1927 & 1930.

Pépin, J. "L'herméneutique ancienne: Les mots et les idées". In *Poétique*, 23 (1975), pp. 291-300.

Perrin, Norman. *Rediscovering the Teachings of Jesus*. New York: Harper and Row, 1967.

Pétrement, Simone. "La notion de gnosticisme". In *Revue de Métaphysique et de Morale*, LXV (1960), pp. 385-421.

——. *Le Dualisme chez Platon, les gnostiques et les manichéens*. Paris: Presses Universitaires de France, 1947.

——. *Le Dualisme dans l'histoire de la philosophie et des religions*. Paris: Gallimard, 1946.

Poortman, J. J. *Philosophy, Theosophy, Parapsychology*. Leiden: A. W. Sythoff, 1965.

Porret, Eugène. "Un Gnostique moderne: Nicolas Berdiaeff". In *Foi et Vie* (1938), 2, pp. 184 ff.

Potter, Charles Francis. *The Lost Years of Jesus Revealed*. Greenwich, Conn.: Fawcett, 1962.

Prucker, E. *Gnosis Theou*. Wurzburg: 1937.

Prümm, K. "Glaube und Erkenntnis im zweiten Buch der Stromata des Klemens von Alexandrien". In *Scholastik*, 12 (1937), pp. 17-57.

Puech, Henri-Charles. "Gnosis and Time". In *Man and Time*. New York: Pantheon (Bollinger Series), xxx, pp. 38-84.

Quispel, Gilles. *Gnosis als Weltreligion: die Bedeutung der Gnosis in der Antike*. Zürich: Origo Verlag, 1972.
      Based on lectures given at the Jung Institute.

————. *Gnostic Studies*, 2 vols. Istanbul: Nederlands Historisch Archaeologisch Institut in het Nabije Oosten, 1974-75.

————. "The Origins of the Gnostic Demiurge". Edited by P. Granfield and J. A. Jungman. Kyriakon: Festschrift Johannes Quasten. Munster: Aschendorff, 1970.

Reicke, B. "Traces of Gnosticism in the Dead Sea Scrolls". In *New Theological Studies*, 1 (1954-55), pp. 137-141.

Robinson, James M. *The Nag Hammadi Library in English*. New York: Harper and Row, 1977. Translated by members of the Coptic Gnostic Library Project of the Institute for Antiquity and Christianity, under the directorship of James M. Robinson. Indispensable tool for all students of gnosticism in the ancient world.

————. "The Jung Codex: The Rise and Fall of a Monopoly". In *Religious Studies Review*, 3 (1977), pp. 17-30.

————. "Basic Shifts in German Theology". In *Interpretation*, 16 (1962), pp. 76-79.

————. *Jewish Gnostic Nag Hammadi Texts*. Berkeley: Center for Hermeneutical Studies, 1972. 28 pages. LC 75-44331.

Robinson, J.M. and Koester, H. *Trajectories through Early Christianity*. Philadelphia: Fortress Press, 1971.

Toques, R. *Structures théologiques de la Gnose à Richard de Saint-Victor*. Paris, 1962.

Rougemont, Denis de. *L'amour et l'Occident*. Paris: Plon, 1956.

Rowley, H.H. *The Relevance of the Apocalyptic*. London: Lutterworth Press, 1963.

Rudolph, Kurt. *Gnosis und Gnostizismus*. Darmstadt: Wissenschaftliche Buchgesellschaft, 1975.

Russell, D.S. *The Method and Message of Jewish Apocalyptic*. London: Student Christian Movement Press, 1964.

————. *Jews from Alexander to Herod*. New York: Oxford University Press, 1967.

Sadhu, Mouni. *Meditation*. London: George Allen and Unwin, 1967.

Sagnard, F. *La gnose valentinienne et le témoignage de saint Irénée*. Paris: Vrin, 1947.

Sandmel, Samuel. *The First Christian Century in Judaism and Christianity: Certainties and Uncertainties*. New York: Oxford University Press, 1969.

Schenke, H.-M. "Hauptprobleme der Gnosis". In *Kairos*, 7 (1965), pp. 114-123.

Scherer, J. *Klemens von Alexandrien und seine Erkenntnis-prinzipien*. Munich, 1907.

Schlier, H., "Das Denken der früchristlichen Gnosis". In *Beihefte zur Zeitschrift für die Neutestamentliche Wissenschaft*, 21 (1954-57).
Schlier sees Christian gnosticism as twin-brother to Christianity, somewhat as Esau to Jacob.

_____. "Der Mensch im Gnostizismus". In *Anthropologie religieuse, Numen*, Suppl. II (1955), pp. 60-76.

Schmithals, Walter. *Gnosticism at Corinth*. Translated by J. E. Steely. Nashville: Abingdon, 1971. Original German edition 1956.

Schmitt, Eugen H. *Die Gnosis*, 2 vols. Leipzig: Diederichs, 1903–07.

Schoeps, H. J. *Urgemeinde Judenchristentum Gnosis*. Tübingen: Mohr, 1956.

Scholer, D. M. *Nag Hammadi Bibliography, 1948-1969*. Leiden, 1971.

Schubert, K. "Jüdischer Hellenismus und jüdische Gnosis". In *Wort und Wahrheit*, 18 (1963), pp. 455-461.

_____. "Gnosticism, Jewish". In *New Catholic Encyclopaedia*, VI (1967), pp. 528-533.

Schulz, S. "Die Bedeutung neuer Gnosisfunde für die neutestamentlich Wissenschaft". In *Theologische Rundschau*, 26 (1960), pp. 209-266 and 301-334.

Simonelli, Manlio. *Testi gnostici cristiani*. Bari: Laterza, 1970.

Suso, Henry, O.P. *The Exemplar*, Vol. II. Dubuque: Priory Press. 1962.
Vol. I consists of a life, Vol. II of the Writings.

Tardieu, Michel. *Trois mythes gnostiques*. Paris: Études Augustiniennes, 1975.

Timothy, H.B. *The Early Christian Apologists and Greek Philosophy*. Assen: Van Gorcum, 1973.

Based on a dissertation for the University of Edinburgh and subsequent more advanced work at Leiden and Utrecht.

Tröge1, Ka1l-Wolfgang. *Gnosis und Neues Testament*. Gütersloh: Güterslohen Verlagshaus, 1973.

Underhill, Evelyn, ed. *The Cloud of Unknowing* (Brit. Mus. MS Harl. 674). London: Stuart and Watkins, 1970.

————. *Mysticism*, London: Methuen, 1911.

————. *Worship*. London: Nisbet, 1936.
All the writings of this remarkable Anglican lady are of interest to the student of gnosticism.

Unnik, Willem van. *First Century A.D. Literary Culture and Early Christian Literature*. Berkeley: Center for Hermeneutical Studies, 1970. 29 pages. LC 75-44025.

————. "Die jüdische Kompenente in der Entstehung der Gnosis". In *Vigiliae Christianae*, 15 (1961), pp. 65-82.

Völker, Walther. *Quellen zur Geschichte der christlichen Gnosis*. Tübingen: Mohr, 1932.

————. *Der Wahre Gnostiker nach Clemens Alexandrinus*. Leipzig: J.C. Hinrichs Verlag, 1952.

Waite, Arthur Edward. *Lamps of Western Mysticism*. New York: Rudolf Steiner Publications, 1973.

Watson, Lyall. *The Romeo Error*. London: Hodder and Stoughton, 1974.
An attempt by a scientist to reconcile scientific investigation with reports on mystical phenomena, more especially on the relation between life and death.

Watts, Alan. *Behold the Spirit: A Study in the Necessity of Mystical Religion*. New York: Pantheon Books, 1971.
Almost all the writings of Alan Watts should be of interest to students of gnosticism.

Welter, G. *Histoire des sectes chrétiennes*. Paris: Payot, 1950.

Werner, Martin. *The Formation of Christian Dogma*. New York: Harper and Bros, 1957. Many passages on Christian gnosticism.

Widengren, G. "Der iranische Hintergrund der Gnosis". In *Zeitschrift für Religions und Geistes Geschichte*, 4 (1952), pp. 97-114.

————. *The Gnostic Attitude*. Translated by B. A. Pearson. Santa Barbara, California: Institute of Religious Studies, University of California at Santa Barbara, 1973.
Consists of an English translation of his *Religionens Värid*, Chapter 16.

Wilson, John Henry. *A Comparative Study of Pauline and Early Gnostic Literature, Demonstrating that Paul was not a Proto-Gnostic.* (Microfilm) Ann Arbor, Mich.: University Microfilms, 1969.

Wilson, R. McLachlan. *The Gnostic Problem.* London: A. R. Mowbray, 1958.

———. *Gnosis in the New Testament.* Philadelphia: Fortress Press, 1968.

———. "Gnostics—in Galatia?" In *Studia Evangelica*, IV, 1 (1968), pp. 358-367.

———. "Some Recent Studies in Gnosticism". In *New Testament Studies*, 6 (1959-60), pp. 32-44.

Winston, David. *Freedom and Determinism in Philo of Alexandria.* Berkeley: Center for Hermeneutical Studies, 1976. 35 pages. LC 76-28773.

Wisse, F. "The Redeemer Figure in the Paraphrase of Shem". In *Novum Testamentum*, 12 (1970), pp. 130-140.

Wlosok, Antonie. *Laktanz und die philosophische Gnosis.* Heidelberg: C. Winter, 1960.

Wolfson, Harry A. *The Philosophy of the Church Fathers.* Cambridge, Mass.: Harvard University Press, 1964.

Yadin, Yigael. *The Message of the Scrolls.* New York: Simon and Schuster, 1957.

Yamauchi, E. M. *Gnostic Ethics and Mandaean Origins.* Cambridge, Mass.: Harvard University Press, 1970.

———. *Pre-Christian Gnosticism: A Survey of the Proposed Evidence.* Grand Rapids, Michigan: Eerdmans, 1973.

Zandee, Jan. "Gnostic Ideas on the Fall and Salvation". In *Numen*, 11 (1964).

INDEX

Abbott, Lyman, 69
Académie Française, 76
Accademia dei Nobili Ecclesiastici, 194
Adam, 144, 170
Adam and Eve, 85
Adelard of Bath, 68
Adoro te devote, 94, 100
Agapē, 4, 18, 71, 94, 106, 117, 119, 124, 143
Agni, 169
Agnosticism in Christian Thought, 112, 121
Ahura Mazda, 22
Alan of Lille, 200
Alberta, 132
Alētheia, 55
Alexandria, Christian School at, 2, 42, 60, 109
Alexandrian Tradition, 201
Albigenses, 61, 174, 183
Allah, 144
Amos, 26
Anabaptists, 34
Ananias, 92
Anaximander, 67
Angelus, 101
Angra Mainyu, 22
Angst, 48
Animals in Latin countries, maltreatment of, 146
Anselm, 18
Apatheia, 123
Apocalypse, 4
Aquinas, Thomas, 25, 58, 61, 68, 94, 100, 113, 121, 124, 145, 159, 186

Arabia, Paul's years in, 92
Arahat, 135
Archetypes in Jung, 56
Aristotle, logic of, 35; recovery of works of, 68; 115, 121, 128
Arnold, Edwin, 101, 152
Arnold, Matthew, 128
Asperges at High Mass, 101
Astrologers, medieval, 66
Atheism, 126
Athens, 8, 16, 54
Augustine, 11, 18, 41, 51, 99, 105, 148, 200; introspective method of, 180
Averroist, doctrine of double truth, 114

Babylon, and Jerusalem, 41; 86
Bacon, Roger, 68, 116
Baha'i, 198
Baker, Derke, 200
Baptism, renunciation of World, Flesh and Devil at, 41
Baptists, 22, 137
Barkley, John, 200
Barrett, C. K., 15, 29
Barrett, W. E., 195
Barton, Bruce, 76
Basilides, 59
Benedict XV, Pope, 194
Benedictine Tradition, 11, 83, 174
Benediction, 100
Berakoth, 101
Berdyaev, N., 51
Berkeley, George, 80

Bernard of Clairvaux, 11, 175
Beyschlag, Karlmann, 12
Bhakti Yoga, 113
Bianchi, U., 37, 51
Blavatsky, H. P., 16
Blind Men, Indian fable of, 10
Boccaccio, 180
Boehme, Jakob, 11
Bogomils, 61
Bonaventure, 58, 132, 145
Bonnat, Léon, 8
Book of Common Prayer, 66, 197
Bornkamm, G., 75
Bosanquet's Logic, 35
Boyd, Zachary, 123
Bremond, Henri, 5, 175, 200
Brombert, Victor, 41
Bronx, 156
Brown, R. E., 89
Browning, E. B., 164
Browne, Thomas, 65
Bruller, Jean, 147
Bruno, Giordano, 180
Buber, Martin, 50, 168
Buddha, Gautama, 50, 162
Buddhism, 10, 44, 96, 174
Bultmann, R., 7, 75
Burgundy, 132
Butler, Cuthbert, 11
Buttrick, George, 165
Byron, 127
Bythus, 54

Cadbury, H. J., 75
Calvin, John, 34, 61, 90; on *cognitio Dei*,
    121; on prayers for the dead, 172
Calvinism, 33
Carmelite Piety, 96
Carrel, A., 166
Carthusians, 181
Cathars, 61
Celibacy, in Judaism, 77
Chadwick, H., 172
Chalcedon, Council of, 44
Charles II, of England, 200
Chartres, 5, 202
Chartres, School of, 131
Chaucer, 126
Chenu, M.-D., 129
Christ of faith and Jesus of history, 44
Christology, 82

Church, decline of spirituality in the,
    188
Chrysostom, John, 183
Cicero, 184
Circumcision of Jesus, Feast of, 1
Cistercians, 175
Clement of Alexandria, 3, 16, 1
    113
Clement of Rome, 16
Codex, 84
Coleride, S. T., 18, 177
Collective Unconscious, in Jung, 56
Coluccio Salutati, 184
Communion of Saints, 172
Confucius, 8, 42
Connaturality, Thomistic doctrine of,
    113
Corpus Mysticum, 105
Credo Quia Ineptum, 17
Credo Ut Intelligam, 18
Croce, B., 110
Cudworth, R., 126
Cullmann, Oscar, 9, 75

Dahat, 3
Daimones, 22
Damascus, 92
Daniélou, Jean, 38
Dante, 8, 99, 162, 184
Darwin, Charles, 69, 139, 146
de Dieu, Louis, 73
Deduction, and induction, 116
Demiurge, 21, 29, 55, 59, 77, 88
Democritus, 128
Determinism, 66
Deus Sive Natura, 126
Devil, 21
Diognetus, 41
Dimnet, Abbé, 39
Dionysius, pseudo-, 5, 145
Dobzhansky, T., 147
Docetism, 45, 59
Docta Pietas, 181
Dominic, 173
Dominicans, 61
Dominium, 90, 189
Donatist Controversy, 105
Dow Jones, 23
Drummon, Henry, 69
Dualism, mind-matter, 29, 43, 56;
    metaphysical, 21; good-evil, 40

Duffy, Eamon, 200
Dujardin, E., 98
Dupont, and the Church, 190
Dynameis, 22

Eastern Orthodoxy, 22
Eaterson, A. M., 180
Eckhart, 11
Einstein, 82, 121, 134
Ekklesia, 55
Elihu, 3
Eliot, T. S., 141
Elitism, in religion, 44
Elohim, 86
Emmaus, 78
Enkrateia, 123
Enlightenment, 130
Epilepsy, 66
Epiphanius, 1
Epp, E. J., 47
Erskine, Thomas, 168
Essenes, 78
Evagrius Ponticus, 4, 123
Everest, Mount, 133
Evil, problem of, 40
Evolutionism, and Gnosis, 138
Ewing, A. C., 159
Ex Opere Operato, 105
Exile, Babylonia, 47
Existentialism, 47
Exodus, 50
Extra-Sensory Perception, 198

Fabian Society, 55
Faith, as correlative of revelation, 19;
    and belief, 107; as inductive gnosis,
    109
Fall, Christian doctrine of the, 21, 45
Federal Reserve Board, 182
Feuerbach, L., 162
Ficino, M., 179
Fideism, 20
Fiske, John, 69
Foss, Martin, 161
Francis, of Sales, 11; of Assisi, 106
Freemasonry, 106
French Revolution, 127
Freud, S., 7, 162
Fundamentalism, 5, 85

Gabriel, Archangel, 143, 170
Genesis, 69, 85, 89
Genetic Pool, deterioration of, 149
General Electric, and the Church, 190
General Motors, and the Church, 190
Genius and Juno, 143
Geneva, 33
George V, King, 139
Gnōsis, in German usage, 8
God and Nature, 126
Goethe, 8
Good Friday, 94
Grace and Nature, 159
Grace, not alien to *karma*, 160;
    prevenient, 203
Gregory, of Nyssa, 5; the Great, 11
Gresham's Law, in liturgy, 174
Grosseteste, 68, 116

Hades, 9
Haemorrhage, woman with, 80
Hagia Sophia, 5, 202
Haggadah, 3
Halakah, 3
Half-Witted Brother, God's, 21
Hamilton, William, 177
Hamlet, 99
Hanson, Virginia, 159
Harvey, W., 72
Heaven, 9
Hegel, G. W. F., 109, 110
Heidegger, M., 49, 128
Heiler, F., 168
Heisenberg, 129
Helen-Ennoia Figure, 12
Hell, 9
Herbert, George, 91
Héring, J., 15
Hillel, 43
Hilo De Amor, 11
Hinduism, 96, 187
Hippocrates, 35
Hosea, 3
Housman, A. E., 48
Humane Society, Royal, 178
Humanism, Christian, 5, 176; origin of
    term in English, 177; and the
    Gnosis, 177
Humanitas, 180
Huss, John, 33
Huxley, Aldous, 120

Huxley, T. H., 6, 69
Hyatt, J. Philip, 10, 21
Hypocrisy, needs a shroud, 95

Ibsen, 140
Icon, importance of, 103
Ignatius, of Antioch, 60
Incarnation, of God in Christ, 59
Independence Hall, 105
Index, Papal. 39
Irenaeus, 2, 61, 66
Irving, Edward, 200
Isaac, 77
Isaiah, 84
Isherwood, C., 120
Islam, 140

Jacob, 77, 104
Jeremiah, 26
Jeremias, J., 75
Jerome, 184
Jerusalem, 16, 90
Jesuit(s), Voltaire on the, 75; piety, 96
Jesus, of history and Christ of faith, 44;
    quest for the historical, 73
Jewish, gnosticism, 8; proselytes, 9
Job, 3, 40
John Damascene, 103
John XXIII, Pope, 196
John, the Evangelist, 29; of the Cross,
    11, 46; the Baptist, 89
Jonas, Hans, 21, 38
Josephus, 78
Joyce, James, 98
Judas, as Church Treasurer, 197
Jung, C. J., 7, 12, 56, 158
Justin, Martyr, 113

Kabbalists, 106
Kant, Immanuel, 20, 122, 158
Karma, yoga, 113, Lords of, 159
Karmic, principle, 48, 154; process,
    139
Kepler, 134
Kerygma, apostolic, 81
Kierkegaard, 17, 19, 24, 26, 37, 43, 49,
    51, 110, 125
Kingsley, Charles, 55
Krause, K. C. F., 127

Krishna Consciousness, 198
Kübler-Ross, E., 144
Kuhn, K. C., 30

Labour Party, British, 2
Lady Philosophy, 202
Lao-Tze, 8, 96
Latria, 170
Layton, Felix, 159
Leonardo, 149, 163
Lightfoot, R. H., 75
Litterae Humaniores, 178
Liturgical, decline in Church, 196
Logos, 55, 87; *spermatikos*, 89
Loisy, Alfred, 200
Longfellow, H. W., 127
Lorenzo de Medici, 179
Lot, and his wife, 148
Lourdes, 166
Lucifer, 21, 57, 144, 176
Lüdemann, Gerd, 12, 13
Luther, Martin, 33, 61, 90, 188
Lutherans, 34

MacDonald, George, 169
Macmurray, John, 24, 117
Macquarrie, John, 49
Macy, John, 91
Mahābhārata, 141
Maimonides, 186
Malebranche, 127
Mandaean, creation myth, 170
Manichees, 18, 183
Manson, Charles, 77
Manual of Discipline, 30
Marcel, Gabriel, 49
Marcion, 55, 59, 77
Marcus Aurelius, 182
Marx, Karl, 7, 110, 156
Mary, 5, 9, 61, 143, 148, 169;
    Magdalene, 80
Mass, Last Gospel at, 89
Maurice, F. D., 55
McCosh, James, 69
McTaggart, 159
Merkabah, 10
Michael, Archangel, 22, 143, 176
Michelangelo, 45, 131, 162
Miegge, G., 38
Mill's Logic, 35

Mimosa Pudens, 95
Modernism, Roman Catholic, 200
Monophysites, 45
Montanism, 17
Montesquieu, 127
Montini, G. B., 194
Moses, 78, 202
Mozart, 149
Muhammad, 50
Muslim Science, medieval, 67
Mysteria (sacraments), 100

Nag Hammadi, 7, 30, 201
Napoleon, 112
Narcissus, 99
Natura, 128
Nature and God, 126
Nazareth, 75
Nestorians, 45
Newman, J. H., 109
Newtonian Physics, 129, 163
Nicene Creed, 163
Niethammer, F. J., 177
Nietzsche, 110, 140
North Sea Oil, Sermon on, 193
Notre Dame de Paris, 127
Nous, 55, 112

Ockham, William of, 57
Ockham's "razor", 58, 111
Ogdoad, 55
O'hEarchaî, Seán, 123
Oratio, ratio et, 166
Origen, 3, 5; on prayer, 171;
    universalism of, 147
Osborn, E. F., 18
Oulton, J. E. L., 172

Pagels, E. H., 89
Palestine, 8
Palladian Architecture, 8
Penentheism, 127
Pantheism, 126; in India, emergence
    of, 40
Pathē, 123
Panthéon, 81
Pantokrator, 22
Papyrus, 84
Parousia, 74

Pascal, Blaise, 17, 51, 132, 141; mystical
    encounter of, 46, 175; Wager of,
    117; Jansenism of, 175
Passmore, John, 161
Pasteur, Louis, 35, 72
Paul, 3, 7, 14, 17, 22, 24, 29, 35, 45, 47,
    70, 91, 99, 106, 120, 124, 143, 176,
    202; to his "infants in Christ", 39;
    on being *en Christō*, 149
Paul VI, Pope, 194
Pelagianism, crypto-, 114
Perfectibility, of man, 161
Petrarch, 180
Pétrement, Simone, 32, 39
Pharisees, 199
Philo, 3, 78, 89
Physis, 128
Pico della Mirandola, 177, 180
Pike, Albert, 106
Pistis, 18, 112; as quest for *gnōsis*, 19, 82
Pitlochry, 193
Pizzardo, Giuseppe, 194
Plato, 26, 42, 89, 128, 131
Platonism, 8
Pleroma, 66, 70
Pliny, 78
Plunkett, J. M., 132
Polygamy, 46
Positivistic Approach, to science, 13
Prayer, as energy, 164
Predestination, and grace, 34
Presbyterianism, 99
"Prince of this world", 21
Prison Motif, 47
Proust, Marcel, 98
Pseudo-Dionysius, *See* Dionysius,
    pseudo-
Ptahil-Uthra, 170
Purgatory, 172
Puritanism, 34
Purity, of heart, 83
Pythagoras, 23
Pythagorean, symbol of soul, 13

Quaker, phrase, 92; silence, 167
Quattrocento, 5, 178, 181
Quiricus, Metropolitan, 153
Qumran, 7, 30
Qur'ān, 67, 91, 144
Qutbs, 140

Reason, Temple of, 127
Redemption, 45
Reformation, Coming, 189
Reimarus, H. S., 73
Reincarnation, as corollary of karmic principle, 158
Religionsgeschichtlicheschule, 11, 32
Resurrection, of Christ, 80
Revolutionary, and conservative elements in religion, 43
Rig-Veda, 169
Robinson, J. M., 30, 75
Romanitas, 185
Romantics, nineteenth-century, 58
Rosary, 101
Rosicrucians, 106
Rousseau, J. J., 127
Roux, Joseph, 64
Ruskin, 103
Russell, Bertrand, 198

Sabatier, Auguste, 20
Sacrifice, 78
Sacrifizio Dell' Intelletto, 195
Saint Patrick's Cathedral, New York, 191
Sainte Chapelle, 134
Saints, and other helpers, 169
Salesian Tradition, 11, 175
Santayana, George, 180
Sartre, Jean-Paul, 48, 50, 162, 181
Satan, 21, 40, 154
Saul, 92
Savage, M. J., 69, 147
Savonarola, 181
Schleiermacher, F., 20
Schmithals, Walter, 47
Schoeps, H. J., 30
Scholem, G., 10
Schubert, K., 30
Schweitzer, A., 74, 168
Scotus, Duns, 58, 61, 68, 145
Scrofula, 66
Second Coming, 74
Septuagint, 3, 15, 70, 87
Shakespeare, W., 18, 99
Shalom Elechem, 81
Shammai, 43
Shaw, G. B., 140
Shekinah, 101
Sige, 55

Simon (Acts), 12
Simonian Tradition, 12
Socialists, Christian, 55
Socrates, 8, 42, 51, 54, 76, 181
Soma Psychikon and Soma Pneumatikon, 91
Sophia, 15
Solomon's Temple, 202
Sophists, 128
Spanish Mystics, 27, 46, 83
Spengler, 49
Spinoza, 126, 130
Stoic Motifs, in the Christian Fathers, 124
Stoicism, 8, 26
Strauss, D. F., 74
Sufi Spirituality, 140
Sufis, 121
Super-Ego, 119
Survival, of fittest, 148
Swadharma, 163
Symonds, J. A., 177
Syncretism, 30

Tantum Ergo, 100
Taoism, in theory and in practice, 96
Taubes, Jacob, 49, 91
Teilhard de Chardin, Pierre, 69
Tennyson, Alfred, 28, 99, 141
Teresa of Avila, 11, 51, 168
Tertullian, 16, 153, 184
Theism, 126
Theodore of Mopsuestia, 183
Theosophia Perennis, 173
Theotokos, 169
Thirty-Nine Articles, 105
Thomas (apostle), 81
Tillich, Paul, 40
Timaeus, 131
Toland, John, 11, 16, 126
Toledo, Council of, 153
Torah, 89, 114, 176
Transcendental Meditation, 198
Trinity, 87, 193
Tripitaka, 91
Tyrrell, George, 200
Ulysses, 98
Umanista, 178
Upanishads, 62, 126
U.S.S.R., 42

Valentine, 54, 59
Valentinians, 3, 7, 54, 66, 107
van Baaren, T. P., 37
van Leeuwen, Arend Theodor, 13
van Ruysbroeck, Jan, 46
Vedanta, 167, 198
Vedantists, 121
Venice, 103, 180
Versailles, 105
Vidler, Alec, 200
Virgil, 184
Visio Beatifica, 124
Voltaire, 75
von Balthasar, Hans Urs, 123
Vercors. *See* Bruller, Jean

Waitingness, 99
Waldensians, 34
Wali, 140
Water, Holy, 101
Weil, Simone, 135
Wesley, John, 104
Whitefield, George, 104
William, of St. Thierry, 5; of Conches, 131

Willis, N. P., 15
Wilson, R. McLachlan, 29
Wisdom, Renaissance of, 188
Woods, Mary, 65
Word, revelatory, 19
World War I, 51, 172
Wren, Christopher, 125
Wyclif, John, 33, 90, 189

Xavier, Francis, 73
Xavier, Jerome, 73
Xenophanes of Ionia, 76

Yahweh, 23, 86; in an ark, 95
Yeretz Israel, 86
Yeshua, 142

Zen, 26, 50
Zendavesta, 91
Zoë, 55
Zoroastrianism, 22

Reincarnation in Christianity

Geddes MacGregor is the author of the much acclaimed Quest book, *Reincarnation in Christianity* in which he questions whether or not there is room for the doctrine of reincarnation in Christian dogma. He asks, "Can Christians possibly accept the rebirth concept while remaining loyal to Bible and church?"

Students of religion, scholars, and laymen alike, will welcome this exhaustive inquiry. It provides a long needed, long awaited critical examination of the pros and cons of this question. Dr. MacGregor cuts through centuries of emotional hyperbole and narrow dogma and analytically reports important comments by some of the world's greatest Christian figures. He offers philosophical, scientific, and Biblical "for and against" evidence in support of his appraisal.

"Professor MacGregor's exciting thesis challenges our traditional orthodoxy."—*Timothy Cardinal Manning, Archbishop of Los Angeles.*

Available from
QUEST BOOKS
306 W. Geneva Road
Wheaton, Illinois 60187